ALSO BY GREIL MARCUS

Mystery Train: Images of America in Rock 'n' Roll Music (1975)

Lipstick Traces: A Secret History of the Twentieth Century (1989)

Dead Elvis: A Chronicle of a Cultural Obsession (1991)

In the Fascist Bathroom: Punk in Pop Music, 1977–1992
(1993, originally published as *Ranters & Crowd Pleasers*)

The Dustbin of History (1995)

The Old, Weird America: The World of Bob Dylan's Basement Tapes
(1997, originally published as *Invisible Republic*)

*Double Trouble: Bill Clinton and Elvis Presley
in a Land of No Alternatives* (2000)

"The Manchurian Candidate" (2002)

Like a Rolling Stone: Bob Dylan at the Crossroads (2005)

AS EDITOR

Stranded (1979)

*Psychotic Reactions and Carburetor Dung: The Work of a
Legendary Critic: Rock 'N' Roll as Literature and Literature as
Rock 'N' Roll* by Lester Bangs (1987)

*The Rose & the Briar:
Death, Love and Liberty in the American Ballad*
(2004, with Sean Wilentz)

THE SHAPE
OF THINGS TO COME

THE SHAPE
OF THINGS TO COME

PROPHECY AND THE AMERICAN VOICE

GREIL MARCUS

FARRAR, STRAUS AND GIROUX / NEW YORK

Farrar, Straus and Giroux
19 Union Square West, New York 10003

Copyright © 2006 by Greil Marcus
All rights reserved
Distributed in Canada by Douglas & McIntyre Ltd.
Printed in the United States of America
First edition, 2006

Library of Congress Cataloging-in-Publication Data
Marcus, Greil.
The shape of things to come : prophecy and the American voice / Greil
Marcus.— 1st ed.
    p.   cm.
Includes index.
ISBN-13: 978-0-374-10438-2 (hardcover : alk. paper)
ISBN-10: 0-374-10438-7 (hardcover : alk. paper)
    1. National characteristics, American. 2. Nationalism—United States.
3. United States—Civilization. 4. Prophecy—Political aspects—United States.
5. Prophecy in literature. 6. Politics in art. 7. Quotations, American. I. Title.

E169.1.M259 2006
973.01'9—dc22

                                                                        2005033139

Designed by Jonathan D. Lippincott

www.fsgbooks.com

            1   3   5   7   9   10   8   6   4   2

Frontispiece: Still from the 1936 film *Things to Come*, from the Wade Williams
Collection, licensed through Corinth Films, Inc.

FOR KATHLEEN MORAN AND SEAN WILENTZ

CONTENTS

PROLOGUE
New York, Washington, D.C., Pennsylvania 3
Massachusetts, Washington, D.C. 19

NEW JERSEY, CALIFORNIA, WASHINGTON, OHIO
Philip Roth and the Lost Republic 41
American Berserk: Bill Pullman's Face 101
American Pastoral: Sheryl Lee as Laura Palmer 147
Crank Prophet Bestride America, Grinning: David Thomas 201

EPILOGUE
Kansas 259

Works Cited 285
Acknowledgments 303
Index 309

PROLOGUE

NEW YORK, WASHINGTON, D.C., PENNSYLVANIA

These are the voices I found when, a few days after terrorists attacked American cities, I was asked to write about what happened. It seemed presumptuous to say anything, and in any case I had nothing to say. I listened instead.

"Where is the building? Did it fall down? Where is it?"
> —Joe Disordo, on the collapse of Two World Trade Center,
> describing his escape from One World Trade Center,
> New York *Times*, 16 September 2001

* * *

Looking down they could see the last convulsions: the lights of the cars were darting through the streets, like animals trapped in a maze, frantically seeking an exit, the bridges were jammed with cars, the approaches to the bridges were veins of massed headlights, glittering bottlenecks stopping all motion, and the desperate screaming of sirens reached faintly to the height of the plane . . .
The plane was above the peaks of the skyscrapers when suddenly, with the abruptness of a shudder, as if the ground had parted to engulf it, the city disappeared from the face of the earth. It took them a moment to realize that the panic had reached the power stations—and that the lights of New York had gone out.   —Ayn Rand, *Atlas Shrugged*, 1957

Everything was absolutely ideal on the day I bombed the Pentagon. The sky was blue. The birds were singing. And the bastards were finally going to get what was coming to them.

I say "I" even though I didn't actually bomb the Pentagon—*we* bombed it, in the sense that Weathermen organized and claimed it . . .
Some details cannot be told. Some friends and comrades have been in prison for decades; others, including Bernadine, spent months and months locked up for refusing to talk or give handwriting samples to federal grand juries. Consequences are real for people, and that's part of this story, too. But the government was dead wrong, and we were right. In our conflict we don't talk; we don't tell. We never confess.

When activists were paraded before grand juries, asked to name names, to humiliate themselves and to participate in destroying the movement, most refused and went to jail rather than say a word. Outside they told the press, I didn't do it, but I dug it. I recall John Brown's strategy over a century ago—he shot all the members of the grand jury investigating his activities in Kansas.   —Bill Ayers, *Fugitive Days*, September 2001

"You don't know where she is?" I asked again. He shrugged again, and I said, "OK." I let the automatic dangle from my hand as I waited for the sound of a jet making its final approach over the motel. "Last chance," I said before the noise got too loud for him to hear. He shrugged again. "You know I'm not going to kill you, don't you?" I said. He shook his head, but his eyes smiled. He might be a piece of shit but Jackson had some balls on him. Either that or he was more frightened of his business associates than he was of me. That was a real mistake on his part. When the landing jet swept over the motel, I leaned down and pumped two rounds into his right foot.
"You didn't have to shoot him twice," Trahearne said.
"Once to get his attention," I said, "and once to let him know I was serious."   —James Crumley, *The Last Good Kiss*, 1978

*   *   *

The terrorist attacks were major atrocities. In scale, they may not reach the level of many others—for example, Clinton's 1998 bombing of the Sudan with no credible pretext, destroying half its pharmaceutical supplies and killing unknown numbers of people.
            —Noam Chomsky, 11 September 2001

Over the years since the seizure of the American embassy in Tehran in 1979, the [American] public has become tolerably familiar with the idea that there are Middle Easterners of various shades and stripes who do not like them . . .

With cell phones still bleeping piteously from under the rubble, it probably seems indecent to most people to ask if the United States has ever done anything to attract such awful hatred.

—Christopher Hitchens, *Guardian* (London), 13 September 2001

What we saw on Tuesday, terrible as it is, could be minuscule if, in fact, God continues to lift the curtain and allow the enemies of America to give us probably what we deserve . . . The abortionists have got to bear some burden for this because God will not be mocked. And when we destroy forty million little innocent babies, we make God mad. I really believe that the pagans, the abortionists, the feminists, and the gays and the lesbians who are actively trying to make that an alternative lifestyle, the A.C.L.U., People for the American Way, all of them who have tried to secularize America, I point the finger in their face and say, "You helped this happen."

—The Reverend Jerry Falwell, *The 700 Club*, 13 September 2001

The responsibility for violence lies with those who perpetrate it.

—Salman Rushdie, *In Good Faith*, 1990

* * *

The water was rising, got up in my bed
Lord, the water was rolling, got up to my bed
I thought I would take a trip, Lord, out on the days I slept.

—Charley Patton, "High Water Everywhere Part II," 1929

I was stranded in Chicago until late last night. On the runway in Newark on Monday at 8 a.m.—that was OK by one day; on the runway at O'Hare on Tuesday at 8.30—that wasn't so great. The airport shut down, and we were left to make our way into a chaotic Chicago of semi-evacuation. After three days and five plane reservations cancelled, I finally found a car and drove home. Eight hundred miles of flags, licenses from everywhere and bumper stickers like MY PRESIDENT IS CHARLTON HESTON and HOW'S MY DRIVING / DIAL 1-800-EAT-SHIT. With my finger on the pulse of the nation, I pulled in about 10 p.m.

—Hal Foster, Princeton, New Jersey, e-mail, 15 September 2001

For the first time in America, except during the Civil War and the World War, people were afraid to say whatever came to their tongues. On the streets, on trains, at theaters, men looked about to see who might be listening before they dared so much as say there was a drought in the West, for someone might suppose they were blaming the drought on the Chief! . . .

Every moment everyone felt fear, nameless and omnipresent. They were as jumpy as men in a plague district. Any sudden sound, any unexplained footstep, any unfamiliar script on an envelope, made them startle; and for months they never felt secure enough to let themselves go, in complete sleep.   —Sinclair Lewis, *It Can't Happen Here*, 1935

Gloom and sadness and bereavement just hang in the air. My local firemen were killed, and the whole area is plastered with missing-people flyers: someone's little daughter who had accompanied her mother to work, endless husbands and wives and daughters and sons and best friends; destroyed people.   —Emily Marcus, Charles Street and Greenwich Avenue,
Manhattan, e-mail, 15 September 2001

High water rising, rising night and day
All the gold and silver are being stolen away
Big Joe Turner looking east and west from the dark room of his mind
He made it to Kansas City, Twelfth Street and Vine
Nothing standing there.
            —Bob Dylan, "High Water (For Charley Patton)," September 2001

*   *   *

"The ship? Great God, where is the ship?"
            —Herman Melville, *Moby-Dick*, 1851

The Barking Dog

America is a place and a story, made up of exuberance and suspicion, crime and liberation, lynch mobs and escapes; its greatest testaments are made of portents and warnings, Biblical allusions that lose all their certainties in American air. "A dog, a dog," as David Lynch wrote in a song called "Pink Western Range," "barking like Robert Johnson."

The story of America as told from the beginning is one of self-invention and nationhood, and before and after the formal founding of the nation, the template, in its simplest, starkest terms, came in the voice of God from the Book of Amos, calling out to the Children of Israel: "You only have I known of all the families of the earth; therefore I will punish you for all your iniquities." From John Winthrop in 1630, with "A Modell of Christian Charity," describing the mission of the Puritans of the Massachusetts Bay Company, to Abraham Lincoln in 1865, delivering his Second Inaugural Address, to Martin Luther King, Jr., ninety-eight years later, speaking on the steps of the Lincoln Memorial, America has told itself that story. Whether America has heard itself in these prophetic voices—voices that were raised to keep faith with the past, or with the future to which the past committed their present—is another question.

The Children of Israel made a covenant with God, to keep his commandments, obey his rules, and follow the path of righteousness; the covenant and nothing else made them a nation. The promises they made were not made to be broken; because one people and no other had made a covenant with God, the stakes were much higher. The promises were made to be betrayed, which meant that when one betrayed the promise, one betrayed God. In the Israel of Isaiah and Jeremiah, as the land fell into misery and sin, prophets stepped forward to speak in God's name, to warn the people that as in their covenant they had been promised God's greatest blessings, should they betray their covenant they would suffer the greatest torments; as they had offered themselves to his judgment, so they would be judged. America began as a reenactment of this drama, Amos's words echoing over Fitzgerald's phylogenetic American memory of "a fresh, green breast of the new world."

The Puritans carried the sense of themselves as God's people to America as they found it; that sense, armed, is what is called American exceptionalism. It re-creates the nation as a voice of power and self-righteousness, speaking to itself in a message broadcast to the whole world. This is an original and fundamental part of American identity; there is no American identity without it, which is also to say there is no American identity without a sense of portent and doom. This is the other side of the story: the urge of the nation, in the shape of a certain kind of American hero, to pass judgment on itself. Israel had the comfort of knowing that should it betray its covenant, God would be the judge; in America, a covenant a few people once made with themselves, a covenant the past made with the future and that every present maintains with both the future and the past, passing that judgment on America is everyone's burden and liberation. It's what it means to be a citizen; all of citizenship, all taxes and freedoms, flows from that obligation. To be obliged to judge one's country is also to have the right to do it.

This story, once public and part of common discourse, something to fight over in flights of gorgeous rhetoric and blunt plain speech, has long since become spectral; it is now cryptic. To the degree that it is worth the telling, it is a story told more in art than in politics, even if it is at the heart of our politics—our ongoing struggle to define what the nation is and what it is for. In the nineteenth century, along with Melville and Hawthorne, Emerson and Harriet Beecher Stowe, Frederick Douglass and Edgar Allan Poe, politicians and preachers asked if the country understood the nature of its covenant. They asked if the country understood the price that would be paid if the covenant were to be broken, or the price to be paid if the fact that the covenant had already been broken, a fact buried under generations of patriotic speeches and prayers, proved to be impossible to hide.

The Jews Are Not the Only People
Who Built the Tombs of the Prophets

"At what point shall we expect the approach of danger?" Abraham Lincoln asked the Young Men's Lyceum of Springfield, Illinois, early in 1838. He was just short of twenty-nine, a first-term representative in the state legislature; he was addressing a self-improvement society.

Shall we expect some transatlantic military giant, to step the ocean, and crush us at a blow? Never! All the armies of Europe, Asia and Africa combined, with all the treasure of the earth (our own excepted) in their military chest; with a Buonaparte for a commander, could not by force, take a drink from the Ohio, or make a track on the Blue Ridge, in a trial of a thousand years.

He went back to his question: "At what point then is the approach of danger to be expected? I answer, if it ever reach us, it must spring up amongst us. It cannot come from abroad. If destruction be our lot, we must ourselves be its author and finisher. As a nation of freemen, we must live through all time, or die by suicide."

From long before Lincoln's time, up to our own and certainly past it, pious and self-promoting denunciations of the corruptions breeding within the republic have been and will be part of the republic's speech: *Unless we rid ourselves of this stain, those parasites, this perversion, these impostors of virtue who claim to speak in our name*—then doom, goes the litany, and deservedly so. The old story—and the heart of what Lincoln was to talk about that night. He was right, as anyone is right when he or she raises this flag. But finally, after more than a century and a half, during which the United States became a world power, and then the most powerful nation in the world, he was proven wrong.

"U.S. Attacked," read the headline in the New York *Times* on 12 September 2001, and it was a remarkable choice of words. It was no matter that the attackers were not Lincoln's army of Europe, Asia, or Africa, but a mere nineteen Muslim terrorists directed from a mountain retreat in Afghanistan. The writer understood that a brilliantly planned conspiracy, an almost perfectly executed, astonishingly spectacular assault, the hijacking and then smashing of planes into the two towers of the World Trade Center in New York, a third into the Pentagon, with the last plane, headed for the Capitol, brought down in Pennsylvania by its passengers after they learned what had already happened, was first of all symbolic. The writer understood that the deaths of thousands of people going about their business, whatever that might be, were necessary to validate the symbolism, and that the intent of the perpetrators was to instantly reveal mere buildings as representative of the country, and thus symbolically enact the destruction of the nation itself. More starkly, more truthfully than any of those who over the next days and weeks gave speeches, wrote essays, or delivered sermons, whoever composed the headline captured all this as if in a two-word poem.

More than any other place on earth, America can be attacked through its symbols because it is made up. It is a construct, an idea, and as from the beginning to this day it is still seeking to construct, to shape, whoever finds himself or herself on its ground. The nation exists as power, but its only legitimacy is found in a few pieces of paper. Take away the Declaration of Independence and the Constitution, and perhaps various public speeches that lie behind those documents or pass them on, and as a nation you have little more than a collection of buildings and people who have no special reason to speak to each other, and nothing to say.

If the nation is a construct, though, as it was made up it can be unmade; the September terrorists may have understood that. As a construct, America exists by means of its symbols, and if those symbols are destroyed—destroy one, destroy them all, the American way, buy one, get one free—the idea is suddenly exposed as nothing more than that. A few agreements made more than two centuries ago make up the contract that binds all Americans to each other and to the nation as such, which is to say they are all that binds them, that they are all the nation is. The notion that people can validate themselves through a few words denying tyranny, affirming equality, and insisting that any individual has rights no power can grant or take away—what we call freedom—is itself as much a symbol as it is a way of life, and so it too can be attacked as a symbol. It's a crude, backward reading—*If your power can be denied so terribly and so swiftly, what is the power of your idea?*—though not so far from our own primitive, backward translation: *Behold our power, tremble before our idea.* In their emptiness, both versions make plain how unlikely and odd the idea is.

The idea is that of a country inventing itself, staging the old play about a chosen people and their covenant with their god—but as the country took shape and announced itself as a nation, the ground shifted. America became a country that was a nation because it had made a covenant with itself. It made certain promises about who its citizens might be, how they might live, and for what purposes. Though the blessings of God were called upon, and intimations of his judgment summoned, it was never about God. If the country betrayed its promises, it would betray itself; each citizen would find himself or herself betrayed by every other.

The promises made in the Declaration of Independence and the Constitution—the promise that all would find themselves free to say what they had to say, the guarantee of equal justice under law, that governments were formed to respect and protect those rights, that citizens owed governments no respect if they did not—were so great that their betrayal was part of the promise. "We're living in this non-fiction culture, we're living in a world that comforts itself with what we believe to be fact," the novelist A. M. Homes said to an interviewer in 2004. "And yet, the history of *this country*, the best *parts* of its history, from its *founding* to its best political campaigns, and so on, we built on *fantasy*—and on promise, and on hope, on an ideal of something rather than on something we could prove." The betrayal of that ideal became the national drama, the engine of American history, from the day the documents were promulgated—the discovery that the promises one had been made were false, the attempt to make them true, battles over slavery and suffrage, property and speech, for all time. As it was inevitable that the promises the nation had made would be betrayed, it was inevitable that America would produce prophetic figures of its own.

They were not there to predict the future any more than the Old Testament prophets were. Predicting the future is soothsaying; prophecy has more to do with the past than the future. America's prophets prophesy one thing: as God once judged the Children of Israel, America has to judge itself. It's a coincidence that *"Love and Theft,"* the album that carried Bob Dylan's song

"High Water," was released on 11 September 2001; albums are released on Tuesdays, and this one could just as well have appeared
on September 4 or September 18. But the mood of the song, the
way it was sung, the words that made up fragments of a story that
remained incomplete—a disaster, people fleeing for their lives,
others seizing on the chance to change their names, make a quick
buck, or settle old scores—were not a coincidence. America makes
its promises and betrays them with great events and muttered
curses, with heroic poses and tiny gestures; its judgments on itself
are sometimes shouted and inescapable, sometimes will-o'-the-
wisp and almost silent.

Before Lincoln all of this was part of political speech. All sorts of
public actors affirmed the American covenant, its promise and its
betrayal; at their best, as with Douglass in his oration "What to the
Slave Is Your Fourth of July?," they explored the betrayal as a drama-
tization of the promise. "Need I tell you that the Jews are not the
only people who built the tombs of the prophets?" Douglass said to
the Rochester Ladies' Anti-slavery Society on 5 July 1852, speaking
both of "your nation" and of "my fellow citizens"—even "Fellow citizens!" "Washington could not die till he had broken the chains of his
slaves. Yet his monument is built up by the price of human blood."
"We need the storm, the whirlwind, and the earthquake," he said of
what it would take to rid the nation of its hypocrisies. "What, to the
American slave, is your 4th of July? I answer: a day that reveals to
him, more than all other days in the year, the gross injustice and cruelty to which he is the constant victim. To him, your celebration is a
sham; your boasted liberty, an unholy license; your national greatness, swelling vanity; your sounds of rejoicing are empty and heart-
less; your denunciations of tyrants, brass fronted impudence." He
called down Isaiah, speaking the word of God:

"Bring no more vain ablations; incense is an abomination unto me; the new
moons and Sabbaths, the calling of assemblies, I cannot away with; it is iniquity, even the solemn meeting. Your new moons and your appointed feasts
my soul hateth. They are a trouble to me; I am weary to bear them; and

when ye spread forth your hands I will hide mine eyes from you. Yea! When ye make many prayers, I will not hear. Your hands are full of blood; cease to do evil, learn to do well; seek judgment."

"Fifty-three years ago, the Fourth of July was a proud day for our country," the abolitionist William Lloyd Garrison said on 4 July 1829. "It clearly and accurately defined the rights of man; it made no vulgar alterations in the established usages of society; it presented a revelation adapted to the common sense of mankind . . . it gave an impulse to the heart of the world, which yet thrills to its extremities." But slavery and "the law and the prophets" made it all a mockery, he said: "Before God I must say that such a glaring contradiction as exists between our creed and practice the annals of six thousand years cannot parallel." He and his audience had "the work" before them, he said; even if "generations of blacks . . . go down to the grave, manacled and lacerated, without a hope for their children . . . victory will be obtained, worth the desperate struggle of a thousand years."

Or, if defeat follow, woe to the safety of this people! The nation will be shaken as if by a mighty earthquake. A cry of horror, a cry of revenge, will go up to heaven in the darkness of midnight, and re-echo from every cloud. Blood will flow like water . . . The terrible judgments of an incensed God will complete the catastrophe of republican America.

"I tremble for my country," Jefferson famously said in *Notes on the State of Virginia* in 1781, in words chiseled on the walls of the Jefferson Memorial, "when I reflect that God is just, that his justice cannot sleep forever." George Mason wrote the Virginia Declaration of Rights, which Jefferson drew on for the Declaration of Independence. "The laws of impartial Providence," Mason wrote in 1774 to the Virginia legislature on the question of slavery, "may avenge our injustice upon our posterity."

After Lincoln—because, one can imagine, he finally went too far, rendering judgment in words so violent and unforgiving it is sometimes hard to credit that they survive at all, let alone that they remain chiseled in huge letters on an inside wall of a giant monument, where they sit, to be read and considered, to frighten or inspire, or gazed at as if they were no more than a verbal statue and just as mute—few politicians or preachers have dared to suggest that the nation was made to judge itself in a court the country would have to convene over and over again. "If we fail to oppose an evil as obvious as torture—it is an evil and it is obvious it is wrong—then as President Thomas Jefferson said, I will 'tremble for my country when I reflect that God is just,'" Harry Reid of Nevada said on the floor of the Senate on 3 February 2005, the day the Senate confirmed Alberto Gonzales, who as White House counsel had advised on the permissibility of torture as the policy of the nation, as attorney general of the United States. There was no reflection on what Reid said; what he said was ignored, and the language in which he said what he said was taken as mere literary allusion, probably dug up by some eager-beaver intern from Elko or Virginia City, the furthest thing from an idea, or even an echo. Since Lincoln, the drama in which the country judges itself, asks itself what it really is, what it is for, measures the promise by its betrayal and the betrayal by the promise, has been played out most intensely in art: in speech and acts that begin with a single citizen—a single imaginary citizen, a character made up by a novelist, a singer, a filmmaker, a performer—saying what he or she has to say, as if there are others attending to those acts and speech, even though there may be none. "I claim my birthright!" Allen Ginsberg said in his 1966 Vietnam War poem "Wichita Vortex Sutra," speaking into a tape recorder in the back of a Volkswagen bus in Kansas, dead center in the U.S.A.: "A lone man talking to myself, no house in the brown vastness to hear / imagining the throng of Selves / that make this nation one body of Prophecy." This book is an attempt to travel through that throng of selves, to listen to what they say— and as much to attend to how they say what they say, to attend to a conversation of gestures, exclamations, whispers, damns and praises and jokes. Out of a throng of selves, what is one body of prophecy? Before it is anything else it is a single American, claiming his or her birthright, as a single body standing in, if only for a moment, for all other Americans. People are out there; someone has to hear. And then what? Then, if the chord is struck truly, "the throng of Selves / that make this nation one body of Prophecy" appears.

For years now, since perhaps the end of the first Bush presidency, when Bill Clinton's election—or the prospect that twelve years of rule by those who never admitted to doubt, for whom American promises were catchphrases and betrayals were always those of someone else, might be ending—gave many people a kind of breathing space, where they could discover that the country was still daring them to act out the country's drama for themselves, this throng of selves has been assembling itself. It leans toward a void: the artist's sense that America must judge itself, that it can describe itself only by judging itself, that it not only admits to but revels in the instability of a place made up out of an idea, that it revels in its own urge toward self-destruction. The stories I will try to follow are from this time, but my bet is that they are not time-bound; again and again, shadowed by the prophetic speeches of a few ancestors, of recent memory or barely known at all, they call up the whole expanse of the country's history, its struggle to tell its story.

These stories can be found in work as self-consciously weighty as the novels Philip Roth published from 1997 to 2004, from *American Pastoral* to *The Plot Against America*, or in efforts as weightless as the facial expressions of the B-movie actress Sheryl Lee—a few seconds on the screen forming the vortex of a play about self-abasement and shame that only the vortex reveals to have been under way at all. They are present in the blocked gestures of the actor Bill Pullman, which together make a picture of a country that has used itself up. They can be found in the country singer Martina McBride's 1994 single "Independence Day" or in the flailing, frightening songs made in the early 1990s by the two-woman punk band Heavens to Betsy. Artists who work as they do don't trumpet betrayals or warn of danger; they sense the presence of such things, and seek them in their roles like moles in the ground. More like Roth—in his fashioning of an America where a settled landscape of virtue and possibility changes back into a frontier of temptation and ruin—others feel for the role of prophet as such; these are the people who can imagine that they actually do embody the nation and, with the proper disguises, that they can speak for it. There is Ginsberg for one, trying desperately to burn off whatever irony his hipster's credentials allow him, speaking in as unimpressed a tone as he can manage without forgetting his post as keeper of the country's laughter and its screams. For another there is the singer and bandleader David Thomas, performing as a buffoon—because the throng of selves, no matter how much it might make one body of prophecy, is also just that, a throng, made up of busy people running in all directions, with no time to stop to sign your petition or take your leaflet or tell you how to get where you're going, and there is something inherently ridiculous in trying to convince the members of the throng that everything they know is wrong, that everything they believe is false. This is, after all, what a prophet does, and it is what the movie director David Lynch does, more heedlessly and more resentfully, with more gaudiness and austerity, than anyone else, here and there more than anything like an evangelist, if one can imagine Elmer Gantry and Aimee Semple McPherson on a joint national revival tour, prefacing their sermons with a screening of their own porn movie.

It is a drama of foreboding. It is first set out, as I will try to set it out here, as an appeal to the community, then to the republic, with all citizens symbolically present, the dead represented by the living, the living taking their legitimacy from the dead, and both standing in for those to follow. Then, as political speakers politely turn their backs or flee in cowardice from the terror the drama places on anyone who dares to face it, the drama is played out in what appear to be smaller theaters, with characters from this or that made-up story now standing for the community, but I think the drama is the same. The country remakes itself again and again by means of the tension between its promises and their betrayal— but a suspicion that one day the country may push its luck too far is what makes the story any kind of drama at all. Everyone I've mentioned, from Lincoln to Sheryl Lee, takes stage directions from D. H. Lawrence: "At the bottom of the American soul was always a dark suspense."

MASSACHUSETTS, WASHINGTON, D.C.

Hear this word that the Lord hath spoken against you, O children of Israel, against the whole family which I brought up from the land of Egypt, saying, You only have I known of all the families of the earth; therefore I will punish you for all your iniquities . . . Shall a trumpet be blown in the city, and the people not be afraid? Shall there be evil in a city, and the Lord hath not done it? Surely the Lord God will do nothing but, he revealeth his secret unto his servants the prophets. The lion hath roared, who will not fear? The Lord God hath spoken, who can but prophesy?

Through three public speeches, from Winthrop, Lincoln, and King, we can hear the prophet Amos's voice taken up again and again. A chain can be made—a golden chain, for the heat of vision in each address, but also an iron chain, because in each case there is an appeal to an absolute: the prophet speaks for nothing else. The American blessing or curse—the terror or embrace that is found as a reward—is to live out that absolute, or live in its shadow.

The three speeches are classics, touchstones, quoted or anthologized everywhere. Winthrop's "A Modell of Christian Charity" was a lay sermon, dated 1630, delivered, it is usually said, in the middle of the Atlantic Ocean, on the ship *Arbella*, to the members of the Massachusetts Bay Company. It was a sermon about the founding they were about to enact—though some words in the text suggest that the sermon was delivered before the Puritans left England ("the times of persecution here in England"), or after they arrived in the New World ("whatsoever we did or ought to have done when we lived in England"). It is possible it was never delivered at all. "Written on Boarde the Arrabella, On the Attlantick Ocean. By the Honorable John Winthrop Esquire. In His passage, (with the great Company of Religious people, of which Christian Tribes he was the Brave Leader and famous Governor;) from the Island of Great Brittaine, to New-England in the North America," the manuscript reads, but the fanfare aside there is no mention in Winthrop's diary of his ever presenting the speech. It may be that as a public address Winthrop's words entered history as a private document, a fantasy of a public event (*How touched they were to hear me that day!*), a speech that created its public out of readers—or whose public was created only by historians, pointing back to an audience that had never been—and then only as the years went on, and the fable of the sermon's supposed event replaced the fact of its life in a drawer.*

Lincoln's Second Inaugural was delivered two hundred and thirty-five years later, as Lincoln stood before the Capitol in Washington, D.C. Lincoln spoke for perhaps six minutes—as his assassin, carrying a knife that, in an early version of the conspiracy to destroy the national government, he planned to use that day, watched from just above, in the best seats: as a dashing, handsome actor, John Wilkes Booth got his ticket from the daughter of a Republican senator. The challenge in these two addresses is to let them breathe—to isolate their familiar phrases until they cease to ring like chisels on stone, until they're more music than static, more unlikely than cliché.

---

*Someone's drawer. The only surviving manuscript copy of the sermon is not in Winthrop's hand, though it was likely copied by his son Forth. There is only one mention of the speech by Winthrop's contemporaries in letters, diaries, or addresses and treatises of their own. Bizarrely, it seems not to have been published until 1838—closer to our time than to Winthrop's. Or just in time, perhaps, for Lincoln to come across it.

King's Address to the March on Washington was delivered ninety-eight years after Lincoln spoke—as King, in his own words, stood in Lincoln's "symbolic shadow," before the Lincoln Memorial, with the entire text of the Second Inaugural featured on an inside wall. King spoke to the three hundred thousand people gathered before him and to the nation at large: "Even ABC," Richard Powers wrote in 2003, in his novel *The Time of Our Singing*, "cuts away from its scheduled soap operas to give the nation its first full look at itself." All three networks—in 1963, television as such—carried King's speech as he spoke, as I watched, as you may have watched, as no doubt his assassin watched. The novelist John Kaye imagined the scene in 1997, in *Stars Screaming*: it's 1969, in a bar in Los Angeles called the Stardust Lounge, where a would-be screenwriter named John Burk kills his afternoons. "Jesus, you better get your ass out there," says Miles, the bartender, after Burk tells him his wife has just miscarried. "As soon as I finish this beer," Burk says. "If that's okay with you."

Miles shrugged. If thirty years behind the bar had taught him anything, it was when to back off if he sensed that a conversation with a customer was beginning to sound peculiar. Burk usually acted like a normal guy, but then so did James Earl Ray, a regular for a while at the Stardust Lounge. Except to order a drink ("Another tall screw, bub"), Ray never uttered a word to anyone, and the only time he left his stool was to play "Tennessee Waltz" on the jukebox. But one day he didn't show up, and the next time Miles saw him, James Earl Ray's ice-cold eyes were staring down from the television screen above the bar. "Can you believe it?" someone said at the time. "All those hours he was sittin' here, that crazy cracker was workin' out how he was gonna bag that jig."

Like those of Winthrop and Lincoln, King's speech too has become part of the American canon, but less as a prophecy, as an attempt to seize the truth and tell it, than as a sort of cultural legend, a rhetorical Woodstock. It is part of the canon of the sound bite, a cliché of a cliché. But that's not all it is. At the end it is fully musical, and the challenge is only to re-create the context of the speech, to present history as the present and the present as its own history, and let the music call its own tune.

The New Jerusalem

What John Winthrop and his fellow members of the Massachusetts Bay Company had set out to found was nothing so grand or permanent as a country. They meant to found a community, which might endure only so long as it took for that community to shine forth, in Winthrop's phrase, as a "model" for the rest of the world: a model of God's truth, or a model of his servants' failure to realize his truth. The Puritans meant to found something smaller and far greater than any mere country: their New Jerusalem would light the world and it would last forever, at least until the last trump sounded, or it would not be at all.

There is an illustration from an edition of *Gulliver's Travels*— published in Germany in 1910—that captures the quest. On a rocky shore, a man of the eighteenth century, dressed in a long coat and leggings, holds a spyglass to his eye. Resting on a solid, circular platform, floating in the sky like a flying saucer (like the mothership in *Independence Day*, the 1996 blockbuster where Bill Pullman plays a president fighting off alien destroyers), is a whole city, with walls and towers and brick buildings. At the edge of the city platform there is a crowd; one man in the crowd points to the lone man with the glass.

In calm and direct language that at once affirmed the authority of the speaker and the speaker's respect for his listeners, Winthrop spoke of salvation and delight, of ruin and damnation. He described the free founding of a society under the greatest authority: of their own free will, Winthrop told the men and women gathered before him, they had joined in a covenant with God and with themselves to create a new society according to God's laws. The first of these laws was that of inequality, of "the variety and differance of the Creatures": the men and women who were to make up the new society. According to God's wisdom, Winthrop said, "in all times some must be rich some poore, some highe and eminent in power and dignitie; others meane and in subjeccion." There were three reasons for this—as the Berkeley professor John Schaar used to say when he lectured on the Puritans, for the Puritans there were *always* three reasons—and it was the third reason that went to the heart of the new town, or the new world, that the Puritans meant to found. God had created difference, Winthrop said, "That every man might have need of other, and from hence they might be all knitt more nearly together in the Bond of brotherly affeccion." The glory of honor or wealth was not that of whoever was wealthy, or judged a figure of honor. Wealth and honor belonged only to God; they were present or absent among men and women for the common good, so that no individual could stand except as part of a whole: "for it is a true rule that perticuler estates cannott subsist in the ruine of the publique."

If the members of the Puritan community were to seek "greate things," Winthrop said in words that would echo into the preamble of the Constitution—if the members of the community were to turn away from one another and seek "greate things for our selves and our posterity, the Lord will surely break out in wrathe against us be revenged of such a perjured people and make us knowe the price of the breache of such a Covenant . . . so he tells the people of Israell, you onely have I known of all the families of the Earthe therefore I will punish you for your Trangressions." The purpose of the community was not to be the piling up of goods or the achieve-ment of renown; it was the spreading of God's laws, by means of their embodiment, "in that Condicion comparable to the exercise of mutuall love": proof that "This love among Christians is a reall thing not Imaginarie." The risk was that they would sink God's laws by embodying their violation—and as Winthrop pauses, you can easily see him in the midst of the Atlantic crossing, warning against the temptations of solid ground.

He was speaking in words that today sound so strange they can barely be fitted into American political speech at all. In almost all times from Winthrop's to ours his words seem to come from some other country. "Now the onely way to avoyde this shipwracke," Winthrop said, the shipwreck after which each member of the community would pillage what was left and set himself or herself against whoever had less or more, "is to followe the Counsell of Micah":

to doe Justly, to love mercy, to walke humbly with our God, for this end, wee must be knitt together in this worke as one man, wee must entertaine each other in brotherly Affeccion, wee must be willing to abridge our selves of our superfluities, for the supply of others necessities, wee must uphold a familiar Commerce together in all meekeness, gentlenes, patience and liberallity, wee must delight in eache other, make others Condicions our owne rejoyce together, mourne together, labour, and suffer together, allwayes haveing before our eyes our Commission and Community in the worke, our Community as members of the same body.

If they kept faith with each other, Winthrop said, "the Lord will be our God and delight to dwell among us, as his owne people and will commaund a blessing upon us in all our wayes . . . we shall finde that the God of Israell is among us." The tale of their endeavor would be on the lips of the world.

But should they fail the same would be true. Winthrop said this in the words that, today, are all that has really come down from him, the only phrase of his that the country has kept.

For wee must Consider that wee shall be as a Citty upon a Hill, the eies of all people are uppon us; soe that if we shall deale falsely with our god in this worke wee have undertaken and soe cause him to withdrawe his present help from us, wee shall be made a story and a by-word through the world, wee shall open the mouthes of enemies to speake evill of the wayes of god and all professours for Gods sake; wee shall shame the faces of many of gods worthy servants, and cause theire prayers to be turned into Cursses upon us till wee be consumed out of the good land whether wee are goeing.

"A city on a hill" was the image so often evoked by Ronald Reagan, during his presidency, as a sign of American triumphalism, of America as God's country, of "You only have I known of all the families of the earth." But as with Amos, the words were found and placed in the American language as a warning, as a prophecy of self-betrayal. The depth of the possible betrayal—"consumed out of the good land," not driven from it, not abandoning it, but the replacement of God by a demon who, as citizens went about their work or leisure, would suddenly devour them—measures the breadth of the possible achievement.

As a warning, Winthrop's shipboard address named the American endeavor as less the establishment of a country than a story to be told. As a warning, he placed the wish and the need for utopia in the American story. Without it—without the *anything is possible* in Winthrop's sermon, the greatest truth, the worst horror—there is really no American history.

The City of Blood

By the time Lincoln took up the tale, the utopia, the city on a hill, had been stood on its head. A community founded on the rock of inequality had changed into a slaveholding nation "dedicated to the proposition that all men are created equal." In the United States, utopia was still where history pointed, even if that history was now splitting in half. The Civil War was in its fifth year: "Turned back upon itself to propagate like a virus into the moral system," the historian Robert Cantwell wrote in his memoir "Twigs of Folly." It's the kind of phrase that seeks its subjects, or like a magnet draws them to it.

The nation, caught up for a long moment in the burden of prophecy that runs through the American voice—in the absolute of prophecy, referring always backward and forward to the New Jerusalem somewhere in the past, somewhere in the future—is what turns back: "It is turned back upon itself to propagate like a virus into the moral system, into every gesture and word, out of the very lifeblood of a society constitutionally hung up on its own contradiction, that actual human difference, and the arrangements arising from it, should ever actually bow to a metaphysically perfect idea, or that people laboring under this contradiction should ever cease trying to appear to be what they are not, or be despised for trying, or failing to try."

In other words, "You only have I known of all the families of the earth; therefore I will punish you for all your iniquities." Therefore I will put the instruments of my punishment in your own hands, so that God's work may truly be your own. The metaphysically perfect idea is American democracy; at Gettysburg, in 1863, Lincoln had already raised the question of its demise. The virus is not only slavery, the contradiction of "all men are created equal"—as Frederick Douglass said, the contradiction drowning in blood—but the prophetic voice as such. The virus was carried by whoever held the promise in one hand and the betrayal in the other. That was what Lincoln did, when on 4 March 1865 he took the oath of office for the second time, and stepped forward to deliver his Second Inaugural Address.

As Booth sat above him, other conspirators—all of whom were later convicted in secret, and four of them hanged—gathered in the crowd directly below. Inside the great national ceremony of continuity and renewal, there was a man walking alone at night through a forest as bats flew through the trees. There are many stories that in the last months of his life, Lincoln talked more and more frequently of death—of assassination, of dreaming of himself as a witness to his own body lying in state. Whether the stories are true or not, this day Lincoln returned to the foreboding of the old Puritans.

He spoke of God—but the deism of Jefferson and Madison, and the skepticism of the frontier towns where he grew up, made Lincoln's god at once all-powerful and indistinct. Winthrop's creator-judge had turned into Providence, the "Nature's God" of the Declaration of Independence—the elemental force of moral harmony that would use all means, the death of one or the death of millions, to achieve its goal, or make its point: that there *was* a force of moral harmony in the universe. As Lincoln spoke, it seemed to him that in this moment the United States of America was the agent of that force, or the field on which its imperatives were to be played out.

In 1862, after the defeat of the Union Army at the Battle of Bull Run, Lincoln wrote what came to be known as "Meditation on the Divine Will":

In great contests each party claims to act in accordance with the will of God. Both *may* be, and one *must* be wrong. God cannot be *for*, and *against* the same thing at the same time. In the present civil war it is quite possible that God's purpose is something different from the purpose of either party—and yet the human instrumentalities, working just as they do, are of the best adaptation to effect His purpose. I am almost ready to say this is probably true—that God wills this contest, and wills that it shall not end yet. By his mere quiet power, on the minds of the now contestants, He could have either *saved* or *destroyed* the Union without a human contest. Yet the contest began. And having begun He could give the final victory to either side any day. Yet the contest proceeds.

The naïveté can seem touching—because whatever else this is, it is not the voice of the twentieth century or the years that have followed it. The whole of that exterminating century did not merely appear in the guise of a whirlpool, it was the whirlpool. For the god of the twentieth century, god of the sanctity of each breath and god of the erasure of peoples and nations, maps and bodies, histories and literatures, nothing was easier than to be for and against the same thing at the same time.

In his Second Inaugural, Lincoln edged closer to this god, to this voice, a modern voice that is also an ancient voice—the voice of God in the most blasted deserts of the Old Testament, the voice of a trickster god no more moral than the weather. As sometimes happened when Lincoln spoke—in the most carefully prepared, written-out speeches—passion rose up with lust and fear. As you read one hundred and fifty years later, you can imagine the speaker's face changing, Dr. Jekyll into Mr. Hyde, the worried man into a werewolf, a nineteenth-century rhetorical trick or the rhetorical cadence of late-twentieth-century Washington state punk, something from Nirvana or Sleater-Kinney: the straight, well-built verse, the chorus in flames, the song blowing up in your face. To follow such upheavals, never denying them, Lincoln would answer the spirit that was already receding with a kind of benediction. "With malice toward none; with charity for all," he said immediately in the Second Inaugural as the spirit left him, just as he had begun his dark retelling of the American story and his dark prophecy of its guilt with lines from the New Testament, but as if searching for its one line truest to the spirit not of Jesus but of Yahweh. "I expect [it] to wear as well as—perhaps better than—any thing I have produced; but it is not immediately popular," Lincoln wrote of the speech eleven days later; he was writing a thank-you note. "Men are not flattered by being shown that there has been a difference of purpose between the Almighty and them. To deny it, however, in this case, is to deny that there is a God governing the world. It is a truth which I thought needed to be told." It's that deceptive calm again: a minister's piety, not the piety of a war president, or a sinner—as if the force of moral harmony actually moves with the regular swings of a pendulum, not in a frenzy. For it was something close to a frenzy that Lincoln offered the country, in his high voice, a voice that was never raised, that moved steadily into the whirlwind. I still find it strange that in Washington, D.C., these words are carved in stone; it's easier to imagine them on the wall of an Egyptian tomb yet to be found.

The Almighty has his own purposes. "Woe unto the world because of offenses! for it must needs be that offenses come; but woe to that man by whom the offense cometh!" If we shall suppose that American slavery is one of those offenses which, in the providence of God, must needs come, but which, having continued through His appointed time, He now wills to remove, and that He gives to both North and South, this terrible war, as the woe due to those by whom the offense came, shall we discern therein any departure from those divine attributes which the believers in a Living God always ascribe to Him?

It's a queer hesitation, that pulling back, if that is what it is: not "we believers in a Living God," but "the believers in a Living God," as if to say, *Whoever* they *might be—and God bless them*. For this is only the preamble to a prophecy so deadly and a judgment so un-forgiving that no nation, let alone a nation known by God as God knows no other, could ever accept it, let alone acknowledge what it is: a call for a reenactment, on a national scale, of an Old Testa-ment sacrifice—of a prize sheep, or, thousands of times over in the war Lincoln made, a firstborn son. "Fondly do we hope—fervently do we pray," Lincoln said, the quiet of the verse promising peace before the bleeding fury of the chorus,

that this mighty scourge of war may speedily pass away. Yet, if God wills that it continue, until all the wealth piled by the bond-man's two hundred and fifty years of unrequited toil shall be sunk, and until every drop of blood drawn with the lash, shall be paid by another drawn with the sword, as was said three thousand years ago, so still it must be said "the judgments of the Lord, are true and righteous altogether."

Again, it's Amos who laid the ground: "Woe unto you that desire the day of the Lord! to what end is it for you? the day of the Lord is darkness, and not light."

The Flood

"I hate," God said through Amos, "I despise your feast days, and I will not smell in your solemn assemblies. Though ye offer me burnt offerings and your meat offerings, I will not accept them; neither will I regard the peace offerings of your fat beasts. Take thou away from me the noise of thy songs; for I will not hear the melody of thy viols. But let judgment run down as waters, and righteousness as a mighty stream."

That last sentence was repeated by Martin Luther King, Jr., on 28 August 1963, at the March on Washington for Jobs and Freedom, at that time the greatest mass meeting in the history of the republic. With prayers and songs, speeches and sermons, it was the sunburst day of the Civil Rights movement. "Until judgment rolls down like waters, and righteousness like a mighty stream": as he spoke these words, King knew they meant not a lovely waterfall, but a flood; not the cool waters of God's grace, but a mortal cleansing of a whole people. A prophet speaking an almost-secret language, his cadences in a declension at once thrilling and comforting, each word descending the steps of its phrase in perfect rhythm—this is what's at stake as King speaks. The curse is disguised as a blessing.

Lincoln spoke of a debt to be paid in blood, to be paid in full. King began on the same terms—and he began stiffly, as his orations often began. His lumbering phrases were too carefully polished. His tone was odd. As he spoke, it was as if the audience were missing; the speech called up not the nation before him but a vacuum, as if King were listening most of all for the echo of his own words. "In a sense we've come to our nation's capital to cash a check," King said to the civil rights workers who had driven from the South in old cars and buses, who had for a few days left behind their burned churches and bullet-riddled communal houses. King was bringing the moral system in which the whole country was caught up down to the level of dollars and cents: "When the architects of our republic wrote the magnificent words of the Constitution and the Declaration of Independence," he said to the Hollywood film stars and affluent white college students who had traveled from New York or California on trains and jets, "they were signing a promissory note—to which every American was to fall heir." As Bob Dylan and Joan Baez looked on along with Josephine Baker, the expatriate singer wearing her Free French uniform and this day the only woman to address the crowd, King went on like that, the metaphor coiled so tightly it made no room for passion, let alone poetry. He was the face and the voice of the movement to renew the nation by leading it to finally keep the promises it had broken.* The whole of the day had come to rest on his shoulders. Nevertheless the day was slipping away from him. King had been told he would be cut off if his speech went a moment over seven minutes, and the speech he wrote was seven minutes long. But he had already used up more than half of his time. "America has given the Negro people a bad check," he concluded, "a check which has come back marked, 'Insufficient Funds.'" The crowd cheered the line, but there was no joy in the cheer.

But as the speech went on, it began to wander back to phrases and cadences King had worked out over the previous year, most crucially at a huge freedom rally in Detroit two months before. There, he announced that he had a dream—a dream that quickly exploded, so that in minutes King was speaking of himself as the romantic egomaniac his critics in the Civil Rights movement said he was: *"De Lawd."* "I-I-I-I-I will go out," he thundered, his voice shaking and shuddering, *"I-I-I-I-I* will go out and carve a tunnel of

---

*The true message of the Civil Rights movement, wrote Mario Savio in 1965, with a fine sense of paradox, was "freedom for all Americans, not just for Negroes!" In 1964 Savio was one of many white northern college students to take part in "Freedom Summer," working in Mississippi against the disenfranchisement of black Americans; in the fall of that year, as a philosophy student at the University of California at Berkeley, he became a leader of the Free Speech Movement, formed to contest a University ban on political advocacy on campus. "The two battlefields may seem quite different to some observers, but this is not the case," Savio said of Mississippi and Berkeley on 2 December 1964, in the midst of the nearly one thousand fellow students who had occupied the University administration building, as they waited for police to drag them out and place them under arrest. "The same rights are at stake in both places—the right to participate as citizens in democratic society and the right to due process of law . . . The university is the place where people begin seriously to question the conditions of their existence and raise the issue of whether they can be committed to the society they have been born into. After a long period of apathy in the fifties, students have begun not only to question but, having arrived at answers, to act on those answers. This is part of a growing understanding among many people in America that history has not ended, that a better society is possible, and that it is worth dying for."

hope through the mountain of despair." Save for this moment, though, the delivery in Detroit was unsteady. The words died in the air. When King spoke of a dream of a better nation it was just a dream; there was no force in the words. When you listen today you hear a man trying to convince you of something of which he has yet to convince himself. But in Washington, when King began to talk about freedom, about integration—a word America no longer uses—calls began to ring out from the crowd and from those around him. "Tell 'em about the dream, Martin!" the great gospel singer Mahalia Jackson shouted from King's side. Hosannas and affirmations, cries of delight that as one listens now seem physical, no more mediated than the reaction to an electric shock, rose up in waves. In this moment, Winthrop's ancient, forgotten call for a people knit together as one, as members of the same body, was in the words now flowing from King's mouth: "with this faith, we will be able to work together, to pray together, to struggle together, to go to jail together, to stand up for freedom together." Now, that was what the word integration meant.

And so he went on, now in his twelfth minute, unstoppable, pulling phrases back from Detroit and merging them with phrases pulled out of the patriotic air of the day. "All of God's children," he said, "will be able to sing with new meaning, 'My country, 'tis of thee.'" "'From every mountain . . . side,'" he said, now pausing with more musicality than drama even in the middle of his words. "From every mountainside, let freedom ring," goes the last line of the first of the four verses that in 1832 the Reverend Samuel F. Smith put to the tune of "God Save the Queen" and called "America"—the first verse being all of the song that is usually sung, or that anyone needs to know—and as the last three words came out of King's mouth they were no longer from the song. They came after a long pause that made it clear that the words were now his—but also as if the song was, too.

He rushed now. "Let freedom ring and if America is to be a great nation, this must become true. And so let freedom ring—"

and he went off, traveling the country from mountaintop to mountaintop, in the most powerful and beautiful minutes of oration the country has ever known. But as with Lincoln's odd, distanced reference to "the believers in a Living God," King's hesitation, his demurral, is also buried, all but lost in the momentum of the words around it. It's shocking and heretical: "If America is to be a great nation." It is not, he is saying. With its blunt, Biblical fanfare, "We hold these truths," it is a metaphysically perfect idea—or a great impulse, some fundamental human instinct, made into an idea.

In the sound bite that since King's assassination has been most often thrown back at his ghost, King had already said, "I have a dream that my four little children will one day live in a nation where they will not be judged by the color of their skin but by the content of their character"—but this nation, he did not have to say in 1963, is not that nation: not that great nation. For all of its promises, in 1963 the U.S.A. was just another country.

It doesn't seem like just another country as King flies like the bald eagle from one end of the American continent to the other, from the Rockies in Colorado to Stone Mountain in Georgia, in an instant raising images of such strength that each mountain takes the shape of the Liberty Bell and rings out the same tune, each bell cracking one after the other in a crescendo that sounds out the truth that the promise of liberty remains as broken as the promise of liberty remains real. It feels like a miracle, this explosion of rhetoric, these flying words, but the pain they now carry is not what propelled them through the air the day King gave them flight. The pain is that the great nation King prophesied so long ago no more exists today than it did then. America raised itself on the rock of a metaphysically perfect idea, and on that rock it broke into pieces: the nation, not the idea.

"I have a dream that one day every valley shall be exalted, and every hill and mountain shall be made low, the rough places will be made plain, and the crooked places will be made straight, and the glory of the Lord shall be revealed and *alllll* flesh! shall see it together." So said Martin Luther King in his most ecstatic moment, the words from Isaiah 40:4–5 all but rendering him as much spirit as he was flesh. In the moment, the transformation he called for took place. The cracks in the mountains closed up; the bells rang true. That every valley should be exalted and every hill and mountain be made low, that the world should turn upside down and yet all people feel at home there, more at home in the world than they had ever been, seemed, for an instant—for the instant one may still inhabit when the speech sounds from the radio or a loudspeaker on Martin Luther King Day—the inevitable result of the ordinary, uncelebrated work some of the people King was speaking to performed every day. And then the moment passed. A few sound bites were chosen, and shaped to fit a different country from the one King sighted, and the moment was passed into history, as if its life could be snuffed out, just like that.

Any Fool Could See This Coming

It wasn't, though: as with the visions offered by Winthrop and Lincoln, King's persists as utopia and bad conscience. Each speech calls up a public, the whole of the nation, the living and the dead. Each speech judges the nation, and calls on each member to judge it in turn. The speech calls on each citizen to weigh the nation's promises against their betrayal, just as the blues singer Otis Spann did the day King was shot.

"On the fourth of April / In the year nineteen and sixty-eight"— Spann is in a storefront church on Forty-third Street in Chicago, the day James Earl Ray killed Martin Luther King as King stood on the balcony of his room in the Lorraine Motel in Memphis, Tennessee. Sitting at a piano, Spann is playing "Blues for Martin Luther King" and "Hotel Lorraine," both made up on the spot. Outside, up and down the street, the riot, the frenzy of revenge, has already started, even if self-destruction is the only form it can take. Buildings are already burning: "The world was all up in flames," Spann sings. Accompanied only by a drummer, he is bringing the day into focus. He pulls his words out of the air; his piano opens "Hotel Lorraine" with the same unanswerable sense of foreboding he had helped put into play ten years before in Little Walter's unanswerable "Blue and Lonesome." As in that song, the piano strikes back at the verse as if every word it holds is a lie, because if words cannot tell the whole truth, words lie, and words can never tell the whole truth, only sound can do that, sound that is not made by men and women but by Nature's God, sound that is not made but found.

Spann's voice is now desperate, now stoic, now as if he has seen it all before, a hundred times, as if any fool could see this coming. With notes trailing down the keyboard like water down a drain, he traces familiar blues runs with such passionate restraint it's as if the blues came into being in anticipation of the need to answer this event. The music is not a representation, or even a version; it is an event in and of itself, a voice in a building that may be burned to the ground before the day is over. "You know, the last words he said," Spann sings, letting "said" slide almost into silence, then shouting back: "'God knows! I'm going to the Promised Land.'" But the promised land was supposed to be America; King had called it up. Spann had heard him; then he heard the news.

One of the people present as King spoke before the Lincoln Memorial was Marian Anderson. "My God," says a man in Richard Powers's *The Time of Our Singing*, sighting Anderson from his place in the huge crowd. "Oh my God. It is her." "Who?" says his daughter. Her name is Ruth; he's David Strom, a German-Jewish physicist who in the thirties escaped the Nazis for America. Twenty-four years before, on Easter Sunday in 1939, in the same spot, he had met his wife, Delia Daley, a young black woman from Philadelphia. Along with seventy-five thousand others, they had come to hear Anderson sing; she was the greatest voice in the land. "*Who*, Daddy?" "The woman who married your mother and me." In Powers's telling, a new America had come into being that day in 1939; as David Strom and Delia Daley met in that new nation, all the laws were abolished, all the laws were made, and so a wedding took place even before they met; they themselves made that new America.

In Powers's pages, time curves. People are present when they are dead and missing when they are alive. "My brother jumped into his own future," says Joseph Strom, the novel's narrator. He is Ruth's brother, Delia and David's younger son; he's speaking of Jonah Strom, his dead older brother, in his time the most gifted singer of his generation. "He posted the message of 1967 forward to a year when he would no longer be able to read it," Joseph Strom says. "With total clairvoyance, he sang about where we were headed, things he couldn't have known as he sang them, things I wouldn't recognize now except for his explanation waiting for me, telegraphed from an unfinished past."

In 1939, Sol Hurok, Anderson's manager, had determined to present the opera singer as a soloist, in the finest halls; in the nation's capital that was Constitution Hall, owned by the Daughters of the American Revolution. They refused, and not for the irony. "Constitution" Hall, the Daughters of the "American Revolution": they made it a certainty that no black American would appear on their premises. Eleanor Roosevelt resigned from the organization; Harold L. Ickes, the secretary of the interior, arranged for Anderson to perform in front of the Lincoln Memorial instead. Wearing a heavy coat in the chill, she began with "America." "My country 'tis of thee," she sang. "From every mountainside." In Powers's book, Delia Daley stands in the crowd: "A mixed crowd, the first she's ever walked in, American, larger than her country can hope to survive, out to celebrate the centuries-overdue death of *reserved seating*, of *nigger heaven*. Both people are here in abundance, each using the other, each waiting for the sounds that will fill their own patent lack. No one can be barred from this endless ground floor." As Anderson sings, Daley's "lips form the words, and her windpipe mimes the pitches: Every valley, exalted."

A balding man about ten feet away from her, ghost white, with the Cumberland Gap between his two front teeth, perching inside a thin gray suit, starched blue shirt, and tie printed with Washington landmarks, hears her sing aloud what she has only imagined. "Bless you, sister!" the ghost man says. She just bows her head and lets herself be blessed.

"Maybe they could make an America more American than the one the country has for centuries lied to itself about being," Delia and David think, after Anderson has married them, before they are married under the laws of the old nation they were forced to return to, after the concert was over.

In 1963, again under Lincoln's "symbolic shadow," David Strom, now with his daughter, is again present in the crowd as, once again, Anderson steps forward. "The hat is bigger, the dress more colorful, the body weighed down by twenty-four more years," but Anderson is singing "America" as before: "the sound is the same, at its core." But then "America" is passed to King. The words "My country 'tis of thee" roll out of Anderson's mouth and into King's; they roll out of King's mouth, all the way through the crowd. In the crowd, Ruth has fallen asleep standing up; her father shakes her. "You must wake up," he says. "You must hear this. This is history."

She hears a swelling baritone, a voice she has heard before, but never like this. *We also have come to this hallowed spot to remind America of the fierce urgency of now.*

Now: the reason why her father wakes her. But the thought nags at her between the rolling baritone thunder: Her father couldn't have known the words were coming until after he shook her awake. Then she forgets, posting the question to a later her. Something happens in the crowd, some alchemy worked by the sheer force of this voice. The words bend back three full times in staggered echoes. Her father is right: history. Already she cannot separate these words from all the times she'll hear them down the years to come.

———

In 1948 Modjeska Simkins was the secretary of the South Carolina chapter of the NAACP, and a fearsome, castigating orator; even at the very beginnings of the Civil Rights movement she did not allow herself a guarded word; she expected no change in the land other than that which she and a few others might make. One day she wrote notes on the Book of Job—notes for a speech:

FIRE FROM HEAVEN—burned sheep an servants . . . Camels slain servants with swords . . . In this confused, disoriented, suddenly frustrated state, the final blow fell, "THY SONS AND DAUGHTERS WERE EAT- ING AND DRINKING IN THEIR ELDEST BROTHER'S HOUSE, AND A . . . GREAT WIND CAME AND STRUCK THE FOUR CORNERS OF THE HOUSE AND IT FELL UPON THEM AND THEY ARE DEAD . . . Each messenger closed his awful news with the words, 'AND I ONLY AM LEFT ALONE TO TELL THEE.'"

Now, in this book, those who in different ways could take those words as their own credo take over the story. It's a story of two na- tions, one made of inequality and love, the other of equality and separation. There is the nation in which all must be as they must, where no one truly belongs except as a member of the community. There is the nation in which one must be as he or she can, and the community is dissolved by the claims of the individual. In one na- tion, the community grants the freedom of the city to the individ- ual. In the other, the individual flees the community even if he or she remains on its streets. The two nations course through the public speeches that made the public space. Regardless of the ten- sion, as the speeches sound, the public space—as a good, as that place where the nation speaks to itself—is never in doubt. But now in these pages, public speeches will be replaced by solitaries trying to get someone to listen to them. The public space will shrink; sometimes it will disappear. But the solitaries will keep looking for it, as if trying to reconstruct last night's dream while on the run from enemies determined to fence them out at any cost.

NEW JERSEY, CALIFORNIA,
WASHINGTON, OHIO

PHILIP ROTH AND THE LOST REPUBLIC

On 23 May 2005, it's nearly 7:00 a.m. in the twenty-fourth hour of the fourth season of *24*, the unspeakable-terrorist-conspiracy-unfolds-and-must-be-stopped-in-the-course-of-a-single-day cliffhanger on Fox. Air Force One has been shot down, but thanks to Jack Bauer of the Counter Terrorist Unit in Los Angeles—who will meet any hardship, pay any price, bear any burden, and kill whoever needs to be killed to ensure the survival and success of liberty—the detonation of a stolen nuclear warhead over the city has been averted. Incompetent and vain, the vice president, who under the Twenty-fifth Amendment has replaced the disabled president, has called in former president David Palmer to manage the entire situation. Now Palmer, whose whole demeanor as the episode unreels has so resembled that of Bill Clinton you can forget that Palmer is black, has been dismissed.

Palmer and Bauer have worked together, and protected each other, for years. Their trust in each other is absolute. Desperate for information about the nuclear attack that was already under way, Palmer had authorized Bauer to lead an illegal raid on the Chinese consulate in Los Angeles to seize a man for interrogation; in the confusion the Chinese consul was shot by his own men. With the new president crumbling under Chinese threats, Palmer has brokered an agreement to turn Bauer over to the Chinese for trial and certain imprisonment in China. He calls Bauer from Washington, offering only the empty promise that, as a private citizen, he will do everything he can to bring Bauer back to "American soil." "I know you will, Mr. President," Bauer says. But the new president, fearing that under torture Bauer will implicate the government—will implicate *him*—has approved Bauer's death. Palmer calls Bauer again: *The Secret Service agent dispatched to take you into custody is to kill you instead.*

In the CTU headquarters, Bauer tricks the agent into opening fire; with the help of CTU comrades, he fakes his own death and escapes. Leaving the White House through a long, elegant corridor, David Palmer takes what he knows will be Bauer's call. "For all intents and purposes Jack Bauer is dead," Palmer says. "This is probably the last time we'll ever speak."

The face on a Lincoln bust stares over Palmer's shoulder. Unlike the faces of Lincoln that in 1962 appeared throughout *The Manchurian Candidate*—on busts, in paintings, as a lamp, with Lincoln forced, always in deep focus, his eyes clear in their sadness, to helplessly witness a conspiracy to destroy the republic— this face, as it approves Palmer's conspiracy to preserve if not the republic itself at least its honor, is deeply out of focus. It barely registers; maybe it's meant to register subliminally if it registers at all. Palmer closes his cell phone.

As Jack Bauer closes his, he is in a rail yard, hidden between piles of slats. With a bag over his shoulder, he turns his back, puts on dark glasses, and steps out, suddenly back in the 1920s, in the '30s, a bum about to board a train and disappear. It's a romantic image; after so many Depression-era movies, it's even more fated than coded. For all of its romanticism, though, the sting of defeat in the image, its picture of complete isolation, of the citizen who in his own country is also his own ghost, is as hard as it could be. The train will arrive soon enough, if, in 2005, on these tracks somewhere outside of Los Angeles, the trains are still running at all.

A Plain Statement of Purpose

Eight years before, in 1997, Philip Roth embarked on a series of books that would put his long and distinguished career as an American novelist in the shadows. These books would draw a line between what Roth had written before and whatever he might write next; setting out to judge his country, to hold it up for the judgment of others, Roth was caught in the game. He was setting a standard against which his own work, his own good faith as a writer and as a citizen, would be judged.

Beginning with *American Pastoral*, then moving on only a year later with *I Married a Communist*, and continuing in 2000 with *The Human Stain*, Roth took up a patriotic literary project that in the United States had no contemporary match in any field: not in the movies, not in music, certainly not in the work of any other novelist, young or, like Roth, old—old but, in his mid- and late sixties, doing his best and most ambitious work. Only Bob Dylan, in 1997, with *Time Out of Mind*, a state-by-state, city-by-city guided tour of an America that has used itself up and a portrait of an American who has used up his country, even came close to occupying the same territory, and Roth stayed longer.

Look back over the last twenty years: in terms of ambition the task Roth set himself might be comparable, as a plain statement of purpose, only to the totalistic remaking of America announced in November 1994 by Congressman and soon-to-be Speaker of the House Newt Gingrich on the occasion of the routing of the Democratic majorities in the House of Representatives and the Senate by a new, morally rearmed Republican army. The new Republicans, Gingrich declared, were going to redefine what it meant to be American—and to define who was, and who wasn't. With political sympathies that could not be more different, Roth's project in a sense emerged from the wreckage of the Gingrich revolution—with Roth's three books completing their arc just before, under George W. Bush, that revolution began again, this time with no gauntlet thrown down, no threats issuing from the Capitol, but disguised in reassuring rhetoric and folksy language. Roth set out to rediscover what it meant to be American, and to explore what it means both to invent a country and, as a moral citizen who in some essential way embodies the country, to invent oneself—even if that means leaving the country itself behind, and abandoning all those whose blocked ambitions and withered aspirations those who invent themselves represent. They enact Cantwell's curse: the solitary's attempt to keep the American promise betrays America as such.

Zuckerman's Ear

In each book, the brooding presence watching over the terrible stories that unfold is the novelist Nathan Zuckerman, son of Newark, New Jersey, and Roth's longtime literary foil, gone mostly missing since *The Counterlife* in 1987. Now in his sixties, the old sexual adventurer, married and divorced again and again, has been left impotent and incontinent by surgery for prostate cancer. He has never had children; now he doesn't have to think about it. He lives alone on a mountain in the Berkshires. He no longer has adventures. "[I'd] come here when I was sixty to live alone," he says, "by and large apart from people . . . But my seclusion is not the story here. It is not a story in any way . . . I've had my story." But chance encounters—with the brother of a boyhood hero at Zuckerman's forty-fifth high-school reunion in 1995, with a ninety-year-old former high-school English teacher in 1997, with a disgraced professor from nearby Athena College in 1998—bring Zuckerman back into the world. He returns as a listener, as a witness, one who, finally, has to reimagine all the stories he is told—and, because in every case these are stories about the discovery of America as the discovery of American identity, to reimagine the country itself. Like a dime novelist tugging at the coat of Buffalo Bill or Wild Bill Hickok in the 1870s, Zuckerman tracks the great characters Roth has invented—in *American Pastoral*, Seymour "The Swede" Levov,

Newark's Jewish high-school hero of the 1940s; Dawn Levov, his Catholic wife, a former Miss New Jersey; and Merry, their daughter, grown up in the 1960s as a teenage bomber who kills four people in her attempts to end the Vietnam War. In *I Married a Communist*, Ira Ringold, in the late 1940s the star of leftist radio plays as Iron Rinn, professional Abraham Lincoln impersonator and secret Communist Party militant, exposed and banished in the Red hunts of the early '50s; Eve Frame, Ira's wife, once an adored actress in silent pictures, then beloved for her roles on Broadway and the radio ("That woman speaks the King's English like nobody's business," says the father of a teenage Nathan Zuckerman), a cultivated, anti-Semitic Manhattan hostess who began life as Chava Fromkin of Brooklyn; and Murray Ringold, Ira's older brother, the English teacher who in 1955 is himself fired from his job for his refusal to testify before the House Un-American Activities Committee about his nonexistent affiliation with the Communist Party. In *The Human Stain*, the seventy-one-year-old Athena classics professor Coleman Silk, an African-American who has passed as a Jew his entire adult life; the janitor Faunia Farley, Silk's thirty-four-year-old lover; and Faunia's ex-husband, Les Farley, the Vietnam veteran ("Had PTSD. I had what they call post-traumatic stress disorder") who, Zuckerman is certain, killed both Silk and Faunia, running them off the road and into a river, who then spread the rumor that the old professor lost control of his car because his girlfriend's head was in his lap. Is that enough? In the house Roth is building, it's no more than the coats you find hanging in the anteroom.

Once the country was a finished story for Zuckerman; full of himself as a young writer, eager to make his mark, to scar the land, he was happy to close the book on the U.S.A. In Roth's first Zuckerman novel, *The Ghost Writer*, published in 1979, where in the book's 1956 Zuckerman appears as a twenty-three-year-old, one can hear him dismiss the New England he will inhabit four decades later as "the *goyish* wilderness of birds and trees where America began and long ago had ended." To this Zuckerman, America was never interesting: "when Oswald shot Kennedy," all that happened was that "the straitlaced bulwark gave way to the Gargantuan banana republic."

He couldn't see past himself; he wasn't ready for the country. Now, as he recedes into his own smallness, the country looms up like the moon, whole and bright. All of its promises, made to each American in turn, his or hers to betray or fulfill, the country's to break or keep, are brought to bear, and it takes all Zuckerman has to bear to listen to the stories the country tells.

U.S.A.

To find the solid ground that Zuckerman will feel crumbling beneath his feet, Roth takes him back to the idealism of his boyhood. In *American Pastoral*, Zuckerman homes in on some of the finest of all American boys' books, John R. Tunis's series of novels about the Brooklyn Dodgers, and especially the toughest of them, *The Kid from Tomkinsville*. Here the story of the country boy who comes to the city is told again—right up to the point of destruction, in an ending so hard, so heroic, that boys all over America put the book down and tried to make it come out differently. But it's in *The Human Stain* that another book, the true inspiration for Zuckerman's quest, and Roth's overarching story, is named.

It's the summer of 1998, and the specter of Bill Clinton's impeachment, brought on by the carefully orchestrated exposure of his affair with the White House intern Monica Lewinsky, is titillating the nation. It has turned the nation itself into the dirty joke it cannot stop telling itself, even as those bent on driving Clinton from office insist that the only way the nation can cleanse itself is to tell the joke again and again, piling up details of saliva and semen on top of newsbreaks about *Leaves of Grass* and phone sex until finally the man who has done the disgusting things he has done will be left naked in the public square—and, lacking any other way to cover himself, will surely run away. To Zuckerman, the country has returned to its beginnings, as if its history never happened—not as if the story can be begun again from its beginnings, but as if the American story never got out of its first chapter, and never will. It's the Puritans and their witch trials all over again. "A virile, youthful middle-aged president and a brash, smitten twenty-one-year-old employee carrying on in the Oval Office like two teenage kids in a parking lot," Zuckerman says with appreciation, with delight and envy, "revived America's oldest communal passion, historically perhaps its most treacherous and subversive pleasure: the ecstasy of sanctimony." "Dreams of witch-burning and barnstorming in their heads," the novelist Meg Wolitzer wrote in 2005 in *The Position* of a crowd marching on a public library "with torches held aloft," demanding a sex manual be taken off the shelves, as if all Americans lie in bed imagining who they might cast out, already knowing how. It's what Nathaniel Hawthorne—"who, in the 1860s," Zuckerman now proudly notes, "lived not many miles from my door"—called "the persecuting spirit." Zuckerman quotes a real William F. Buckley column: in gilded literary allusion, the deacon of the American right argues that Clinton's proper punishment is not removal from office but castration.

Zuckerman himself dreams "of a mammoth banner, draped dadaistically like a Christo wrapping from one end of the White House to the other and bearing the legend A HUMAN BEING LIVES HERE." "It was the summer in America when the nausea returned," Zuckerman says, "when the joking didn't stop, when the speculation and the theorizing and the hyperbole didn't stop"—as with three young Athena professors ragging obscenely on How the President from Arkansas Met the Girl from Beverly Hills. "If Clinton had fucked her in the ass," says one of the professors, "she might have shut her mouth . . . Had he turned her over in the Oval Office and fucked her in the ass, none of this would have happened." "Still," says one of the others a bit later, after the philosophical implications have been disposed of ("She was totally corrupt and totally innocent . . . The extreme innocence *was* the corruption"—ponder that the next time someone trots out the American-innocence dead horse), "you have to admit that this girl revealed more about America than anybody since Dos Passos. *She* stuck a thermometer up the *country*'s ass. Monica's *U.S.A.*"

It's a signal homage, especially since it's hard to imagine a young professor in 1998 referring so casually to John Dos Passos's once epochal, now mostly forgotten trilogy about America tearing itself apart as it emerges from the nineteenth century as a world colossus, about the murder of an America made of decency and justice ("the old free America," as the poet Kenneth Rexroth once said) by an America made of power and greed ("I can hire one half of the working class to kill the other half," the financier and fixer Jay Gould said in 1886): Dos Passos's novels *The 42nd Parallel*, from 1930, *1919*, from 1932, and *The Big Money*, from 1936, collected as *U.S.A.* in 1938.

U.S.A. opens with a two-page prelude: a movie image, a long tracking shot, a man in a city making his way through the crowds until the streets empty and he seems headed for the river, the harbor, the rail yard, the story of the country written on his back as he fades into the distance:

The young man walks by himself, fast but not fast enough, far but not far enough (faces slide out of sight, talk trails into tattered scraps, footsteps tap fainter in alleys); he must catch the last subway, the streetcar, the bus, run up the gangplanks of all the steamboats, register at all the hotels, work in the cities, answer the wantads, learn the trades, take up the jobs, live in all the boardinghouses, sleep in all the beds. One bed is not enough, one job is not enough, one life is not enough. At night, head swimming with wants, he walks by himself alone.

No job, no woman, no house, no city.

Pulling back from that last shot of Jack Bauer in the Los Angeles rail yard, you can see this figure as Henry Fonda in John Ford's 1940 film *The Grapes of Wrath*, but harder, more beaten, angrier, veteran of all the strikes, victim of all the strikebreakers, someone who gave as good as he got and bears the scars, part Jeffersonian farmer Tom Joad, part drifter mass killer Richard Speck, who in 1966, looking for money to get to New Orleans, broke into a house in Chicago and murdered eight of the nine young female occupants, leaving one alive only because he lost count of how many there were to kill. In a single sentence, Dos Passos takes his unnamed man from the docks in Seattle to Market Street in San Francisco, from a hot summer in Washington, D.C., to the oceanfront in San Diego, from a flophouse in New Orleans to the dank, ugly street that runs under the glittering shops of Michigan Avenue in Chicago, and this is not just Everyman, posing for the cover of *The Masses*. This is the American without a country, because he has yet to find the country he wants—the American trying against all odds to discover his country, the Ishmael, the isolato, his hand raised against every man and every man's hand raised against his.

A Riot of Modernism

"U. S. A. is the slice of a continent," Dos Passos finishes his introduction, making "U.S.A." more an idea, a concept, than a place or a thing, then running a string like somebody reeling in a U.S.A. made of Norman Rockwell paintings of the Pledge of Allegiance and birthday parties and Fourth of July parades and high-school sweethearts in a jalopy and a fireman getting a cat out of a tree. "U. S. A. is a group of holding companies, some aggregations of trade unions," Dos Passos went on flatly, "a set of laws bound in calf, a radio network, a chain of moving picture theatres, a column of stockquotations rubbed out and written in by a Western Union boy on a blackboard, a publiclibrary full of old newspapers and dogeared historybooks with protests scrawled on the margins in pencil. U. S. A. is the world's greatest rivervalley fringed with mountains and hills, U. S. A. is a set of bigmouthed officials with too many bankaccounts. U. S. A. is a lot of men buried in their uniforms in Arlington Cemetery. U. S. A. is the letters at the end of an address when you are away from home. But mostly U. S. A. is the speech of the people."

The sentimentality of the last sentence is typical of *U.S.A.*—a certain failure of nerve in the face of the flatness. It's also why even if decades have passed since you read the book a single page can bring it all flooding back.

Beginning with the beginning of the twentieth century, Dos Passos's *U.S.A.* is the story of the U.S.A. as an enormous upsurge of energy and industry, desire and terror, with the subterranean current of social revolution pushing against the surface of capitalist everyday life, the demands of the republic pulling back against the temptations of empire. The heroic possibility of change, of a new world, of new men and new women—the promise of the American Revolution, among other moments when the world did change, was changed—is dramatized by the fate of the Industrial Workers of the World: the IWW, the Wobblies. It is the anarchist One Big Union, determined to give birth to "a new society in the shell of the old." The same story is everywhere across the fourteen hundred pages of *U.S.A.*—with Americans speaking out against the nation's entry into the First World War or demanding an eight-hour workday or protesting the shooting of strikers as they themselves are shot, beaten, lynched, arrested, deported, sent to prison in mass trials with twenty-year sentences for committing the crime of public speech. "For more than a century this nation has been a world power," William Jennings Bryan said in 1908 in Indianapolis, responding to the notification that, as in 1896 and 1900, the Democratic Party had made him its nominee for president of the United States. His dating may have seemed odd to students of war and diplomacy, but Bryan was not speaking to the likes of Bismarck or Disraeli. He was speaking to Washington and Jefferson as they spoke to Pericles and Cicero. "For ten decades," he said, the U.S.A. "has been the most potent influence in the world."

Not only has it been a world power, but it has done more to shape the politics of the human race than all the other nations of the world combined. Because our Declaration of Independence was promulgated others have been promulgated. Because the patriots of 1776 fought for liberty others have fought for it. Because our Constitution was adopted others have been adopted.

Now, though, Bryan said, the country was faced with the prospect that its place as a world power might mean no more than it meant for any other nation. The nation was on the verge of betraying itself in the embrace of its own power, or in power's embrace. "This nation can do whatever it desires to do," he said frighteningly.

But it must accept responsibility for what it does . . . The young man upon reaching his majority can do what he pleases. He can disregard the teachings of his parents; he can trample upon all that he has been taught to consider sacred; he can disobey the laws of the State, the laws of society and the laws of God. He can stamp failure upon his life and make his very existence a curse to his fellow men, and he can bring his father and mother in sorrow to the grave; but he cannot annul the sentence, "The wages of sin is death."

And so with the nation. It is of age and can do what it pleases; it can spurn the traditions of the past; it can repudiate the principles upon which the nation rests; it can employ force instead of reason; it can substitute might for right; it can conquer weaker people; it can exploit their lands, appropriate their property and kill their people; but it cannot repeal the moral law or escape the punishment decreed for the violation of human rights.

Of course it can, Dos Passos replied two decades later. In *U.S.A.* the Bill of Rights is a children's story, the Constitution a rumor. Power is everything, and for those who own the country, the official story of equality and the pursuit of happiness, freedom, and justice, is no more than a hoax played on the world—a screen behind which those who have made the nation what it is, and know it for what it is, do business.

Nevertheless, in the pages of *U.S.A.* the message that from the first the country sent to the rest of the world is received by itself. You can feel the nation within the nation, the new society within the shell of the old, as a country whose declaration of independence remains to be made and whose constitution remains to be written. The energy of transformation that is the real fuel of the new factories cannot be stopped—and it is this energy, as much a wellspring of liberty as of power, that convinces people the world can be changed, and that they can be, too.

The book is a riot of modernism. Dos Passos sets out to re-create the novel itself, interrupting the thousand pages of his conventional narrative of love and struggle with episodes of "The Camera Eye," snippets that seem to have been taken at random from film libraries and albums of family snapshots; with absurdist, cut-up "Newsreels" taken from movie theaters with dada projectionists (No. 43: "the placards borne by the radicals were taken away from them, their clothing torn and eyes blackened before the service and ex-servicemen had finished with them: 34 Die After Drinking Wood Alcohol / Trains in France May Soon Stop / (GERARD THROWS HIS HAT INTO THE RING) / SUPREME COURT DASHES LAST HOPE OF MOIST MOUTH . . . *America I love you* [a song plays under the headlines] *You're like a sweetheart of mine . . . Just like a little baby / Climbing its mother's knee* / MACHINEGUNS MOW DOWN MOBS IN KNOXVILLE / *America I love you"*). Most memorably the narrative is seized by brittle, sardonic biographies of the celebrated and reviled of the times, among many more Isadora Duncan, Thomas Edison ("In Detroit there was a public library and he read it"), J. P. Morgan, Luther Burbank, Eugene Debs ("*I would not lead you into this promised land if I could, because if I could lead you in, someone else would lead you out*"), Henry Ford, Bryan ("his voice charmed the mortgageridden farmers of the great plains, rang through weatherboarded schoolhouses in the Missouri Valley, was sweet in the ears of small storekeepers hungry for easy credit, melted men's innards like the song of a thrush"), Joe Hill ("forming the structure of the new society within the jails of the old"), Rudolph Valentino, Frederick Taylor ("He never loafed and he'd be damned if anybody else would"), Thorstein Veblen ("He turned up there in the office of the head of the economics department wearing a coonskin cap"), Wilbur and Orville Wright ("taking off again and again all day from a big dune named Kill Devil Hill"): inventors and industrialists, social theorists and political radicals, artists and financiers, scientists and politicians, heroes and villains. The historical and the imagined fight over the book for its own airtime.

The riot of modernism parallels the riot that was modern America. As one of the demonstrators in the 1999 Seattle protests against the World Trade Organization put it, "The WTO are the real anarchists; we're the ones who believe in laws." Dos Passos's America is America at its absolute worst, a racket, a fixed game where the First World War is nothing more than a con to protect the House of Morgan and an excuse to smash revolution, in the U.S.A. and everywhere else. It is America as brute force, monopoly capitalism, official lawlessness. It is America as one great sneer at whoever can't pay: a place, as the critic Charles Taylor wrote of the country in 2005, "where contracting has replaced the social contract." Against all this, the fictional characters passing through Dos Passos's pages, his invented men and women, share one attribute: youth. As they fight for the right, as they fall back, as they surrender, as they don't, they hear the trumpet blowing. *Defeat! Defeat! Defeat!* the book screams again and again—and as such the book is inspiring, elevating, heroic. It's not the last trump. As the clubs pound down and people are shoved into police vans and the dead lie in the streets in the rain, every defeat is somehow a victory: proof that the nobodies, the men walking alone in the cities, the women huddling in rooming houses, the social revolutionaries, are as dangerous as they mean to be. Every defeat is proof that the revolution they are desperate to make—a revolution where miners and loggers, like bankers and generals, have dignity even more than power—is not taking place only in their hearts.

As Though They Had Never Been Born

The genius of the whole sweeping story barely contained by the covers of *U.S.A.*—and it doesn't seem quite real, that this is a mere book, something you can hold in your hands, put down, forget

where you put it—is in the way that Dos Passos, forty-two when
the story was finished, makes the sweep whole. As you read you
may feel as if you are inhabiting the entire country, every state at
once. You may feel that you are inside the skin of every American,
rich and poor, famous and those who (as in the Biblical Apocrypha
quoted by James Agee at the end of *Let Us Now Praise Famous
Men*, his and the photographer Walker Evans's 1941 study of three
Alabama tenant farmers and their families) "are become as though
they had never been born"—even though in *U.S.A.* there are really
no black Americans, no Asian-Americans, no Hispanics, no Italian-
Americans, almost no Jews—and it all comes to a verge at the end
of *1919*, with "Paul Bunyan," the five-page biography of the real-
life Wesley Everest, who in 1919 was a logger back from the war.
He was an IWW organizer in Centralia, Washington, some twenty
miles down the road from Olympia, the state capital.

"Wesley Everest was a logger like Paul Bunyan," Dos Passos
writes—as if the hundred-foot-tall Bunyan were real, or Wesley
Everest, twenty-nine in 1919, was not. Dos Passos runs his hand
over Everest's American grain: "His folks were of the old Kentucky
and Tennessee stock of woodsmen and squirrel hunters who followed the trail blazed by Lewis and Clark into the rainy giant
forests of the Pacific slope." He quickly runs statistics on the tim-
ber monopolies: you see a gnat, a Red U.S. Army infantryman,
buzzing at a grizzly's nose—but, Dos Passos says over and over,
"Not a thing in this world Paul Bunyan's ascared of." The tone is so
strange, unstable, the writer mocking his own hero, as if he must
be all parties to the story at once, not allowing the reader a moment
of spectatorship, putting the reader in the action, inside every role,
forcing the reader to choose sides and then to act or flee.

The IWW wants the workers who create the wealth to have it;
they want loggers to be worth more than their tools, to be more
than tools. Commies, say the good people of the town. Skirmishes
break out. The IWW hall in Centralia is attacked by the American
Legion; loggers and their allies are beaten and dumped outside the

county lines. But the union grows, and on Armistice Day in 1919, under cover of a parade, the hall is raided for good. Legionnaires fire their pistols from the street; sharpshooters fire from the hills. The Wobblies try to defend themselves; Wesley Everest and a few others shoot back. Legionnaires fall. Overwhelmed, Everest runs for the river. Waist-deep in the water, Dos Passos writes, he "turned to face the mob with a funny quiet smile on his face . . . The mob was at him. He shot from the hip four times, then his gun jammed. He tugged at the trigger, and taking cool aim shot the foremost of them dead . . . Then he threw his empty gun away and fought with his fists. The mob had him. A man bashed his teeth in with the butt of a shotgun. Somebody brought a rope and they started to hang him. A woman elbowed through the crowd and pulled the rope off his neck. 'You haven't the guts to hang a man in the day-time,' was what Wesley Everest said." Casting Lincoln's shadow, with Lincoln's forebears along with Everest's tracking the Kentucky forest, Dos Passos merges the past with his present, as night falls on Centralia, as the power line is cut and Everest is pulled out of the Centralia jail to be lynched. In the backseat of the car taking him to the bridge where he will be hanged and torn apart by a barrage of bullets, a businessman castrates him: "For God's sake, men, shoot me . . . don't let me suffer like this." "Nobody knows where they buried the body of Wesley Everest," Dos Passos says, "but the six loggers they caught they buried in the Walla Walla Penitentiary."*

---

*After the lynching, Everest's body was cut down and dumped in the Centralia jail cell holding other IWW members arrested in the raid. Seventeen National Guard troops forced four Wobbly prisoners to build Everest's casket and dig the grave; a stunning photograph, with a backdrop of barren trees and a gray sky, shows them lowering the box into an unmarked grave in the local cemetery. As for "the six loggers they caught," one can listen to William O. Douglas. He was twenty-one in 1919; when he read the papers in his hometown of Yakima, Washington, one hundred and twenty miles east of Centralia, he wrote in 1974 in *Go East, Young Man*, "my impression was that as the legionnaires were parading peacefully, they were wantonly shot down by the IWW's." He learned later that Centralia was precisely Dos Passos's America as racket. As a poet,

There it is: the best America can produce and the worst, the cowardly empowered by power and the heroic empowered by heroism—and by the writer.

Where the Past Is

Forty-three years later, in 1962—forty-three years after Wesley Everest was murdered, thirty years after Dos Passos knit Everest's story into that of the country, when Dos Passos, by then a star of

---

Dos Passos didn't need the details; writing as a justice of the Supreme Court, Douglas did. "The local Bar Association pledged its members not to defend an IWW no matter what the charge. A Seattle paper, called the *Union Record*, pleaded for common sense and urged that the IWW's be allowed to present their side of the case. This led to the arrest and indictment of four members of the staff of the paper by the federal government and the closing down of the plant by federal authorities." And that was only a warm-up: "Ten IWW's involved in the Centralia episode were tried the following March. The courtroom and town were filled with legionnaires in uniform. The federal government had two dozen or more troopers present. When the jury returned a verdict, finding two of the defendants guilty of manslaughter, the judge refused to accept the verdict because it was not stiff enough to suit him. On further deliberation, the jury acquitted two, found one to be insane, and found seven guilty of second-degree murder. The jury recommended clemency, concluding that there had been a conspiracy to raid the hall and that the defendants had acted in self-defense. The jury also protested that the IWW's did not receive a fair trial. The trial judge, however, disregarded the jury plea for clemency and imposed maximum sentences ranging from twenty-five to forty years. The Washington Supreme Court affirmed that verdict."

A statue of a doughboy, named *The Sentinel*, memorializing the legionnaires who were killed in Centralia, was set up in the town square shortly after the event; on 13 December 1997, the labor muralist Mike Alewitz unveiled *The Resurrection of Wesley Everest*, painted on the former Centralia Elks Building, directly across from the statue, despite protests from the American Legion. "Everest is the focal figure of the mural," Mary L. Stough wrote in 1999 in *Columbia* magazine. "He is drawn symbolically with his arms raised triumphantly, dressed half worker in overalls and half veteran in a World War I uniform. Black cats are shown as the Wobbly symbol of defiance; a pig representing the profiteers of war is leaning on bags of gold. Angels on the top of the mural are hanging from a long saw—the 'misery whip' of the loggers—and below that is a pie denoting 'pie in the sky,' the happiness that workers could look forward to when they died . . . Across the bottom of the picture flames lick up, consuming workers who are shown as prisoners. As grim as this scene is, the artist is not without a sense of humor. A small volcano emitting a plume of smoke and sporting a pair of glasses was Alewitz's thank-you to the mural committee's co-chair, Helen Lee, director of the Evergreen State College Labor Center. He called it Mount Helen Lee!"

the extreme right, could share a stage with John Wayne and Strom Thurmond to be honored by the Young Americans for Freedom at Madison Square Garden—I was a member of Boys State in Sacramento, California. Two students from, we were told, every high school in the state had been selected by local chapters of the American Legion to gather together in a grand convention to learn about government. Following that, two students from each state would be selected to travel to Washington, D.C., for Boys Nation—the next year, it was Boys Nation that brought Bill Clinton from the Arkansas Boys State in Little Rock to stand in line with the ninety-nine other boys to shake the hand of President John F. Kennedy. So there we were, in a stupor of camaraderie, seated in the chambers of the California legislature in the Capitol building, delivering thrilling patriotic speeches to each other, listening to each other quote from Kennedy's Inaugural Address, from the Gettysburg Address, even, I think, from Martin Luther King's "Letter from Birmingham Jail," written only months before.

On the last night of Boys State, with the Pledge of Allegiance made, with our Boys State governor elected (Santiago Garza, whose campaign speech about the American dream was so heartrending some of his opponents conceded even before the ballots were cast, but who got nowhere with the same number at Boys Nation), an American Legion commander took the podium. He announced that he was there to commemorate a great event. It was his task, he said, to make us understand that as we were gathered together now, we were part of this great event from long before—when, in Centralia, Washington, the American Legion, like the unofficial militias of Lexington and Concord, fired the first shots on American soil in the war in which we were still engaged: the war against Communism. And, he said, it was the first victory in a long struggle: though they were still out there, on that day in 1919 the Reds got their first taste of American lead.

As the Legion commander told the story, there was no lynch mob, no one begging to be shot, no one hanging from a bridge. But

that was not what shocked me. What was so shocking was the realization that I had taken Dos Passos's elegiac true-crime sketch of
Wesley Everest, which I had read aloud in a high-school rhetoric
class earlier in the year, as an art statement. The moral symmetry
of the tale as Dos Passos told it rendered the horrible story beautiful; the perfection of the story as Dos Passos told it rendered the
story finished, complete, protected, a history that was immune
from history. I walked out of the class and took a train to Boys State
and found the story wasn't finished at all. As the man said, it was
still going on.

Words on a Page

The war in *U.S.A.* can be summed up in a word: hurry. The momentum of the biographies, the there-and-then-it's-gone rhythm of
the "Camera Eye" sections, the panic, flight, and hiding in the fiction proper, the hurry especially of the countless compound words
Dos Passos throws across the pages, "workingstiffs" "machinegun-
fire" "policedepartment" "CongressoftheUnitedStates" "wholosthis-
lifeduringtheworldwarandwhoseidentityhasnotbeenestablished"—
and with all this hurry, this panic, the book seems short. Just like
that it's over. You have no idea, as the stories of Joe Williams and
Eveline Hutchins and Charley Anderson and Margo Dowling and
Richard Ellsworth Savage unroll, how anything is going to turn out;
with Dos Passos's made-up heroes experiencing nothing but defeat
and his invented enemies barely noticing they are under assault,
you don't even know who won. You forget that when you reach the
end of the story told in *U.S.A.* most of the century is yet to come.
There's no sense of a future; it seems as if the American Century,
stopping short even of the stock market crash, is already over, suspended forever in battle. "An orator haranguing from the capitol of
a lost republic," Dos Passos writes of Fighting Bob La Follette,
U.S. senator from Wisconsin, he and a few more standing against
America's entry into the First World War, "the little group of willful

men expressing no opinion but their own," as their opponents condemned them and Dos Passos celebrates them: "They called it a filibuster but it was six men with nerve straining to hold back a crazy steamroller with their bare hands."

That's it: from the first appearance of the young-man-alone on its first page, the book is absolutely suffused with romanticism—the same romanticism of defeat, of the best laid low, that in the forties and fifties brought boys raised in New Deal households to John R. Tunis, and then to Dos Passos's *U.S.A.*: boys like Nathan Zuckerman, as he remembers those years in *I Married a Communist*—"My idealism (and my idea of a man) were being constructed along parallel lines, one fed by novels about baseball champions who won their games the hard way, suffering adversity and humiliation and many defeats as they struggled toward victory, and the other by novels about heroic Americans who fought against tyranny and injustice, champions of liberty for America and for all mankind. Heroic suffering. That was my specialty"—and boys like myself. It's the ennoblement of defeat, of preordained defeat; it quickens the heart as only an adolescent heart can be quickened, as only an adolescent heart can be opened and, for some, never quite closed. It's *stirring*.

Back to Earth

Roth's own version of *U.S.A.* breaks with Dos Passos's modernism first of all. Dos Passos's experiments in form are a way of saying that America is an experiment in form, that it can be unmade at any moment, that the language everyone uses is really babble, that to say even the simplest thing a new language must be found. In *American Pastoral* and *The Human Stain*, Nathan Zuckerman creates his own novels out of the lives of now-dead acquaintances by imagining both the external events and the inward thoughts of those lives; in *I Married a Communist* he relates what he remembers and what, in perfect, loving, furious detail, he has been told.

But you forget all that as you read. You are sucked all the way into a reconstructed, emblematic world, with Jewish Newark from the beginning of the twentieth century to its end embodying America itself and Nathan Zuckerman its Boswell, writing down everything it has to say.

As the hero in those of Roth's novels that told Zuckerman's own story—from his pilgrimage to a revered older writer in *The Ghost Writer* to his flaming notoriety as the author of the reviled, best-selling *Carnovsky* in *Zuckerman Unbound* in 1981 to his middle-aged breakdown (in the course of which he tries to pass himself off as a pornographer, specifically the publisher of a magazine called *Lickety Split**) in *The Anatomy Lesson* in 1983 to the conflicting adventures in love and death in *The Counterlife* in 1987—Zuckerman was not very interesting. His stories always seemed made up. But now, when he no longer acts but only listens, he begins to speak both for himself and for the country; his wound is his bow. You follow his voice. As with all great novels, you are so completely seduced by the novelist's invented realities—the stories Nathan Zuckerman has made out of the stories he has been told, listening both to the stories and to the murmur of the country as it, too, listens, opening doors and shutting them, the country saying to any solitary citizen that he or she can be president, that in some essential way he or she already is, the country at the same time saying the game is up, you have gone too far, that you never existed at all—you forget the novelist exists.

As the modernism of form is gone in Roth's *U.S.A.*, so is the modernism of revolutionary politics, because each is a mirror of the other: both are an acting out of the faith that anything, everything, can be changed. That faith is further away, now, than the likes of Murray Ringold's lovingly detailed, street-by-street reconstruction of immigrant Newark as it was early in the twentieth century in *I*

---

*A great joke then; a sex video store on Third Avenue in Minneapolis thirteen years later.

Married a Communist, or the Swede's equally loving, equally detailed account in *American Pastoral* of the creation of the Levov glove business in the years before the war, or his worker-by-worker, stitch-by-stitch description of every stage in the passage of a glove from animal to hand. It is further away than the horribly precise, slowed-down details of Les Farley fighting the Vietnam War twenty years after the fact in a series of visits to a Chinese restaurant with his veterans' support group—and all of those details are very far away. Even as they suck the reader in, such details are, in the strictest sense, alienating, creating an overwhelming sense of how social life is made: how it is produced.

In each case there is a tremendous apprehension of place and time. In these pages this is the root of patriotism, a particular home and a particular past joined to the shared place and past of the nation—but the sense of the past is really a sense of what has disappeared. It is a way of presenting America as at once familiar and foreign, so that, like a foreigner, you have to think about it, cross-examine its assumptions, and take nothing for granted.

As a reader you listen with doubting ears. As Roth puts speech into Ira Ringold's mouth and pulls it out, when he does the same with Rita Cohen, the fugitive Merry Levov's go-between for the Swede, both of them lecturing with perfect rationality about exploitation and oppression, false consciousness and revelation, it is speech that flames up and dies on the page. The lessons about dignity and self-respect, heritage and legacy, that Coleman Silk's parents try to pass on to their son—their account of the America whose rejection of them they will never accept, their portrait of the country that to answer to itself will have to accept them, speech that is erased by Silk's rejection of his parents, his vow to live as if they had never been born—seem in *The Human Stain* to be from another world.

It all seems further away than it is, because Roth is telling a different kind of story; Zuckerman, listening to his own memories, is moving at a pace that turns the great energies of social transformation, as mass movement or solitary exemplary act, into the hare that can't outrun the tortoise. Instead of the hurry of Dos Passos's novels, in Roth's books the slowness, the tentativeness of the cancer survivor in his sixties is patent. And rather than seeing social history as a great drama taking place on a stage as big as the country itself, where finally no single individual stands out from the multitude, Roth has taken the social history of postwar America into himself, or rather into Zuckerman—who you can imagine not as Roth's alter ego (in Roth's term, his "alter-mind") but as Roth's best, imaginary friend. Roth has brought that history into Zuckerman in order to return it to America at large in the form of singular characters pursuing a drama that is at once unique and held in common; a drama that is perverse, as only individuals can be perverse, but which implicates whoever might presume to come to it as an innocent spectator.

The Iron Rinn

Dos Passos's U.S.A. comes to life most directly as Ira Ringold of *I Married a Communist*, the giant Jewish roughneck, the secret Communist, who is a pigheaded version of Mac, the rail rider, journalist, and IWW militant who is the hero of *The 42nd Parallel*. Ira is the long-dead brother of Nathan Zuckerman's ninety-year-old Weequahic High School English teacher, Murray Ringold, now speaking late into the night in the Berkshires, telling the tale of Ira's tragedy—imploding in 1952, after the breakup of his marriage to Eve Frame, when she publishes the bestselling exposé *I Married a Communist*, "as told to Bryden Grant," the right-wing gossip columnist who parlays the destruction of the imitation Lincoln into a successful run for Congress and a seat on the House Un-American Activities Committee—but Zuckerman has his own memories. In 1948, Ira had taken the young Nathan under his wing: to recruit him into the Party, as Nathan now realizes. But as a teenager Zuckerman was overwhelmed by a man who could introduce him to the great baritone and Negro activist Paul Robeson, to Henry Wallace, vice president under Franklin Roosevelt before Harry Truman, now running for president on the Communist-dominated Progressive ticket—a Newark boy overwhelmed by a New York radio star, but also by a man who, in the 1930s, as the Depression raked the nation, had been a vagrant, dug ditches, who like Dos Passos's Mac had lived in the belly of the whale. "I had never before known anyone," Zuckerman remembers, "whose life was so intimately circumscribed by so much American history, who was personally familiar with so much American geography."

They would spend nights in Ira's hideaway cabin, the giant and the boy, and as Ira retraced his steps across the country, speaking of what he'd done and where he'd been, it "aroused," Zuckerman says, "exalted patriotic cravings to know first-hand an America beyond Newark." Ira comes to Weequahic High to perform as Abraham Lincoln; at six feet six he is two inches taller than Lincoln himself. "He'd appeared on the stage in costume," Zuckerman remembers, "and, standing all alone, delivered Lincoln's Gettysburg Address and then the Second Inaugural, concluding with what," as Murray Ringold would tell Zuckerman's English class, "was as noble and beautiful a sentence as any American president, any American *writer*, had ever written (a long, chugging locomotive of a sentence, its tail end a string of weighty cabooses, that he then made us diagram and analyze and discuss for an entire class period)." This sentence: "With malice toward none; with charity for all; with firmness in the right, as God gives us to see the right, let us strive on to finish the work we are in; to bind up the nation's wounds; to care for him who shall have borne the battle; and for his widow, and his orphan—to do all which may achieve and cherish a just, and a lasting peace, among ourselves and with all nations." The echo of Winthrop's "A Modell of Christian Charity" was deep, quiet, and inescapable—"wee must be knitt together in this worke as one man, wee must entertaine each other in brotherly Affeccion"—and whether Lincoln knew the sermon, or if it had simply come down to him in the grain of his own language, what it all was, Zuckerman understands, was "something large that we were all, however small, a part of . . . the reality of the myth of a national character to be partaken of by all."

"The reality of the myth"—it's that reality, that myth, that *American Pastoral*, *I Married a Communist*, and *The Human Stain* take as terrain to fill in, as a still-new country to inhabit. That is because, with the reality of a myth of social revolution now part of the American past, the drama Roth fixes on is the drama of American self-invention, a drama in which every American is his or her own Columbus, discovering America as he or she invents it: the drama of people laboring under the contradiction of a democracy in which each must be the same and each must be different, with none ever seeming to appear what they are not—"or be despised for trying, or failing to try." And part of the drama is Zuckerman's drama, though he is not discovering himself ("I've had my story"), but rather discovering America by attending to those who lost themselves in the quest. The adolescent who in the 1940s understood why and how the world should be changed now faces the horror that awaits those who merely try to create themselves.

"What they had here was a steel-making operation," Zuckerman recalls in *I Married a Communist* of a trip he made as a college student, down from Chicago to Gary, Indiana, to visit Ira's Communist Party mentor Johnny O'Day, hanging on as an organizer in a room so small and bare that it offers Nathan a version of heroic suffering so stark he can almost smell it. It is a passage that word for word, rhythm for rhythm, could come straight from *U.S.A.* "Miles and miles of it stretching along the lake through two states and vaster than any other in the world, coke furnaces and oxygen furnaces transforming iron ore into steel, overhead ladles carrying tons of molten steel, hot metal pouring like lava into molds, and amid all this flash and dust and danger and noise, working in temperatures of a hundred degrees, men at work around the clock, men at work"—and all this sealed with a phrase that hammers a bell as thick as the Liberty Bell and fails to crack it, a phrase that calls up Dos Passos's opening country-in-a-sentence and goes it one better, as much in less—"that was never finished."

"This," Zuckerman says, "was an America that I was not a native of and never would be and that I possessed as an American nonetheless"—and that might be a watchword for the stories he tells of Seymour and Merry Levov, Ira Ringold and Eve Frame, Coleman Silk and Faunia Farley. All, as he says of Coleman Silk in *The Human Stain*, were part of "the great frontier tradition, accepting the democratic invitation to throw your origins overboard if to do so contributes to the pursuit of happiness." Merry Levov becomes a terrorist murderer, disappearing into the fugitive underground and leaving behind her face and name; Ira Ringold pretends to be Abraham Lincoln, in moments even to himself; Coleman Silk, born into a proud, striving, educated African-American family in East Orange, New Jersey, masquerades as a Jew, almost by accident the closest he can come to all-American white. Never mind that given Silk's true ancestry, mixing slaves and slaveholders, English colonists and pioneers, Indians and Scandinavians, he could not be more truly all-American if he were descended from Thomas Jefferson and Sally Hemings. The first black professor hired by Athena College, he enters as the first Jew. He becomes a great teacher; as the dean of faculty he upends a third-rate institution and transforms both the college and the town around it. But it is the secret he keeps all his life from his wife, his children, his friends, his colleagues, the secret that obligates him to keep his mother in the shadows, ensuring that she will die without ever meeting her daughter-in-law or even seeing her grandchildren, that is the true heroism of his life; his escape to his internal Western frontier is that, in Zuckerman's words, "Every day you woke up to be what you had made yourself," and that self would, as the story that was never finished continued, help define what it meant to be American. "Being Jewish immigrants in Britain means you don't have any part to play in making a contribution to the construction of the national identity," the British writer Linda Grant said in 2000 of her parents, who grew up in Liverpool, "because the identity is constructed already." It was not, she said, a story that could be compared to those told by "Philip Roth about the Americans."

Johnny Appleseed

Like *U.S.A.*, *American Pastoral* more than its fraternal novels revels in scope. It is less alive to its own rhythms than *I Married a Communist*, less brazen in its imagining than *The Human Stain*, but more thundering than either. "There is the grand truth about Nathaniel Hawthorne," Melville famously wrote to Hawthorne in 1851. "He says NO! in thunder; but the Devil himself cannot make him say *yes*. For all men who say *yes*, lie; and all men who say *no*,—" In *American Pastoral*, within a personal drama, the country is discovered, and discovered whole, at war with itself. As with *U.S.A.*, the country that remains when you close the book seems bigger than the country that was present when the book was opened—and this happens in a book where the great project of self-invention and national discovery is rendered essentially in the negative. The tragedy of Seymour Levov is that he does not invent himself—he wants nothing more than to inherit the role he will play, to act out a role prepared long before he was born and that will endure long after he is dead. That might seem like one America, but it isn't Roth's. The country Seymour Levov acts out, that he portrays as if his success were a stage and all decent people his audience, might be somebody's somewhere; Roth's judgment is that it can never really be anyone's America.

Seymour Levov, "the Swede," was "the greatest athlete in the history of Weequahic High." He was the U.S. Marine so handsome he could have stepped out of a recruiting poster, the husband of Miss New Jersey 1949. As the Swede takes over Newark Maid, the glove company his father started, manages it brilliantly and fairly and becomes rich, as he finds his way to the sylvan glade of Old

Rimrock, New Jersey, almost a theme park of American Protestant taste and decorum, as his and Dawn's daughter, Merry, grows up amid cows and trees and a big sky and "the village," the Swede imagines who he really is: Johnny Appleseed. That's his secret self. As at the beginning of the nineteenth century John Chapman traveled west from his native Massachusetts into the Ohio River Valley, giving away apple seeds and seedlings to pioneers along the way, so the Swede wants only to scatter the fruits of his good fortune, the American promise both made and kept, to scatter his blessings all around himself, so that he is both benefactor and recipient; striding in giant steps as he walks from the village to his eighteenth-century stone house, he mimes the movements, his arms swinging wide. The pursuit of happiness is a national drama played out before an imaginary audience, an audience that includes all Americans, living and dead. As an actor, one seeks oneself; one also seeks to fulfill the aspirations of all those less brave, knowing that to fail one's own quest means the betrayal of everybody else.

All Seeds Bear Fruit

"Of the few fair-complexioned Jewish students in our preponderantly Jewish public high school," *American Pastoral* begins, "none possessed anything remotely like the steep-jawed, insentient Viking mask of this blue-eyed blond born into our tribe." "A voice and a smile unsullied by even a flicker of superiority," Zuckerman goes on, "the natural modesty of someone for whom there were no obstacles, who appeared never to have to struggle to clear a space for himself." Man or boy, the Swede was someone "whose natural nobility was to be exactly what he seemed to be," "exempted from all self-doubt by his heroic role." As the twentieth century began, Newark's first Jews laid claim to their part of the city "like audacious pioneers to the normalizing American amenities," and the Swede, Zuckerman realizes, is their best inheritor: "He is our Kennedy."

In 1995, at his forty-fifth high-school reunion, Zuckerman imagines himself addressing his fellow alumni, his comrades in place and time, the valedictorian of their journey through history. He looks back to their graduation day. It was 1950, the war was over, the Depression was over, and "Americans were to start over again, en masse, everyone in it together . . . We had new means and new ends, new allegiances and new aims, new innards—a new *ease*, somewhat less agitation in facing down the exclusions the goyim still wished to preserve," Zuckerman says to himself. "And out of what context did these transformations arise—out of what historical drama, acted unsuspectingly by its little protagonists, played out in classrooms and kitchens looking nothing at all like the greater theater of life?" He's echoing Cassius's great speech in *Julius Caesar*: "How many ages hence / Shall our lofty scene be acted over / In states unborn and accents yet unknown!" It was this destiny the Swede was meant to fulfill, for all around him.

But when Zuckerman, who in high school barely knew the older Seymour Levov—the young Nathan entering the Levov house principally to be regularly beaten at Ping-Pong by Jerry Levov, the Swede's unbearable younger brother—meets the Swede again in 1995, "what he has instead of a being, I thought, is blandness—the guy's radiant with it. He has devised for himself an incognito, and the incognito has become him." The hint was there in the first description, the hint or the destiny of such a hero: "blond," "blue-eyed," "steep-jawed," but even more so "insentient" and "mask." As the Swede is "wandering deeper and deeper into an American's life, forthrightly evolving into a large, smooth, optimistic American," as Dawn Levov evolves into a vibrantly genteel country wife, breeding prize cattle and keeping a perfect home, their daughter was evolving too, seeking her own country: evolving into a large, jagged, fatalistic American, discovering a country where nothing was as it seemed. The "Mr. Smooth-It-Away" of Hawthorne's 1843 story "The Celestial Railroad"—"This is the famous Slough of Despond—a disgrace to all the neighborhood; and the greater that it might so easily be converted into firm ground," Mr. Smooth-It-Away says in the voice of the can-do American from Ben Franklin to Sam Walton—produces as heir the Gothic American sketched out in the century before as Hester Prynne, Roderick Usher, Captain Ahab. Johnny Appleseed scattering seeds behind him produces a terrorist who leaves behind bodies.

The Mob Comes for Wesley Everest

Well, these things happen. Everyone comes from somewhere. You can't blame everything on the parents. Everyone has to take responsibility for herself, even an angry, stuttering teenager with all the best lessons who gets involved with big-city radicals and blows up the post office, because that's the outpost of the Federal government, that's Old Rimrock's battlefield in the Vietnam War, the post office in the general store in the village—even an angry teenager who accidentally kills beloved Dr. Fred, and then goes underground. It happens.

But what happens in *American Pastoral* is less a drama of events than a drama of revelation. While all Americans who discover themselves must assume a mask—must "throw your origins overboard if to do so contributes to the pursuit of happiness," not merely one's own pursuit of happiness, in Roth's phrasing, but the pursuit as such—the American who does so must understand that he or she is playing a dangerous game. Like the Communist Abraham Lincoln Ira Ringold, or Navy enlistee Coleman Silk unmasked in a white whorehouse in Norfolk, Virginia, in 1945 ("You're a black nigger, ain't you, boy?"), you become the purloined letter, hiding in plain sight, even if the only one who can see you is yourself. You become a fugitive the rest of the country does not even know it is pursuing—not yet. The mob that came for Wesley Everest can come for anyone at any moment, as soon as it is revealed that he or she is not one of them, that you are not who you appear to be.

It's 1968. Merry blows up the post office; she vanishes. The Swede, who never thought he had anything to hide, or that in his public or private life he was hiding anything, never thought that his face as he saw it in the mirror every morning was a mask, now no longer lives his life as it was meant to be. Like a pitcher aiming the ball rather than throwing it, he acts it out. As Zuckerman will imagine the story after the Swede is dead, the Swede's wife breaks down and is institutionalized; the Swede hides from her in an affair with Merry's speech therapist. It's 1970, and Merry is still missing; in California, Angela Davis, the black professor accused of supplying the guns used in the Marin County shoot-out, an attempted prison break, is awaiting trial for murder, kidnapping, and conspiracy. Night by night, alone, the Swede talks to her, conjuring up conversations in which Davis, sitting in jail or on the run before she was caught and brought back in chains, can tell him where Merry is, who Merry is, why Merry is, a spirit who can calm his heart and relieve his guilt. The Swede, the Swede—even his own real name now sounds false. "Flushing him out of hiding as if he were a fugitive—initiating the Swede into another America entirely": that's what Merry meant to do, that's the role that like the role of Johnny Appleseed the country itself had prepared for him, but the insentient man can only hear the messages he's heard before, and he can't hear this one. He can't hear the "daughter who transports him out of the longed-for American pastoral" where he raised her, where she grew up, "and into everything that is its antithesis and its enemy, into the fury, the violence, and the desperation of the counterpastoral—into the indigenous American berserk."

Another America comes into view: not the America of "With malice toward none; with charity for all," but the America prophesied in the same American minute, in the sentence before, the America where every blessing contains its punishment, where the real civil war would and should "continue, until all the wealth piled by the bond-man's two hundred and fifty years of unrequited toil shall be sunk, and until every drop of blood drawn with the lash, shall be paid by another drawn with the sword"—but that is not an America the Swede can ever countenance.

Coming Soon to Your Local Theater

Others could—easily. Lincoln's words are strange in their context: a president, speaking to the nation of the soul it may deserve to lose. But let the words loose and they can infuse anyone with heroism and fate, reduce anyone to pettiness and sin: diagram *that*. The magic of the characters in *American Pastoral* is that they are capable of generating the infinite detail of the individual while at the same time generating their own magnetic fields—drawing anyone's details to themselves, which is to say they are at once utterly unique and absolutely generic. In 2000, after a walking parlor game with friends, I asked a class of nineteen college students to cast the movie of the book—using any figures, dead or alive, real or fictional, actors from any stage of their careers. Robert Redford as the only possible Swede, I assumed, but after that . . .

The students had devoured the book; now they rewrote it. Some put genre on genre, casting the Swede, Dawn, and Merry by pairing them to characters from *To Kill a Mockingbird* (Atticus Finch cast as the Swede by his daughter, Scout, who casts herself as Merry), *Apocalypse Now*, *American Beauty*, or by matching them with Greek gods, dogs, figures from the 1988 presidential campaign, or one student's family members and the denizens of her hometown. "My friend Cory would be the 'young Swede' and my dad would be the 'grown-up Swede,'" wrote Cameron Siewert, a sophomore from Perryton, Texas. "Cory, simply enough, was the God of High School Sports, which in the Panhandle of Texas is also God, period. Like the Swede, much of his persona has been created by others' expectations—and like the Swede, my father is very simple in his ideas of how to live, how to interact with others, and how to achieve happiness and success. They share the same passion, insatiable interest, and mistaken belief that everyone wants to hear about it." After a single vote for Robert Redford, plus John Elway, Michael Dukakis, Lance the Surfer from *Apocalypse Now*, Zeus, the Incredible Hulk, and a golden retriever mutt, most strikingly there was Rock Hudson. "The Rock Hudson of this film would of course be brought back from the dead," Tanya Kalivas wrote. "What will lend Hudson the ability to play this role more convincingly than any contemporary actor is that the audience will know the course of his life. We will know that despite his performance as a heterosexual macho icon, he hid his homosexuality from the public world and died a victim of the AIDS virus."

For fully half the class, Dawn was Meg Ryan—but also Martha Stewart, Sharon Stone, Natalie Portman (as Queen Amidala from *Star Wars*), Robin Wright, Annette Bening from *American Beauty*, Kitty Dukakis, a standard poodle, and "Cami Skaggs, wife of our local veterinarian." Merry was Angelina Jolie, Parker Posey, Linda Blair from *The Exorcist*, Juliette Lewis, Thora Birch from *American Beauty*, a German shepherd mutt, Marlon Brando's Col. Walter E. Kurtz, again the Incredible Hulk, and Athena. "Neither my sister nor I have bombed any convenience stores as of yet," Siewert wrote, "but as with anyone, there have been events in our lives as a family that have made us all question who we are to ourselves and each other." Jerry Levov was Danny DeVito, Steve Buscemi, Kevin Spacey from *American Beauty*, Hades, and Rodney Dangerfield. Rita Cohen, Merry's poison-tongued terrorist mouthpiece, posing as a student and conning the Swede into giving her a tour of Newark Maid before coolly announcing that Merry "wants her Audrey Hepburn scrapbook," who sets him up and knocks him down, toys with him, forces him to meet her in a hotel room to pass money to his daughter and then lies back on the hotel bed with her legs open ("Let's f-f-f-fuck, D-d-d-dad"), anything to crack not just the mask but now the Swede's entire plaster body, is Christina Ricci, again Angelina Jolie, the Bush-Quayle campaign, Dennis Hopper's manic photojournalist from *Apocalypse Now*, and, blowing away the competition, Daria from *Beavis and Butt-head*. And even this carnival was merely an entryway to a hall of mirrors in which the country itself took on a different cast.

For Olivia Ford, *American Pastoral* was a family mystery finally solved—or at least set down in print. After swiftly handling the Swede

(Gene Hackman—"a smug sort of strength and self-assurance, an assumed power, that mingles with a far-underlying knowledge that power is fleeting and perhaps even artificial"), Dawn Levov (Patty Duke), Rita Cohen (Courtney Love), and Zuckerman himself (Robin Williams), Ford hit a wall. Zuckerman has to make up many of the characters in his putatively real story. Seymour Levov he knew from high school, but Dawn Levov is just a name and a news clipping from Atlantic City '49, Merry Levov Zuckerman knows only from what Jerry Levov has told him at their high-school reunion, and Rita Cohen and many other characters are altogether invented—and for all of them, Ford wrote, "Zuckerman has a great deal more freedom and flexibility. He may turn them into the full, complex individuals that" the Swede could never be. And there was a deeper reason Ford's Hollywood casting call came to a halt: "Some characters were impossible to cast with actors, because I had the feeling I *knew* these people—not simply through Zuckerman's detailed narration, but because I had met them before, in some other form. The task of casting these roles had become comparable to the impossible task of casting the roles of your own family members."

Thus after casting Merry with a high-school friend of her own, she moved on to the Swede's parents: his tyrannical father, founder of the family business, arbiter of all disputes, forbidding the Swede's attempt to marry a Protestant woman and, with the Catholic Dawn, all but forcing her to sign a religious prenuptial agreement before allowing his son his own life, and the Swede's compliant mother. "Lou and Sylvia Levov were of particular interest to me," Ford said flatly. "To portray them I chose to cast Mickey and Addie Goldstien, the brother-in-law and late sister of my maternal grandfather: my great aunt and uncle."

I have built my knowledge of them much in the way that Zuckerman's characters have come to life—through impressions, snippets of extremely biased character sketches, exaggerations grown up from shards of information. I never met these two members of my family: my grandfather's brother-in-law promised, in 1949, that if my grandfather married my grandmother—a black woman—that they would never speak again, and my grandfather would never be allowed to see his sister again. He made good on that promise. Forty-nine years later, after watching my grandfather mourn the loss of that same sister three thousand miles away from her funeral, and then pass away himself that same year, I still have not set eyes on this man, who to this day still runs his business and the remains of his family with uncompromising severity; who inspired respect and fear in those too weak or indoctrinated to see through his bullshit; who has grown in my mind to represent the ultimate perversion of the American dream. Through *American Pastoral* and Lou and Sylvia Levov, I feel that I have finally met this man, and the wife who for their entire married life obediently followed his every lead and forgot her own flesh and blood in the process.

As for Angela Davis, Ford cast herself.

"As times change, prejudices change as well," Sara Isani wrote. "Now Jews have spread all over New Jersey just as they have moved through all dimensions of society. Blacks, on the other hand, were still in segregated schools until 1958 in towns as close to Newark as Princeton. They were barred from even low-middle-class-income housing establishments such as Levittown, and if a black family were to buy a home in a place like Old Rimrock, the white families would clear out of the town." Thus Seymour Levov was Denzel Washington. As the Jewish Swede's wife will be Meg Ryan, this Swede's wife will be Meg Ryan, too. There was no Merry ("She is not so much a character as a catalyst acting as a dose of the reality that the Swede had seemed to elude"). Morgan Freeman was Nathan Zuckerman, and Jerry Levov was Ice-T.

The Fugitive

The riot of the casting of *American Pastoral* opens into the stranger drama of Ira Ringold casting himself as Lincoln—or casting Lincoln as himself. This was a drama that took the form of the 1940s radio play, where history, in the war years made on the radio as you listened, now came to life again.

"America had been scaled down and personalized," Zuckerman says, thinking back to V-E Day, 8 May 1945, when he was twelve, and he and the rest of the country listened spellbound to *On a Note of Triumph*, Norman Corwin's hour-long radio play. The drama—music by Bernard Herrmann, more than twenty-five voices, a hard-boiled narration by the actor Martin Gabel, a veteran of Orson Welles's Mercury Theatre—was written over several months and produced the day that Germany surrendered. It lit up the sky. "We sat there transfixed," Studs Terkel said. "The single greatest— and we use 'greatest' in its full meaning—radio program we ever heard," one could have read in the traditionally hyperbolic *Billboard*. "That prayer at the end," the film director Robert Altman once said, "I know like little children know the Lord's Prayer." "One of the all-time great American poems," said Carl Sandburg.

Lord God of test-tube and blueprint . . .
Appear now among the parliaments of conquerors and give instruction to
    their schemes.
Measure out new liberties so none shall suffer for his father's color or the
    credo of his choice.
Post proofs that brotherhood is not so wild a dream as those who profit by
    postponing it pretend.
Sit at the treaty table and convey the hopes of the little peoples
    through expected straits,
And press into the final seal a sign that peace will come for longer than
    posterities can see ahead,
That man unto his fellow man shall be a friend forever.

"You flood into America and America floods into you," Zuckerman says, echoing Ecclesiastes 1:7. "All the rivers run into the sea; yet the sea is not full." The specter of America as idea, as faith, rises up before him in the memory of that night in 1945: "The mere citing, on the radio, of American cities and states ('through the nippy night air of New Hampshire,' 'from Egypt to the Oklahoma prairie town,' 'And the reasons for mourning in Denmark are the same as they are in Ohio') had every ounce of the intended apotheosizing effect." He quotes from memory, calling up Gabel's voice as it has stayed with him down the years, "the determined, compassionately

gruff, slightly hectoring halftime voice of the high school coach—
the coach who also teaches English," which is to say, for Zuckerman, his high-school English teacher Murray Ringold. "Take a bow,
G.I.," Gabel says. "Take a bow, little guy / The superman of tomorrow lies at the feet of you common men of this afternoon." "I
wouldn't care to judge today if something I loved as much as I loved
On a Note of Triumph was or was not art," Zuckerman says to himself more than half a century later: "it provided me with my first
sense of the conjuring *power* of art."

This was the world where Ira Ringold did his work. The show
was *The Free and the Brave*. It had all started back in Chicago, for
a union fund-raiser, with the huge man got up in a fake beard, a
stovepipe hat, high-button shoes, and an old black suit, reading
from the Lincoln-Douglas debates, "one of Lincoln's most telling
condemnations of slavery," and, Zuckerman says, "he got such a big
hand for giving to the word 'slavery' a strong working-class, political
slant—and enjoyed himself so much doing it—that he continued
right on with the only thing he remembered by heart from his nine
and a half years of schooling, the Gettysburg Address. He brought
the house down with the finale, that sentence as gloriously resolute as any sounded in heaven or uttered on earth since the world
began"—and a reader can soar with the pleasure Zuckerman finds,
that Roth must have found, producing a cadence to match Lincoln's own: "that government of the people, by the people, for the
people, shall not perish from the earth." "Raising and wiggling one
of those huge hairy-knuckled, superflexible hands of his," Zuckerman writes, "plunging the longest of his inordinately long fingers
right into the eyeball of his union audience each of the three times,
he dramatically rasped 'the people.'"

But that was only the beginning. On the radio in 1948, Iron
Rinn plays working-class characters in daily soap operas; in patriotic or historical sketches he is Orville Wright or Wild Bill Hickok
along with Lincoln. The producer of *The Free and the Brave* comes
up with the idea of an Ira Ringold "Life of Lincoln" one-man

show—"Three hours. No intermission. Leave them speechless in
their seats. Leave them grieving for what America might be like today,
for the Negro *and* the white man, if he'd served his second term
and overseen Reconstruction. I've thought a lot about that man.
Killed by an actor. Who else?"—but the point is not really Iron Rinn
as Lincoln. As a member of the Communist Party who will flatly tell
the New Deal father of a twelve-year-old Nathan Zuckerman that he
is not, Ringold onstage is using Lincoln as a mask that is also a mega-
phone. In costume, "with Lincoln's high-pitched country twang,"
this Lincoln stands up for the union shop, attacks laws outlawing
the Communist Party, and denounces a racist senator from Mississippi. At the Progressive Party rally where Henry Wallace and Paul
Robeson along with Nathan Zuckerman watch, Lincoln attacks
Democrats and Republicans alike, "the warmongers in both political parties: 'Supporting reactionary regimes all over the world, arm-
ing Western Europe against Russia, militarizing America . . .'"

In 1949, *I Married a Communist* was a Hollywood melodrama,
remembered today more for the left hook of its title (later changed
to *The Woman on Pier 13*, though probably not out of fear of losing
the Communist audience) than for anything it put on the screen;
it starred Robert Ryan as Brad Collins, former stevedore, now vice
president of Cornwall Shipping in San Francisco. But Communist
Party members—who with their sophisticated surveillance equipment and person-by-person files seem more like FBI agents—
know Collins as Frank Johnson of Jersey City, just another dumb
lug when he joined the Party, "typical of that lost generation of the
thirties." The Party used him as muscle; on its orders, he killed a
shop steward, and then he ran. Now they've caught him. Here the
Party operatives are indistinguishable from Murder, Inc.: a swarthy
boss, a blond moll, blackmail, torture, homicide. Party defectors
and even merely suspected turncoats are drowned or thrown from
windows. There's a fancy cocktail party: a well-dressed guest talks
to a neophyte about "the theory of a scientifically organized state"
as others nod; on the wall is a knock-off of Diego Rivera's *The*

Flower Carrier, a picture of a stooping Mexican peasant. Collins is about to negotiate an agreement between the shippers and the longshoremen; the Party forces him to sabotage it. Ryan is a master of the hard face, the frozen mouth, the cruel gesture, and his whole personality changes as he mouths the lines the Party has fed him. He becomes a pod, acting out *Invasion of the Body Snatchers* seven years in advance. In the end he kills his Party master: he dies fighting, but he has to die for his sins.

In Roth's novel, it's Eve Frame's exposé that takes the title *I Married a Communist*: suddenly the whole country is reading the inside story of Iron Rinn, the Abraham Lincoln impersonator taking his orders from Moscow. But characters change shape in culture; one person turns into another, just like that. Iron Rinn is the flip side of the Red-hunting U.S. Senator John Iselin in *The Manchurian Candidate*, biding his time until the conspiracy plotted by his Communist masters in Moscow and Beijing will catapult him into the White House. There he is, dressed as Lincoln from head to foot at a costume party, his supporters at the party nomination convention wearing Lincoln hats and Lincoln beards as they scream and shout, all of them, knowing and unknowing, traitors, star or bit players in a great drama whose purpose is to wipe Lincoln's words from the memory of mankind. "It wasn't as though a book had been thrown at him—the book was a bomb that had been thrown at him," the ninety-year-old Murray Ringold tells Nathan Zuckerman on his Berkshire porch in 1997, when Murray Ringold is "the last person alive who knows" Ira Ringold's real story, and Nathan Zuckerman is "the last person who cares." "McCarthy, you see," Murray explains,

would have the two hundred or three hundred or four hundred Communists on his non-existent lists, but allegorically one person would have to stand for them all. Alger Hiss is the biggest example. Three years after Hiss, Ira became another. What's more, Hiss to the average person was still the State Department and Yalta, stuff far, far away from the ordinary Joe, while Ira's was popular culture Communism. To the confused popular imagination, this was the democratic Communist. This was Abe Lincoln. It was very easy to grasp: Abe Lincoln as the villainous representative of a foreign power, Abe Lincoln as America's greatest twentieth-century traitor . . . Iron Rinn was Everyman's Communist in ways that Alger Hiss could never be.

Didn't the impersonation always rub against the cultural memories that each member of the audience for Ira Ringold's Lincoln carried like a keepsake? For Ira Ringold, Lincoln was transparent; for Woodrow Wilson, he emerged from a fog, and never all the way. "I have read many biographies of Lincoln . . . but I have nowhere found a real intimate of Lincoln's," Wilson said in 1916, dedicating Lincoln's birthplace in Hogenville, Kentucky. "That brooding spirit had no real familiars . . . This strange child of the cabin kept company with invisible things, was born into no intimacy but that of his own silently assembling and deploying thoughts." When one cheers and shouts for a falsity—for Abraham Lincoln telling you exactly what you want to hear, for an Elvis impersonator singing "My Way" while you grab for one of the sweat-stained scarves he's throwing to the crowd—are you still thrilled when you turn off the lights, or embarrassed, or shamed? Playing with Lincoln is playing with fire. Jesus's voice may sound in the Second Inaugural, but so does John Brown's; Lincoln's Second Inaugural is a version of John Brown's last testament, set down on 2 December 1859, the day Virginia hanged him: "the crimes of this guilty land: will never be purged away; but with Blood. I had as I now think: vainly flattered myself that without very much bloodshed; it might be done."

Playing with Lincoln may be playing with fire, but who can resist? In American iconography, no one changes shape like Lincoln. During the Super Bowl broadcast on 6 February 2005, there was a slightly cracked commercial: a guy eating at McDonald's with his wife finds a French fry that looks like Lincoln in profile. He shows it around. Some scorn him: "Now you're a big shot." But girls mob him, and one looks like she's going home with him. It's the all-American version of the Virgin Mary on a tortilla; the wife puts the French fry on eBay. There's a follow-up commercial later in the game: a "Japanese gentleman" writing "I have always been fascinated by your Mr. Lincoln." We see him dressed up as Honest Abe, and a new McDonald's sign: HOME OF THE LINCOLN FRY.

At the Venice Biennale in 1999, the Ohio installation artist Ann Hamilton's *Myein* was the American entry. As you approached the American Pavilion, crossing a flagstone courtyard, you noticed that the stones were stained red, as if someone had spilled paint. The neoclassical building was small and low, with two rectangular wings coming off a dome. The place, a sign in the entryway between the wings said, had reminded Hamilton of Jefferson's Monticello; she decided to orchestrate the place as an American metaphor. The sign explained further: the bumps one would see on the walls of the wings would be renderings in Braille of accounts of the torture and murder of slaves, taken from the lawyer and poet Charles Reznikoff's *Testimony*, his 1934 rendering of court records,* while the whispering voice one would hear emanating from the ceilings would be Hamilton reciting Lincoln's Second Inaugural in something called the International Phonetic Code.

In the wings the information dissolved into suggestion, like the title of a song translating words you can't make out. The sense of suggestion changed the dots on the walls from poems you couldn't read anyway into an abstract version of the Second Inaugural as it's chiseled on a wall of the Lincoln Memorial—because, in the realm of suggestion, it was now that building, not Monticello, that the pavilion matched. Hamilton's voice-over was precisely a song where you couldn't understand the words, done in the style of the sort of female heavy-breathing number—Jane Birkin and Serge Gainsbourg's 1974 "Je t'aime . . . moi non plus" is the template—that's

---

*One case concerned a woman who, after her son was taken from her, refused to follow orders; she was continually resold, again and again escaped, was found and beaten, and again resold. Reznikoff's version of her punishment by a new owner, one Spencer: "He had her stripped and staked down on the ground: her feet and hands spread and tied to the stakes, her face downward. Mr. Spencer was calm and took his time; he whipped her from time to time with a plaited buckskin lash about fifteen inches long. He drew some blood, but not a great deal, and then he took salt and a cob and salted her back with it."

good for a hit every ten years or so. The few words that came through, if they did ("Oscar," "November," "Sierra," "uniform," "triumph"), seemed not to belong to the Second Inaugural, even if one of them does. In this surrealist memorial, you noticed the difference between Lincoln's and Hamilton's: in hers, the walls moved.

Down every wall, streams of dark pink powder fell to the floor, sometimes in slivers, sometimes in gushes, like the bleeding walls in *The Shining*. The powder piled up on the floor, inches deep; as people walked through the rooms, causing drafts, the powder spread across the floor, and people picked it up on their shoes. When they left the U.S. Pavilion for those of other nations, they carried a trail of blood—not, you could think, the blood of conquest, but of crime and punishment, the crime and punishment acted out in Lincoln's time in the country the pavilion represented and ever since. The Lincoln fry walked out of that building; Ira Ringold walked out of it; Abraham Lincoln walked out of it.

The Dark End of the Street

In *American Pastoral*, five years have passed since Merry's disappearance—five years during which the Swede has, as a businessman, as a husband, and as a father without a daughter acted out an even more upstanding life than before. Now the Swede receives another message from Rita Cohen. Merry is in Newark. He can meet her.

"Your children will wander looting the shopping malls / for forty years, suffering for your idleness," the poet Donald Hall wrote in 1988 in *The One Day*, "until the last dwarf body rots in a parking lot . . . I shall prophesy through millennia / of Jehovah's day until the sky reddens over cities." The Swede meets his daughter on a terrible, ruined Newark street, and she, just a young woman now, is a ruin as well. The place where she lives is worse. It is any parent's nightmare—worse than a child's death—to see a child living for death. Merry tells her father that, in the blank years, she continued her life as a terrorist. She killed three more people. She was

raped. But now in the filth and squalor of her hideous room, she
says she has found herself. She is now a Jain, a follower of the most
ascetic of all Hindu sects. It's something she read about in a library;
for all she knows she may be the only American Jain there is, but it is
her whole life. To her it all makes sense: Jainism was founded in the
sixth century B.C. as a negation of the caste system. From its insistence on the absolute sanctity of all life came Gandhi's faith in passive resistance as the answer to all violence. From Gandhi came
Martin Luther King, Jr., and the opening of the path from the Civil
Rights movement to the movement against the war in Vietnam. She
is simply a moment in the great circle of justice and time.

Merry talks like a cult member. Covering her face is a veil made
out of the foot of a nylon stocking, meant to protect the tiny or-
ganisms in the air around her from the predations of her own
breath. She is being devoured by her own purity. Frantic, the
Swede imagines this is all a trick, some humiliating play staged just
for him. "They," the terrorist underground, Merry's kidnappers, the
real bombers, anybody, "they wanted to kill him off with the story
of a pariah exiled in the very country where her family had triumphantly rooted itself in every way"—and so for one moment
only the Swede steps out of the pastoral America, out of the sylvan
glade into which he stepped as if by nature, and into the other
America, a place of killing and no words. Like Ahab demanding
that his crew break the blank face of the white whale—"All visible
objects, man, are but as pasteboard masks. But in each event—in
the living act, the undoubted deed—there, some unknown but still
reasoning thing puts forth the mouldings of its features from behind the unreasoning mask. If man will strike, strike through the
mask!"— the Swede rips off his daughter's veil. But then he smells
her, a smell of foreignness, of flesh that is already dying, his flesh,
dying his death, and so the father helplessly vomits into his daughter's face. "The veil was off," Zuckerman says almost coyly, imagining the scene, "but behind the veil there was another veil. Isn't
there always?" The Swede leaves.

Again, as Roth would know as well as anyone, with Zuckerman imagining the old American as his neighbor, Hawthorne was there first. As if stepping out of *The Scarlet Letter*, Merry is Pearl, the uncontrollable spirit made by Hester Prynne and Arthur Dimmesdale. She is perhaps even named for Hawthorne's 1836 story "The May-Pole of Merry Mount," where the Puritans' devil lures his prey. But in these pages Merry is more than anyone else the preacher in a Hawthorne tale from the same year, "The Minister's Black Veil."

One Day

One day, without a word, a Puritan preacher assumes a black cloth and becomes a figure of horror. "Each member of the congregation . . . felt as if the preacher had crept upon them, behind his awful veil, and discovered their hoarded iniquity of deed or thought." It's the child covering her eyes with her hands, "You can't see me but I can see you!" a game everyone remembers, a reality turned inside out that no one can explain away. "There is an hour to come," the minister tells his terrified wife, "when all of us shall cast aside our veils": the end of time. Death.

As he rejects the affections of the world, like Merry the minister becomes a kind of saint. The dying especially seek his blessing, to be "with him behind the black veil." And when his own death approaches and all beg him to remove the mask, he sits up straight in his bed like a dead man sitting up in his coffin at his own wake, shouting: "When the friend shows his inmost heart to his friend; the lover to his best beloved; when man does not vainly shrink from the eye of his Creator, loathsomely treasuring up the secret of his sin; then deem me a monster, for the symbol beneath which I have lived, and die! I look around me, and, lo! on every visage a Black Veil!"

The Swede cannot shout out like the minister; he can't speak this strange and unacceptable language, merely the pidgin of the American Gothic, because he has only become who he was meant to be: the great athlete, the successful businessman loved by his employees and respected by his peers, the virtuous citizen, the good husband, the devoted father. The Swede was invented, made up out of the whole cloth of honest American cotton, but he was invented by others, not by himself. Were he to take off his own mask as he has ripped off his daughter's, there wouldn't be another mask behind it, there would be nothing at all.

Merry is the Swede's Moby-Dick, but the Swede is not Ahab, the mad pantheist captain, but Starbuck, the pious, law-abiding first mate. He cannot be unreasonable. He cannot purposefully do wrong. He cannot defy. Desperate after his daughter has sent him away—"How strongly," she says in horrible, stiffened language, less alive in her speech than in her smell, "you still crave the idea of your innocent offspring," anticipating the reversal in *The Human Stain*, where "the extreme innocence *was* the corruption," as if to say that despite her foulness it is her father and not she who is corrupt, and who for his crime of innocence will have to pay— desperate to save his daughter, unable to force, demand, rescue, or kill, the Swede calls his brother Jerry.

The Swede is the good son; Jerry is the bad son. A surgeon, he marries and divorces one nurse after another. He says exactly what he thinks, if he even thinks at all, if he ever does more than strike out, strike through the mask, or whatever else is handy. Seymour calls Jerry for reassurance: Did he do the right thing? He gets a rant at first seemingly not out of Hawthorne or Melville but out of the ground: "Go back to the room and get her . . . drag her out of that fucking room by her hair." But she killed four people, the Swede says. "*Fuck* the four people. What's the matter with you?" It's not morals, it's not respect, Jerry thunders, and now it is Hawthorne and Melville, Hawthorne as Melville heard him, pressing through the page: "Oh, if someday you could become conscious of why you are doing what you are doing. Do you know why? Do you have any idea? Because you're afraid of creating a bad scene! You're afraid of letting the beast out of the bag!" The Swede's insentient answer is the answer of the American who does not invent himself or herself, who is not hiding in the public square, who doesn't know enough to hide, to be afraid, as if he has already forgotten who he has just seen, what she looked like, how she spoke, what she has done, where she came from: "What are you talking about? What beast? What beast?"

"What are you?" Jerry slams back. "Do you know? What you are is always trying to smooth everything over . . . What you are is always trying to find the bright side of things. The one with the manners. The one who abides everything patiently. The one with the ultimate decorum. The boy who never breaks the code. Whatever society dictates, you do. Decorum. Decorum," says Jerry, in a line that could sum up the ambitions of Roth's career from his first book, *Goodbye, Columbus*, in 1959, to whatever and whenever its end may be, "is what you spit in the *face* of. Well, your daughter spit in it for you, didn't she? Four people? Quite a critique she has made of decorum."

"You think you know what this country is?" Jerry says—and now he is on the hunt, now he is truly Ahab, rallying for the assault on the whale that could be his brother ("Out there playing at being Wasps," he says of his brother and his wife in Old Rimrock. "*I* would have thrown a bomb. *I* would have become a Jain and live in Newark"), or his niece ("Are you going to break with appearances," Ahab says to Ishmael and everyone else gathered on the deck of the *Pequod*, "and pit your will against your daughter's or aren't you?"), or the U.S.A. itself. "You have no *idea* what this country is. You have a false image of *everything*. All you know is what a fucking glove is. This country is *frightening* . . . You wanted Miss America? Well, you've got her, with a vengeance—she's your daughter! You wanted to be a real American jock, a real American marine, a real American hotshot with a beautiful Gentile babe on your arm? You longed to belong like everybody else to the United States of America? Well, you do now, big boy . . . The reality of this place is right up in your kisser now. With the help of your daughter you're

as deep in the shit as a man can get, the real American crazy shit."
It's as if Jerry is saying that the Swede's confrontation with his
daughter is his real bar mitzvah: *Now*, Jerry is saying, *you are an
American*.

"He got caught in a war he didn't start, and he fought to keep it
all together, and he went down . . . My brother was the best you're
going to get in this country, by a long shot," Jerry tells Nathan
Zuckerman after his brother's death. But "the best" isn't in the
charter; the pursuit of the good isn't in the Declaration of Independence. Sacrifice and virtue aren't there. Not even justice is
there. What there is is anarchy: "Life, Liberty, and the pursuit of
Happiness," a license to do whatever it takes.

How Do You Know?

In a motel situated inside an Egyptian pyramid, where he has registered as Mr. and Mrs. John Smith of Anytown, U.S.A., a man
named Babe—he's just bought a new car and switched the climate
control to "Land of the Pharaohs"—meets a couple of American
tourists in the Do Da Room. It's 1969: we're in the middle of "How
Can You Be in Two Places at Once When You're Not Anywhere at
All," an absurdist, generic, and instantly recognizable version of
On a Note of Triumph—for those Americans of a certain age, even
those born too late to have heard the old radio play, a version coded
in their very beings.

The guys in the Do Da Room, Joe and Eddie ("I'm not Joe," Joe
confides after Babe admits he isn't really Mr. and Mrs. John Smith.
"And he's not Ed," Ed says mysteriously), have a good head start on
Babe; so apparently does the desk clerk. Soon enough they fall into
a drunken celebration of their country, retelling the national story
again and again. "We needed the Hope, the Faith, the Prayers, the
Fears," announces Joe in the rat-a-tat-tat Good-Evening-Mr.-and-
Mrs.-America-and-all-the-ships-at-sea voice of Walter Winchell as
Morse code runs under his lines. "The Sweat, the Pain, the Boils,

the Tears!" answers the desk clerk without missing a beat. "The Broken Bones!" says Joe. "The Broken Homes!" answers the desk clerk—though at the speed they're going whatever they say sounds like patriotic static and the revelry in their tone turns every 1969 Vietnam no back into a 1945 V-E Day yes. "The Total Degradation of—" "Who?" says Babe, thrilled by the drama. "YOU!" Eddie shouts, beside himself. "THE LITTLE GUY!"

One after another, or all at once, they break into song, from the jaunty "You're an American Well So Am I" to the stentorian "I Was Born an American" to the Woodyguthried "This Land Is Made of Mountains"* to the barbershopped "Candied Apples and Ponies with Dapples." "That's America, buddy!" the desk clerk says with ringing satisfaction. "Just remember: Abraham Lincoln didn't die in vain—he died in *Washington, D.C.*" "I *see*," says Babe, suddenly confused. "Well . . . who *am* us, anyway?" You can feel the others take a step back from him. Eddie, puffing his chest: "We're one of you, and you're one of us," Eddie says. "I think—" "Maybe—" says Joe. "Possibly—" says the desk clerk. "How do you tell?" Babe asks desperately. "How do you know for sure? How do you ever really know?"

The Country Vanishes

In a country based on a document, made up, not merely the Declaration of Independence promulgated and the Constitution adopted but the nation promulgated and adopted, you don't know. As captured in a few of Lincoln's words even more than in its founding documents, America is an idea—an idea that mapped the landscape and shaped the people in it, or failed to.

---

*"A little song I learned upstream at prison!" Babe says. "Everybody sing along! 'This land is made of mountains / This land is made of mud / This land is made of everything / For me and Elmer Fudd.'" Horrible, even as a parody—but not that far from "Folksong" in *On a Note of Triumph*: "Hitler went to the Russian front / Where every bullet missed him / But he caught a dose of Stalingrad / That spread all through his system."

The country charges its citizens with the mission to create themselves, just as the republic was created—but if each American carries the republic within himself or herself, then each American can become a lost republic. "This country is *frightening*": part of what is frightening is the apprehension that the republic itself can vanish in an instant, leaving each American unknown to every other, with nothing in common, in a state of nature, "a war of all against all," where the mob can come for anyone at any time. Jefferson opens a continent; it is filled up with great cities bursting with speeches and commerce. Blink your eyes and it is filled up with the zombie cities of *Invasion of the Body Snatchers*—the Central Valley town of Santa Mira, California, in 1956, in Don Siegel's original film, San Francisco in 1978, in Philip Kaufman's remake, and Washington, D.C., the capital itself, in the remake titled *The Visiting*—with the citizens bent on the destruction of liberty even as an idea.

In 1849 Melville was writing to his editor Evert Duyckinck about the devil and Plato and Ralph Waldo Emerson, all in his usual jocular, self-mocking tone: "I would to God Shakspeare had lived later, & promenaded in Broadway. Not that I might have left my card for him at the Astor, or made merry with him over a bowl of the fine Duyckinck punch; but that the muzzle which all men wore on their souls in the Elizabethan day, might not have intercepted Shakspeare from articulation. Now I hold it a verity, that even Shakspeare, was not a frank man to the uttermost. And, indeed, who in this intolerant universe is, or can be? But," Melville said, changing his voice, flattening it, as if he were saying something very great in the shape of something very small, "the Declaration of Independence makes a difference." But what if it doesn't? What does Melville's sentence mean in a time when, should the president come to your city, people who might want to make their voices heard against him are placed out of sight, in a parking lot temporarily designated a Free Speech Zone, which, our documents remind us, is what the country itself is supposed to be? In 1989 the critic

Howard Hampton was writing about the band Pere Ubu, their song "Chinese Radiation," and the demonstrations that over the spring of that year Chinese students had mounted in Tiananmen Square— until the government brought in the army, which shot the students down as the boys and girls rushed forward, shouting "Fascist, fascist, beast, beast." "*It can't happen here*, go the reassuring passwords," Hampton said. "The massacre, or the uprising?"

In 1935 *It Can't Happen Here* was the name of a novel by Sinclair Lewis. The book put the phrase into the air of the country, made it common coin. *It Can't Happen Here* is the story of the U.S.A. as the lost republic that for Dos Passos, writing about the way his hero Robert La Follette "sat firm" in the Senate with "an undelivered speech on his desk," the U.S.A. already was; Lewis's book is the story Roth reached back for in 2004, when in *The Plot Against America* he put aside the parables of the republic in each American, and tried to see the country bucking and reeling as a single body. Roth reimagined 1940: the heroic aviator, isolationist, anti-Semite, and Nazi sympathizer Charles Lindbergh gains the presidential nomination at a deadlocked Republican convention, defeats Franklin Roosevelt with the slogan "Vote for Lindbergh or Vote for War," and sets the nation on a course toward fascism. "A willful man expressing no opinion but his own," Dos Passos called La Follette; in *The Plot Against America* the only man willing to stand against Lindbergh is the Jewish radio broadcaster, gossip columnist, and low-life Broadway hustler Walter Winchell, announcing a mad candidacy for president in 1942, a full two years before the next presidential election, setting out with an actual soapbox from New York to Boston, then up and down the Eastern Seaboard and into the Midwest, met by rioting mobs in city after city, shouted down, threatened, beaten, and finally, like so many before him, killed for what he said or what it was believed he meant, shot to death in Louisville, Kentucky. At Winchell's funeral in New York, Roth has Mayor Fiorello La Guardia say the words with which Roth nods to the writer who was there before he was. "It can't happen here?"

Roth's La Guardia says, he himself turning his head to Sauk Centre, Minnesota, where Sinclair Lewis sat. "My friends, it *is* happening here."

A Cautionary Tale

"It was a town of perhaps ten thousand souls," Lewis writes of Fort Beulah, Vermont, where *It Can't Happen Here* begins, "inhabiting about twenty thousand bodies." That sets the tone: the novel is funny, sour, wisecracking, amazed at itself.

It was supposed to be a cautionary tale. It was meant to wake the nation, to stop what it was predicting: in 1935 there really were fascist movements abroad in the land, in the Midwest, in New York, in California. Both American Nazis and American Apollonians—like the young architect Philip Johnson, a leader, in 1934, of the Gray Shirts—were convinced that government of the people, by the people, for the people was a sewer of immorality. They were certain the nation needed a leader with the power to make his every word come true: a leader, American fascists such as Johnson imagined, because an American fascist was still an American, like himself.* Along with the Silver Shirts, the Black Shirts, and the Khaki Shirts, the German-American Bund, the Black Legion, businessmen's groups armed to break unions, and the politicians that might try to ride their waves, this is what Lewis set out to stop.

---

*Front page of the New York *Times*, 18 December 1934: "REICH SEIZES 600 IN MORALS DRIVE—STORM TROOPS ARE CHIEF TARGET IN CLEANUP OF PUBLIC BATHS AND BARS." It's the Night of the Long Knives—the night the SS began the extermination of the Brown Shirts, the night the Gestapo consolidated its power. To the side: "28 MORE ARE SHOT IN SOVIET ROUNDUP"—Stalin is wiping out the last traces of "leftist" dissent. A few inches away, William Green, head of the American Federation of Labor, "URGES LAWS TO RESTRICT REDS."

On page 12, there's a story about the Louisiana state legislature and Huey Long— a Democratic Party threat to Roosevelt from the left, or maybe the right—to many the very incarnation of an American dictator. As a U.S. senator, Long of Louisiana has no official role in the legislature whatsoever; nevertheless the former governor owns it. "With Senator Huey P. Long cracking the whip," the *Times* reports, "the Louisiana

On the back cover of a 1940 edition of *It Can't Happen Here*, you see a white, middle-class family gathered around the oversized radio that in ten years or so would be replaced by a TV set. Both the father and son are wearing ties; the mother and daughter are

---

House today advanced the last step before the final passage of thirty-four of the thirty-five edicts"—note the word "edicts," not "measures" or "laws"—that Long had presented the previous night, "when his special session of the legislature convened." The *Times* explained that the thirty-fifth edict had been dropped on Long's own orders; every one of the remaining thirty-four increased Long's personal power in the state. He was present on the floor of the Louisiana House to intimidate the two legislators who dared to vote against him; also present, the *Times* noted, were Long's armed bodyguards, state troopers, and perhaps a score of unidentified thugs.

A few pages on there was a story about a new fascist party. "TWO FORSAKE ART TO FOUND A PARTY," read the top headline. "Museum Residents Prepare to Go to Louisiana at Once to Study Huey Long's Ways—GRAY SHIRT THEIR SYMBOL." "A new and still nameless political party has plunged into the American political arena under the generalship of two young officials of the Museum of Modern Art," the story read. "The founder of the party is Alan Blackburn, 27, who graduated from Harvard in 1929. His companion in political adventure is Philip Johnson, who completed his studies at Harvard in 1927. For three years the young men dedicated themselves to the advancement of American culture through art and architecture, Mr. Blackburn as Executive Secretary of the Museum of Modern Art and Mr. Johnson as head of its architecture department. Recently they became convinced that, after all, abstract art left some major political and economic questions unresolved. Consequently both have turned in their resignations and will leave as soon as practicable for Louisiana to study the methods of Huey Long." "We know we see something, but its outlines are not yet clear," Blackburn said. "We feel that there are 20 or 25 million people in this country who are suffering from the inefficiency of government. We feel that there is too much emphasis on theory and intellectualism. There ought to be more emotionalism in politics. After all, life isn't intellectual. I think that what people want to do is eat, sleep, and play."

Rebuffed in Louisiana, Blackburn and Johnson, now calling themselves the National Party, attached themselves to the National Union for Social Justice, a proto-fascist party organized by Father Charles Coughlin of Detroit, a radio preacher whose anti-Semitic, anti-Roosevelt broadcasts reached across the country. Blackburn and Johnson saw the National Party as an elite group, taking in the higher type of American fascist—Lindbergh, Ezra Pound. They bought their way into the Union for Social Justice with a five-thousand-dollar contribution—a huge sum for the time—but they were again ignored, and drifted back to their smaller careers. Johnson eventually returned to the Museum of Modern Art—as a member of the board of trustees. Long was assassinated in Louisiana in 1935. Father Coughlin supported the Axis conquests; even after the American entry into World War II, when he went off the air, his Christian Front initiated violence against American Jews. "Probably the most disastrous doctrine Satan has disseminated through his earthly leaders was 'government by the people,'" he wrote in 1969.

dressed up as well. "IF AMERICA GETS A DICTATOR," reads the
scare headline, "Will your husband be put in a concentration camp?
Will you have to stop going to church? Will your son have to join the
Storm Troopers? Will your property be confiscated? Will your
daughter lose her job? Will you lose freedom of speech? THESE
ARE SOME OF THE QUESTIONS WHICH THIS EXCITING
NOVEL ANSWERS"—the answer being in every case *yes*.

As a cautionary tale it was also a great yarn, a real American tall
tale. It's 1936, just one year into the future of the 1935 bestseller;
with the nation still trapped in the Great Depression, a cowboy
senator from the West takes the Democratic Party nomination
from FDR and is elected president on a platform promising the
suspension of the Constitution and the immediate imposition of a
racist, fascist dictatorship. But it hasn't happened yet when Lewis's
hero, a newspaper editor in his early sixties named Doremus
Jessup—his wife calls him Dormouse—lets loose with his first
speech. "There's no country in the world that can get more
hysterical—yes, or more obsequious!—than America," he says to a
gathering of local businessmen after a Rotary Club dinner. "Look
how Huey Long became absolute monarch over Louisiana, and
how the Right Honorable Mr. Senator Berzelius Windrip owns *his*
state. Listen to Bishop Prang and Father Coughlin on the radio—
divine oracles, to millions," he rants. "Remember the Kuklux Klan?
Remember our war hysteria, when we called sauerkraut 'Liberty
cabbage' and somebody actually proposed calling German measles
'Liberty measles'?"

Lewis is having terrific fun with his story. Buzz Windrip is president, the Chief. The man behind him, one Lee Sarason, is running
the country. The nation changes overnight—or, on Doremus Jessup's terms, an America always present inside the America of the
Declaration of Independence and the Constitution emerges out of
the nation almost everyone had taken for granted, and replaces it.

Now it's 1937: sharecroppers in Arkansas rise up. They are captured, told to run, and machine-gunned in the back. In San Fran-

cisco, dockworkers attempt a strike; their leaders are tied up and set on fire as their fingers and ears are shot off. In Kansas, rebels are blown up with grenades: "an altogether intelligent move," Lewis writes, maintaining his supercilious tone, "since there was nothing of the scoundrels left for sentimental relatives to bury." But then, as if Lewis has suddenly heard his own voice, the tone changes, and the writer begins to scare himself. People stop talking, afraid of what someone, anyone, might hear, afraid of who might tell whom what someone said; if they speak at all they speak in code.

People who could not resist talking politics spoke of Windrip as "Colonel Robinson" or "Dr. Brown" and of Sarason as "Judge Jones" or "my cousin Kaspar," and you would hear gossips hissing "Shhh!" at the seemingly innocent statement, "My cousin doesn't seem to be as keen on playing bridge with the Doctor as he used to—I'll bet sometime they'll quit playing . . ."

Daily—common now as weather reports—were the rumors of people who had suddenly been carried off "under protective arrest," and daily more of them were celebrities . . . Now, incredulously—for these leaders had seemed invulnerable, above the ordinary law—you heard of judges, army officers, ex–state governors, bankers who had not played in with the Corpos, Jewish lawyers who had been ambassadors, being carted off to the common stink and mud of the cells.

Never silent, always a creature of his own exasperation, his Yankee rectitude, Jessup ultimately joins the underground resistance, and as the republic disappears in a series of coups, as massacres spread across the country like plague, that is where the story leaves him, but it is passages like those that stick with a reader—and though the tone is never sarcastic and the story never a comedy, the same is true of *The Plot Against America*. Roth is raising the specter of "another America entirely," insisting that the nation remains as it was from the first: unstable, unfixed, like its citizens capable of anything.

In *The Plot Against America* it is an America ruled by a godlike figure who travels the land alone, in his Lockheed Interceptor if not in the *Spirit of St. Louis* itself, shooting out of the clouds like something out of ancient myth, landing in a town here, a city there, to deliver oracular pronouncements, speeches of less than a hundred words. "Our country is at peace," President Lindbergh says in Louisville after the assassination of Walter Winchell, refusing to even mention the name of his rival or the act that took his life. "Our people are at work. Our children are at school. I flew down here to remind you of that. Now I'm going back to Washington to keep things that way."

The Lonesome Ace

Lifting off in the *Spirit of St. Louis* from Roosevelt Field on Long Island on 20 May 1927, and landing at Le Bourget Field in Paris thirty-three hours later, in the first solo flight ever made across the Atlantic Ocean, Lindbergh became a singular American hero— part Babe Ruth (who in that same year hit sixty home runs and made the number magic) and part Davy Crockett, part Douglas Fairbanks and part Sergeant York. Then came his charmed marriage to Anne Morrow, the nationally celebrated birth of their first child, a son, in 1930, the boy's kidnapping and murder in 1932, and the trial and execution of Bruno Hauptmann—"The Crime of the Century," it was called, and aside from the assassination of John F. Kennedy it probably was. The man of lightning struck by it: "the boldness of the world's first transatlantic solo pilot," Roth writes, "had been permeated with a pathos that transformed him into a martyred titan comparable to Lincoln." And what could be more irresistible, or more dangerous, than a living martyr?

Imagining the Lindbergh-Roosevelt campaign in 1940, Roth imagines himself as he would have been, seven years old, part of a family of dedicated Newark Jewish Democrats, striving, serious, informed, patriotic, his father a true village explainer of seemingly every facet of American history. But now that history itself is slipping away, and so early on under Lindbergh's presidency, the Roth family—Herman Roth, Bess Roth, eight-year-old Philip, and his older brother, Sandy—make a trip to Washington, D.C. Lindbergh—who in real life had proudly worn the Nazi Service Cross of the German Eagle, who had attacked America's Jews for supposedly attempting to maneuver the country into joining the European war, for being a traitorous class loyal not to the U.S.A. but only to themselves—has now already signed ententes with Germany and Japan. He accepts the Axis conquests in Europe and Asia and leaves Britain to its fate—"and the only ones against him, people said, are the Jews." The Roths drive into the heart of the nation that is in the process of casting them out: to erase them from its story, to deny them any chance to claim it as their own. That's not how Roth's parents, and Philip, who has brought his stamp collection with him, with all of its pictures of national heroes and monuments, see it as they arrive; they have come to prove that they do belong. They are American born. They are passionately caught up in the great public issues of the day, and for them the great issues of the American past—from the adoption of the Constitution to the *Dred Scott* decision, the Civil War to the winning of the West, the emergence of the labor movement to every detail of the New Deal—are alive in the present. Like anybody else, they think, they are the American story, and without America they would have no story worth telling, even to themselves.

In their days in and around the capital, their hotel reservations will be canceled when the hotel discovers they are Jews. They will hear slurs against Jews in general and against themselves. But now they are simply driving into town. "Immediately upon entering Washington," the Philip Roth who has made himself a character in the novel remembers,

we made a wrong turn in the heavy traffic, and while my mother was trying to read the road map and direct my father to our hotel, there appeared before us the biggest white thing I had ever seen. Atop an incline at the end of the street stood the U.S. Capitol, the broad stairs sweeping upward to the colonnade and capped by the elaborate three-tiered dome. Inadvertently, we had driven right to the very heart of American history; and whether we

knew it in so many words, it was American history, delineated in its most inspirational form, that we were counting on to protect us against Lindbergh.

But symbols like the Capitol are mute. In the shadows of the
inner chambers of the Lincoln Memorial—"What ordinarily passed
for great just paled away, and there was no defense, for either an
adult or a child, against the solemn atmosphere of hyperbole"—
Herman Roth begins to despair of "what this country does to
its great men." "Thank goodness we have President Lindbergh," a
woman says. "Compare Lincoln to Lindbergh?" Herman Roth says.
"Boy oh boy." "Something bothering you about what the lady just
said?" says a man. "No sir. Free country." "Loudmouth Jew," the man
says to his party. "The best friend of the president of the United
States is Adolf Hitler," Herman Roth rages. "Read that," he says to
Philip, pointing to the tablet in the memorial bearing the Gettysburg Address. "Just read it. 'All men are created equal'"—as if reading the words out loud, uttering the magic incantation, could call
up the dead and make it true. "Herman," Bess Roth says, "I can't
go on with this." "We came back out into the daylight and gathered
together on the top step," Roth writes.

The tall shaft of the Washington Monument was a half mile away, at the
other end of the reflecting pool that lay at the base of the terraced approach
of the Lincoln Memorial. There were elm trees planted all around. It was
the most beautiful panorama I'd ever seen, a patriotic paradise, the American Garden of Eden spread before us, and we stood huddled together, the
family expelled.

Roth moves the story forward slowly, inch by inch. Detail accu-
mulates, reality builds, people try to accommodate themselves to
it, and when that reality is violated people try to accommodate
themselves once more. For Herman Roth, the alterations in the
country—for one, Lindbergh's creation of an Office of American
Absorption, supposedly meant to make "emerging Americans," that
is, Jews, into real Americans, in fact meant to scatter Jewish com-

munities, divide Jewish families, and mark off those Jews whose innate skills in finance and manipulation might be useful from the majority of Jews who will not be needed—seem unimaginably threatening and definitively un-American. But he tries to make sense of them. To Sandy Roth, who becomes an Absorption poster boy, the changes in the country are thrilling. To the country at large, they are of no account, because for real Americans life goes on as before, and the nation is not at war: Joachim von Ribbentrop, the Nazi foreign minister, who in real life would be executed for war crimes in 1946, dines at the White House in the novel's 1942. The real horror in the story, Roth knows, is to make it all seem reasonable, seductive, fated, so that anyone who stands up to say no will do so not as a hero but as a madman.

In the presidential campaign of 1940, the Roth narrating *The Plot Against America* is remembering the Roosevelt who was passed on to him throughout his childhood by his parents: someone, his parents would explain, who in his patrician words fought fear and gave hope. The family would gather around the radio cabinet: "There was something about the decorum of the delivery that, alien though it was, not only calmed our anxiety but bestowed on our family a historical significance, authoritatively merging our lives with his as well as with that of the entire nation when he addressed us in our living room as his 'fellow citizens.'" But against Lindbergh this memory is a parlor game. Lindbergh was himself "American history delineated in its most inspirational form." The cut of his jaw, his flaxen hair blowing in the wind, his pilot's jacket, the goggles he did not even bother to remove when he stepped from his plane to address a crowd, leaving them on his forehead as a sign of readiness—he was "normalcy raised to heroic proportions, a decent man with an honest face and an undistinguished voice who had resoundingly demonstrated to the entire planet the courage to take charge and the fortitude to shape history." Dissolving Roosevelt's radio community, Lindbergh is the man alone, not only able to shape history but free from it, as the heroes of the past seem to rise out of history and hover over it. And so, in Roth's hands, he acts out the fascist creed, standing for all those Americans, living and dead, who never believed that the U.S.A. was more than a field for dominance, the last best place where one man could prove his superiority over another, and another, and another one after that.

It is the creed that democracy is a fraud and the idea that "all men are created equal" is degenerate, that "government of the people, by the people, for the people" is a fairy tale for the worst, an insult to the best, placing the lowest over the highest, reversing the natural order and the will of God. It is the creed where true nationhood means the will of the people, unknown to the people themselves, embodied by a single leader, who will draw the whole of the people into himself, the whole of the true people—and expel or, the suggestion is never far from the fascist surface, exterminate the rest. With the leader embodying the true will of the people, it becomes possible to see who belongs, and who doesn't. "How do you tell? How do you know for sure? How do you ever really know?" Now you know. Those who do not belong become the enemy; with the leader comes the scapegoat. In action, the will of the people becomes a celebration of destruction. The determinate *purpose* of the Nazi regime, the political theorist Hannah Arendt once wrote, was the committing of previously unheard-of, unimaginable crimes—and now, in Roth's hands, the same story begins to play out in the United States.

That it all ends with Lindbergh vanishing into thin air and the cavalry riding over the hill to save the day—with the whole of the Lindbergh years leaving no imprint on America whatsoever, shifting the nation's time frame or its moral geography not at all, so that in *The Plot Against America* Robert F. Kennedy is still assassinated in the kitchen of the Ambassador Hotel in Los Angeles on 5 June 1968—perhaps only means that Roth, trapping himself in his own fictional body, had to retreat from his own story. There is a moment in *The Plot Against America* where Herman Roth feels the black hole the novel leaves in the American chronicle with his whole being, the republic replaced by "the huge American cult that worships the president." For the way the line slides by, its echo sounding far more loudly than its actual words, the idea of America as a cult perhaps staying with you long after the details of the story Roth tells are forgotten, it is the most frightening moment in the book. But it does slide by. Here the lost republic is inevitably found again. It is not so simple in the stories Zuckerman tells, because he is telling stories of the republic each of his characters carry within themselves, and there is no cavalry.

The Last Trump

When he reached the age of sixty, his adventures behind him, the life remaining to him seemingly no more than a receding shore of contemplation, Nathan Zuckerman thought he understood the Red Scare, the upheavals of the Civil Rights movement, and the Vietnam War. After that he thought he understood the mob that among the public at large never materialized, the mob that was supposed to come for Bill Clinton: it was, he was sure, just that familiar "persecuting spirit," those bad old Puritans who never went away. *American Pastoral, I Married a Communist,* and *The Human Stain* are his account of how little he understood, how what was right before his eyes he never saw: how, whatever else it might be, the U.S.A. is a place and an idea and a speech of the people that always maintains its power to surprise and shock anyone who thinks he or she has seen it for what it is, because in the tales Zuckerman tells, American identity cannot be taken away any more than it can be granted. It is found, discovered, made up, a declaration that each must make.

Too late to reimagine himself, Zuckerman reimagines the stories of others who passed through his time. Inside the Lincoln costume, a dumb Communist; inside Johnny Appleseed, a withered pip; inside a white man, a black man. Instead of a subterranean current of revolutionary change forcing its way into the public square, there is the uncovering of secrets that, in emblematic form, have hidden the true shape of public affairs, of history as we think we have lived it.

This is the American prospect as Roth defines it: the secrets that lie at the root of American identity tell the story of how the burden of creating a new nation, a new society, has shifted into the thrilling, terrifying obligation to create a new self. That obligation in turn shifts back to the social: it shifts into the obligation to connect the personal drama to the nation's drama, so that the story becomes at once specific and shared, perverse and common, the outcast the insider. The American's personal drama must always become American—and in this sense, while everything that matters is secret, can never really be known even to those who carry the secrets, nothing is private. Everything must be made public— and that can be done, Roth's argument may be, only by imagining the times we have lived through as if we have not, with Roth, speaking through his own veil, his own invented self, as the Tocqueville of the American heart, and a few Newark Jews convincingly standing in for the whole of the great expanse of place and people.

It is at this point that the romanticism of Dos Passos's *U.S.A.* returns, the great sense of experiment, of preordained defeat—and because in Roth's dramas the solitary individual who can sin stands in front of the rolling canvas of history, rather than, as with Dos Passos, the other way around, there is also tragedy. *Defeat!* says Zuckerman of Ira Ringold; *Defeat!* he says of the Swede; *Defeat!* he says of Coleman Silk—and the verdict is almost as thrilling as it is in *U.S.A.* as Roth too throws in his lot as an orator haranguing from the lost republic he has made, like anyone else asking Lincoln to witness and to judge, to take the last word.

AMERICAN BERSERK:
BILL PULLMAN'S FACE

I always saw something in his eyes," David Lynch said in 1998, talking about Bill Pullman, the not-the-star of *While You Were Sleeping* and *Sleepless in Seattle*. "Playing these mild-mannered, guy-next-door characters who most of the time don't get the girl—but I saw the possibility for rage, for insanity. For a leading man. His eyes—it was his eyes. There was a lot more going on there than he was being asked to play."

Sometimes you can see the country you're living in by the face you're looking at. In moments, Roth's American berserk has been present in Bill Pullman's face—a face out of a Western at times, but the Old West landscape upended and cracked by earthquakes and drought, the landscape now present simultaneously as a story and a ruin. Far more often, Bill Pullman's face has been so ordinary, so forgettable—or rather nearly impossible to remember, to pick out of the crowd of the movies of the last twenty years—that if anything it has stood for a country that has no need to recognize itself, for the zombie nation that is Roth's American pastoral when it has swallowed the country whole.

The country had a history; now it is just a place. Have a nice day is the limit of its conscious struggle, which is not nothing; its citizens shoulder on, their weapons an eagerness to please and a submerged resentment of the apparent fact that the country does not give back what its history promised. So ordinariness rules, and an actor who can catch it gets work.

You can see that ordinariness as a stage on which a certain drama can be played out, if the drama hidden in the face can change the stage, or burn it down. This couldn't happen if the face came weighted with portent and significance, or even the clichés that come with fame: Jack Nicholson's raised eyebrow, the sign of someone who's always in on the joke. This isn't a matter of playing against type; it's a matter of playing an unknown against nothing.

Maniacs in a Building

It's a question of a drama in a single face; to get to that question, to get to the face, it's necessary to look into the career of the person who found it. As if he were looking for it, too, knowing, by some sense of its gravitational pull, that such a face was present, even if he couldn't see it, even if he didn't yet know where it was.

If the Bill Pullman who appears in David Lynch's 1997 *Lost Highway* is an all-too-modern Gary Cooper, trapped in Cooper's Western gestures but also trapped in Cooper's doubt, unable to extend the gestures of the quick draw and the resolute stare without a flicker of madness, for thirty years Lynch has been as much a frontiersman as Natty Bumppo or Davy Crockett: an extremist, autonomous filmmaker who has both a subject and an audience, and who, working in Los Angeles, has been neither worn down by Hollywood nor marginalized by it. Wearing his shirts buttoned to the neck without a tie, he posits a moral and social wilderness and plunges into it; the rest of the country may turn away or pretend it doesn't notice, but Lynch's bet is that the rest of the country is already there, ahead of him. "Neat," he might say. "Nifty."

Lynch's great subject is instability and displacement: what happens when the ground disappears from beneath your feet, when you find yourself in the wrong place at the wrong time. "I like the nowhere part of America," he has said, but in his films nowhere is where you find it, or make it. Lynch was born in 1946 in Montana, the least populated and least governed state in the U.S.A.; his family moved to Idaho when he was two months old, but Montana remains his touchstone. When anyone asks him where he's from, Montana is what he says. For Lynch the state stands in for an original America, where you can do what you want and no one can tell you different. Lynch admired Ronald Reagan as an Old West anarchist, a libertarian cowboy, the kind of man who'd do what a man's gotta do, like the hero of Owen Wister's 1902 novel *The Virginian*, the source of so many Western shoot-outs and stone faces. "Son of a bitch," says a cowboy to the Virginian across a poker table; it's 1885, in a Medicine Bow saloon in the Wyoming Territory. "When you call me that," says Dustin Farnum in 1914 in the first movie version, Kenneth Harlan in 1923, Gary Cooper in 1929, Joel McCrea in 1946, or Bill Pullman in 2000, "smile." Someday, the Virginian's cattle boss says in Pullman's TV movie, there'll be courts, judges, laws, but for now . . . and he doesn't need to know every last detail. So the Virginian goes out after his cattle-rustling best friend and hangs him in a barn.

Lynch was a guest at the White House during Reagan's presidency; stories have circulated about his ties to operatives on the far right. "It would be beautiful to have a great leader who inspires people from the top down," Lynch told the journalist Kristine McKenna in 1992. "Not some goody-goody guy either." For many years he has supported the Natural Law Party, a creation of the Maharishi Mahesh Yogi, onetime guru to George Harrison, Paul McCartney, and John Lennon, which advocates the precepts of Transcendental Meditation as the solution to all problems ("One change of attitude," Lynch has said, "would change everything"); in 2000 he directed a campaign spot for the physicist John Hagelin, the Natural Law candidate for president. It was so flat it could have been directed by the TV set; there was the odd sense that you were watching an atom scientist delivering radiation warnings in one of the grade-Z science-fiction pictures that ran on television all through the late 1950s. Lynch's politics, such as they may be, seem to have nothing to do with his movies, unless it's politics as Sinclair Lewis defined it for Buzz Windrip: not FDR's "integrity and reason," addressing questions of "monetary systems and taxation rates," but a leader communicating the sensations of "baptism by immersion in the creek, young love under the elms, straight whisky, angelic orchestras heard soaring down from the full moon, fear of death when an automobile teeters above a canyon." "I don't know what I want to say to people," Lynch said in 1986. "I get ideas and I want to put them on film because they thrill me." There is no sense that as an artist he tells his characters what to do, or that they would hold still if he did. "I used to think that the president of the United States had some sort of control over what happened over my neighborhood but now I know that isn't true," he said to McKenna. "We're in a time when you can picture these really tall, evil things running at night, just racing. The more freedom you give them, the more they come out and just race, and they're running in every direction now." At their strongest his characters are those creatures, in flight both from the country and from themselves; they never escape, but the noise churned up by the suspense they generate is deafening. "It's like being locked in a building with ten maniacs. You know there's a door somewhere and there's a police station across the street where they'll take care of you, but you're still in the building. It doesn't matter what you know about the other places if you're still stuck in the building."

Lynch grew up in Boise, Idaho, the factory town of Spokane, Washington, the college town of Durham, North Carolina, and in Alexandria, Virginia. He started out as a painter, which he still is; he began working in film at the Pennsylvania Academy of the Fine Arts in Philadelphia in 1965. By 1970 he was in Los Angeles, with a grant from the American Film Institute. Places send messages, Lynch says, but you can find the country he has mapped anywhere. "I want to make films that occur in America," he told the documentary filmmaker Chris Rodley, "but that take people to worlds where they may never go; into the very depths of their being." This is pure art speech; Lynch's movies rarely speak the language. Despite behind-the-veil-of-illusion effects that go back to 1930s radio plays—the "Who knows what evil lurks in the hearts of men? *The Shadow knows!*" shock-horror of an unreadable boogeyman face, characters replaced by doubles or characters who double themselves, the camera eye disappearing into holes where all the secrets are, holes in the ground or holes in a head—often what is most alive in Lynch's films, what's most compelling, the scene or the image you can never get out of your mind, is right on the surface.

Sex Crime

Lynch's first feature film, *Eraserhead*, appeared in 1976 after five years of nearly budgetless struggle: a grimy little horror movie about a monstrous baby, its father, Henry Spencer, a young man who seems made more out of fear than flesh and blood, and a woman whose cheeks look like tumors and who lives in Henry's apartment, or rather in his radiator, from which she periodically emerges to do a vaudeville shuffle and sing a song. Lynch wrote the lyrics, as he would do for tunes in the films that followed. "In heaven, everything is fine / You got your good things, and I've got mine," the radiator woman crooned, putting a little-girl voice on a 1920s-style blues. The song ended with one tiny change in the words that had gone before: "You got your good things, and you've got mine." That meant that as Henry listened to the weird apparition, he had to realize that it was him; whatever the woman had, he had too, like a second heart, or a second spleen.

The movie was about a person dissolving like sugar in water, though it was also about a haircut: the six or nine inches of hair standing straight up from the head of Jack Nance, who played Henry, and who, beginning ten years after *Eraserhead*, after Nance had come out of a decade of degenerate alcoholism, could be found around the edges of various Lynch projects, playing a gunsel, a grease monkey, a betrayed husband. There, with gray hair and a little mustache, he would look mean, quizzical, beaten down, and most of all small; as Henry, walking through the ruins of some nameless industrial slum with slag streets and soot walls, he towered. "His particular kind of hair would just *lock in*," Lynch said in 2002, six years after Nance died following a drunken, early-morning fight in a Winchell's doughnut shop. The haircut, maintained daily for all the years it took to make *Eraserhead* by the actress Catherine Coulson, at the time Nance's wife, made Henry look like he lived in a wind tunnel. He looked as if at any time his head might leave his body and fly off into the sky.

The hair took away Henry's humanity, or suspended it; it made Nance's squat, round Irish face appear squished down by a hydrocephalic skull. You couldn't bear to look at Henry, because you could imagine that this was what his monster would look like when it grew up; you couldn't look away. "'You know, Jack,'" Nance would remember Lynch telling him, "'one of these days guys are going to be *trying* to get their hair to look like that.' 'At which time,' I told him, 'that's when I'm going to leave the country.'" But Henry never left the movie. Finally his head did fall off. It rolled right down the street, where it was picked up, brought to a factory, drilled, and made into erasers.

Eraserhead was a cult hit; it brought Lynch the studio projects *Elephant Man* (1980) and *Dune* (1984). In 1990, on his own, he made the picaresque *Wild at Heart*, starring Nicolas Cage in the best of his many Elvis impersonations, at least until 2002, when he was briefly married to Lisa Marie Presley. From 1990 to 1991 Lynch was, with Mark Frost, the creator and executive producer of the TV series *Twin Peaks*, named for the imaginary northwest town where the various residents pursue or flee the mystery of who killed the beloved homecoming queen Laura Palmer, a secret prostitute and drug addict, who turns up dead in the premier show, which Lynch directed along with other crucial episodes. "We then get to know the secret lives of all the people in the town as an FBI agent attempts to unravel the crime," Lynch said; *Twin Peaks* was a version of *Peyton Place* where everyone is reading "The Fall of the House of Usher." In

1999 Lynch offered *The Straight Story*, seemingly named for more than its main character, Alvin Straight: an old man who rides a lawn mower hundreds of miles across Iowa and into Wisconsin to visit an estranged brother. After years of controversy, disgust, celebration, condemnation, and dismissal, approval was almost unanimous; as Herman Melville originally described *Pierre*, the picture was "a rural bowl of milk." The real work, and the celebration and disgust, much of it seemingly ritual, is elsewhere, in Lynch's strongest pictures: *Blue Velvet* (1986), *Twin Peaks: Fire Walk with Me* (1992), *Lost Highway*, and *Mulholland Dr.* (2001)—films that as a set could just as well be called "SEX CRIME." There's a vision in these movies: a vision of an America where all boundaries—of familiarity, belief, place, body, and identity—can and will be used against you, where they will be torn up and plowed under.

By means of lurid, sometimes soul-chilling scenes of incest, rape, dismemberment, and murder, through brutal comedy and moments of drama so austere they recall the most indelible moments of silent film, Lynch has pursued this vision where it led, sometimes so heedlessly that the speed of his passage has burnt up whatever trails a viewer might follow. The concessions he has made to flattering or comforting an audience—the happy (or at least resolved) endings of *Blue Velvet* and *Fire Walk with Me*, which can seem to have grown out of the stories that have been told even as they can also seem to be secured with thumbtacks, satisfying resolutions or insulting non sequiturs—are few and mostly hidden. As in *Mulholland Dr.*, in *Lost Highway* there appear to be none.

Gold Rush

"The fifties are still here," Lynch said to Chris Rodley a few years ago. "They're all around. They never went away."

"It was a fantastic decade in a lot of ways," he went on. "Cars were made by the right kind of people. Designers were really out there with fins and chrome and really amazing stuff . . . Now, because they got a computer to aerodynamically design the car, it cuts through the air better and you get better gas-mileage and you don't get the back end of the car rising up when you go a hundred miles an hour. Old cars would weather a crash but the people inside them would just be like, you know, *mutilated!* But I'm telling you now, the thrill is *gone*. B. B. King might have been singing about this *crap* that we drive around now!"

In 1998, onstage in London as part of *Mirror Man*, David Thomas's *Disastodrome!* production, the American poet Daved Hild said the same thing in different words. "Don't get me started," he said, as if he couldn't wait to get started. "Like, those were the days of *non-stop*, kid . . . vision . . . utopia . . . words. Those were the days of gold flowing, shiny black concrete, building the land itself. Speed limits, hell. A time of *speed without limits*, of time without end, just like the river that flowed out back by the porch, the rails that sang over the bridge, the highway that started in the backyard and rolled out, a prescient shadow." Gold flowing, shiny black concrete: America as pure freedom, measured only by sections of broken yellow line running down the middle of a straight black road.

Written by Lynch and the Berkeley novelist Barry Gifford, *Lost Highway* opens from behind the wheel of a car speeding on a black road, a broken line down the middle—a yellow line, here, as in an almost identical shot in *Blue Velvet*, like the broken white line on the black roads in the countless noir films of the 1940s and '50s that used the same device.

Bill Pullman's Fred Madison is a Los Angeles jazz saxophonist in his forties, tortured by fears that his wife—Renee, played by a dark-haired Patricia Arquette—is seeing other men. One morning she finds a video on their front steps, and they play it. Someone has taped the exterior of their house. Maybe a realtor, they say. They find a second video; its eye moves inside their house. From an impossibly high angle, the camera shows Fred and Renee asleep in their bed. They call the police, who advise them to turn on their burglar alarm.

At a party, a drunken Renee hangs on to the host, a sleaze named Andy; she tells Fred to get her another drink. At the bar Fred throws down two quick shots, and as the noise of the party—talk, laughter, and a horrible jazz version of the Classics IV's already pretty terrible "Spooky"—fades to silence on the soundtrack, he is approached by a man with slicked black hair, red lipstick, and white pancake makeup. Played by Robert Blake, the never-named character looks so much like a sixty-year-old Mickey Mouse you half expect him to be wearing three-fingered white gloves; he claims to be inside Madison's house. He hands Fred a cell phone; when Fred calls his own number, he hears the voice of the man standing in front of him answering. The man turns and leaves; the noise of the party comes up, "Spooky" still right in place, as if time hasn't passed. Madison asks Andy if he knows the man, now climbing stairs out of the room. Something to do with Dick Laurent, Andy says.

In an angry panic Fred grabs Renee and drags her home. There is a shot of the two of them outside their house, Renee leaning on a railing in a glamorous long dress, Fred at the front door. Though filmed in real time, the shot seems to play in half-time, and in some other time: in the Aztec-Deco Hollywood exterior of their house, there's a filmy mirror of the Babylonian-Deco sets for D. W. Griffith's *Intolerance*, from 1916. Moments later, when Renee is at her washbasin, taking off her makeup, looking up from under hooded eyes, her dark hair like a fur hat, she herself is suddenly back in the same lost world: in an instant she's the junkie silent-film actress Alma Rubens, Valentino's wife Natacha Rambova, the Hollywood bohemian queen Alla Nazimova of the Garden of Allah. She's all in one: their look on her face is a look of utter allure, a look of power. Renee's self-possession, her ability to possess other selves, is a measure of the weakness of her husband, his inability to stop his own self from splitting in half. With a sense of unutterable desperation and hopelessness, of movement without purpose, every gesture a surrender to the shadows folding around the couple, their return home is made in postures of escape and flight, hatred and loss, self-loathing and contempt. It is so visually intense it seems less like part of a movie than a series of still photographs set in motion. You want to stop every frame as it passes, and the queer tango on the screen makes it seem as if you can.

Alone, Madison plays a third video that has turned up. Like the first two, it opens in black and white; then in color it shows him kneeling on his bedroom floor. There is terror on his face; there are pieces of his wife, butchered like an animal, scattered all over the room. Not on the video, back in the real time of the movie, Madison is interrogated by the same two cops he'd called to his house. "Tell me I didn't kill her!" he begs them; one slugs him in revulsion. His trial is a formality; soon he is on death row.

In his cell Madison has a vision of a house on stilts set in sand, burning; then the smoke and fire are sucked back into the house with a snap. The man in the makeup, plainly Fred's doppel-gänger—short, balding, ugly, and grotesque, as Madison, tall and handsome, believes his hidden, doubled self to be: believes in his subconscious, though the blues term "second mind" is better—is beckoning from the door. Madison sees a broken yellow line as a car rushes down a black road; there is a man standing by the side. Madison's head begins to ache, and he begs his guards for aspirin; then he is possessed by a violent seizure, a thousand silent screams, his head ripping from side to side as if instead of giving him aspirin the guards have decided to give him shock treatment. When it's over, Fred Madison is no longer himself; the man in his cell is twenty years younger, an auto mechanic named Pete Dayton, played by Balthazar Getty as a present-day James Dean. The baf-fled prison officials release the young man to his parents. Baffled himself, but too young to care—or, with his greased hair and black leather jacket, too cool to care—Pete takes up his life where it ap-parently left off. Neither his parents nor his girlfriend, who wit-nessed the vanishing that brought him to Fred Madison's cell, will tell him anything. Pete has sex with his girlfriend—pushing the James Dean connection, she's played by Natasha Gregson Wagner, the daughter of Dean's *Rebel Without a Cause* co-star Natalie Wood—and goes back to his job.

Mr. Eddy—the gangster who, when Bill Pullman is on the screen, is called Dick Laurent, played by Robert Loggia under either name—arrives at the garage where Pete works; Pete is his favorite mechanic. Mr. Eddy has Pete get into his black Mercedes: there's a sound in the motor he doesn't like. Pete takes care of the problem, and they go for a ride; when Mr. Eddy pulls over to let a driver who's tailgating him pass, the man flips him the bird. Mr. Eddy runs him off the road and beats him to a pulp with a huge silver pistol. Mr. Eddy is screaming, but it's a civics lesson: "I want you to get a fucking driver's manual! I want you to study that motherfucker! I want you to obey the rules! Do you know how many fucking car lengths it takes to stop a car at thirty-five miles an hour? Six fucking car lengths! Fifty thousand fucking people were killed on the highway last year!" "I'm sorry about that, Pete," Mr. Eddy says to the terrified mechanic. "But tailgating is one thing I can't tolerate!" Mr. Eddy is a funny guy; he's also dangerous. Pete can't say a word; back in the shop, he's all nerves. Playing a fellow mechanic, Jack Nance has Fred Madison on the radio, blowing frenzied bop; Pete can't stand the music. He snaps it off. "I *liked* that," Nance says, giving Pete the eye, as if he can see the curse that's already on him.

As Lou Reed's jumpy version of the Drifters' once-soaring "This Magic Moment" plays on the soundtrack, Mr. Eddy pulls a Cadillac into the garage, and Pete sees Alice, Mr. Eddy's girlfriend: Patricia Arquette as a gorgeous blonde. She steps out of the car in slow motion, her eyes on Pete, her expression distant and impenetrable, her whole face glowing with a pure film noir sheen, and just like that Pete's life spins out of control. Alice seduces him. Mr. Eddy picks up the scent, and Alice offers a plan. They have to run, they need money, Alice knows a porn merchant named Andy they can rob, they'll steal his car, she'll set it up. When Pete sneaks into Andy's house, he is greeted by a giant projected image of Alice acting in a porn film, grimacing as the penis of an unseen man plunges into her anus. When Andy—the same Andy at whose house Fred Madison met Mr. Makeup—comes down the stairs, Pete knocks him out. Alice comes down to meet Pete; revived, Andy attacks them and Pete hurls him into the air. When he turns to look, he sees Andy on his knees before a glass table, its corner driven five inches into his forehead. "Wow," says Alice, turning into a Manson girl. Pete's nose begins to bleed; he goes upstairs to find a bathroom, moving in a fog down a corridor with a motel's cheap numbered doors. When he comes back down the stairs, the porn movie is still playing, the penis is still plunging into Alice's anus, but now her face on the screen is smiling; off the porn screen, sitting behind Andy's desk, she holds Mr. Eddy's silver pistol on Pete, then brings it to his face: "Don't you trust me?" The stoned Manson girl turns into Barbara Stanwyck in *Double Indemnity*.

Alice hands Pete the pistol. They leave for the house Fred Madison saw in the vision he had in his cell; naked, they make love in the sand, bathed in the headlights of Andy's car. "I want you, I want you," Pete calls out to Alice above him, as if she's miles away. "You'll *never* have me!" she hisses in a disembodied roll of sound, her white body all but disappearing into the blinding white light. She lifts herself off Pete and strides away into the house—and when the man in the sand rises, he is no longer Balthazar Getty as Pete Dayton, but once again Bill Pullman as Fred Madison. He puts on Pete's clothes—the black leather jacket giving him a power in his walk, a sexual confidence, he never had before—and follows Alice into the house. Inside there is no Alice, only his doppelgänger in the bad makeup.

Madison moves off to discover the rest of his story. In a desert motel he moves down a line of numbered doors until he finds Dick Laurent in bed with Renee. She leaves; Madison seizes Laurent and throws him into the trunk of Laurent's own black Mercedes and drives off. When Madison opens the trunk, Laurent attacks him; the doppelgänger hands Madison a knife, and he cuts Laurent's throat. The doppelgänger hands Laurent a tiny TV monitor, where Laurent can see himself and Renee at a party, laughing as a snuff movie plays. "You and me, mister," Laurent says, trying to hold back the blood dripping from his neck, "we can really out-ugly the sumbitches, can't we?"—just before Mr. Makeup shoots Dick Laurent with his own gun. Fred returns to his own house, the house where, long ago, he and Renee played their videotapes, then flees when he is spotted by police. Heading back into the desert, he leads a long line of police cars as the yellow line down the middle of the road rushes at him faster and faster and his face breaks apart in a scream: the same silent scream that on death row turned Fred Madison into Pete Dayton, and that at the end of the chicken run in *Rebel Without a Cause* comes out of the mouth of Buzz Gunderson, James Dean's rival for the affections of Natalie Wood, when he goes over the cliff.

American Pastoral

The beauty in *Lost Highway* is at war with its absurdity, and the beauty—the ability of the film to find a tone and sustain it, to extend it, until you cease to care about anything but the depth of the image before you, its lack of limits—wins. As a friend said, with *Mulholland Dr.*—which is superficially confusing, because its tale of a would-be Hollywood actress reaching Hollywood's deadest dead end is superficially a reversal, where a glamorous fantasy version of the actress's fate precedes the squalid reality it is supposed to replace—the more times you see the picture, the more sense it makes, but with *Lost Highway* each time you watch everything makes less sense. Each time it makes less sense as a narrative— even if as a drama of desire and fear it makes more sense, which is to say that it becomes less possible to dismiss as a narrative absurdity. "We endlessly repeat stories that falsely reassure us that the social is also the real," the film scholar Martha Nochimson says of the perspective Lynch's movies fight off, or mean to destroy.

Certain images in *Lost Highway* take the story that produces the images so far outside of the social that the story ceases to seem real, yet the images are so complete in their familiarity they can convince you that the story contains a plain and simple truth. Just as *Eraserhead* can in moments be about nothing but a pound of hair—hair so bizarre it can make everything around it seem ordinary—there is a way that in *Lost Highway* the story unfolds solely to get Fred Madison to that point where he can take a car down a broken yellow line on a black road at night as fast as the car will go, never mind what's behind him.

That road was the American thing itself, Walker Evans wrote of *U.S. 285, New Mexico*, one of Robert Frank's photographs from his 1959 collection *The Americans*. With its distancing "The," the title of the book signaled that Frank, who came to the United States from his native Switzerland in 1947, still saw Americans as Americans might see "The French," a strange people who could be summed up in a few images and put on a shelf, or that Frank thought that was how Americans understood themselves. But Evans saw the image. With the picture coming right after *Car Accident—U.S. 66, Between Winslow and Flagstaff, Arizona*—four people huddled in the cold and standing over a body covered with a blanket—and mixed in with the Swiss immigrant's doubting portraits of lunch counters, funerals, patriotic displays, jukeboxes, store windows, and bitter, angry faces, Evans was talking about the most ordinary and mythic shot imaginable: U.S. 285, a flat road in the middle of the night in the middle of nowhere, a broken white line running down the right side of the black road, a solid white line on the left, one black car approaching. But it said everything, Evans said, everything he hadn't managed to get into the indelible photographs he himself had made of tenant farmers in Hale County, Alabama, in 1936, the photos that open *Let Us Now Praise Famous Men*, or that he hadn't found in any other picture he'd ever made. "In this picture," Evans said, "you instantly find the continent. The whole page is haunted with American scale and space, which the mind fills in quite automatically—though possibly with memories of negation or violence or of exhaustion with thoughts of bad cooking, extremes of heat and cold, law enforcement, and the chance to work hard in a filling station." In 1972, in his novel *Mumbo Jumbo*, Ishmael Reed raised the ante, but the pull of the image was the same: "Deluxe Ice Cream, Coffee, 1 cent Pies, Cakes, Tobacco, Hot Dogs and Highways," says a Haitian voodoo priest to the Harlem hoodoo detectives PaPa LaBas and Black Herman; it's the early 1920s. "Highways leading to nowhere. Highways leading to somewhere." The sort of highways the U.S. Marines built when in 1915 they occupied Haiti, he says, "to speed upon in their automobiles, killing dogs pigs and cattle belonging to the poor people. What *is* the American fetish about highways?" Reed's Americans answer:

> They want to get somewhere, LaBas offers.
> Because something is after them, Black Herman adds.
> But what is after them?
> They are after themselves. They call it destiny. Progress. We call it Haints.
> Haints of their victims rising from the soil of Africa, South America, Asia.
> Well at any rate I am getting away from our story.

This drama of the iconic—the idea, or the faith, that certain images, certain acts and postures, expressions and movements, framed and allowed to hold a moment of time, can embody very nearly the whole of a country's identity, or its fantasy, its received but still felt and imagined self, the self the country believes it has, the self the country suspects it has, the way a detective might suspect he or she is his or her own culprit—is played as if from a field in Kansas, on a surface as flat as the plains; in *Blue Velvet* the drama is a door that opens onto the country itself. The opening sequence in *Blue Velvet* seems to parody the American fantasy—that is, what's advertised as the all-but-trademarked American dream—but what's happening on the screen may be without any satiric meaning at all, and impossible to immediately understand.

The title sequence has shown a blue velvet curtain, slightly swaying from some silent breeze, calling up the black-and-white

velvet or satin backgrounds used to provide a gloss for the title se-
quences of forties B pictures; the music, Lynch's first collaboration
with the composer Angelo Badalamenti, is ominous, alluring or-
chestral film noir music, at first suggesting Bernard Herrmann and
Vertigo, then a quiet setting where predictability has replaced suspense, then horns cutting off all hints of a happy ending. Bobby
Vinton sings "Blue Velvet," his soupy number-one hit from 1963,
but with the sound hovering over slats of a white picket fence with
red roses at their feet, the song no longer sounds soupy, or for that
matter twenty-three years in the past. It sounds clean and timeless,
just as the white of the picket fence and the red of the roses are so
vivid you can barely see the objects for the colors. In an instant, the
viewer is both visually and morally blinded by the intensity of the
familiar; defenses are stripped away. "A house on a tree-lined block
with a white picket fence, pink roses in the backyard," Bob Dylan
wrote in 2004 of what, in the late sixties, he says he would have
traded his fame and legend for, a visionary unable to imagine the
American iconography of real life any other way.

In slow motion, a fireman on a fire engine moving down a well-
kept middle-class street waves at you, a warm smile on his moon
face. Another picket fence, now with yellow tulips. Children cross
a street in an orderly manner as a middle-aged female crossing
guard holds up her stop sign. There is a house with a white picket
fence and a middle-aged man in a little hat to keep the sun off his
face watering the lawn. Inside the house two middle-aged women
sit on a sofa; there's a Pierrot doll on the lamp table behind them.
They're drinking coffee and watching an old-fashioned TV set, a
small screen set in a blond wood box with legs, a set from the fifties,
when a television was sold as a piece of furniture, an element of interior design, in this case an object reflecting values of taste and
modesty: the box looks Swedish Modern, and also simple enough
that the man in the yard might have made it himself. A noir hand
holding a noir gun moves across the TV screen in noir black and
white, signaling action: signaling the end of the pastoral reverie.

Outside, the man watering the lawn seems to sway with Bobby Vinton; the camera shows the faucet where the garden hose is attached leaking spray. The hose catches on a branch. The sound of water coming from the hose and the faucet rises to a rumble that seems to be coming from out of the ground; every predictable act is about to explode from the pressure it is meant to hide. The man clutches his neck and falls to the ground. He drops the hose; a dog rushes up and, planting its feet on the prone man, drinks from the spray. The rumble grows stronger, and the camera goes down to the ground, to the grass, beneath the grass, to reveal a charnel house, the secret world, where armies of hideous beetles, symbols of human depravity, of men and women as creatures of absolute appetite, banishing all conscience, appear to rise up and march out of the ground to take over the world like the ants in *Them!* Then the hero finds an ear in a field and the detective story begins.

But it is the pastoral that stays in the mind, not nightmare bugs and things-are-not-as-they-seem. Lynch's picture of things-as-they-ought-to-be is elegant; it feels whole, not like a cheat, not like an advertisement for anything, but rather like a step out of the devices of a movie, for a moment a step out of the theater and into an idea of real life. And when you look at the source of the sequence, or at the very least its anticipation, the working out of its account of American life before the *Blue Velvet* fact, you can see that the slightly stiff nature of Lynch's framing and timing of the fireman, the children, the crossing guard, the too-bright images of the fences and the flowers, are not a matter of making the familiar strange, but of getting at how familiar the familiar actually is. Like these first moments in *Blue Velvet*, Bruce Conner's short films *Take the 5:10 to Dreamland* (1976) and *Valse Triste* (1977) dramatize more than anything how inescapable and complete a picture the familiar can make. They capture the familiar as a kind of black gravity, so strong it can seem that no other kind of light, no other kind of image, can escape from it.

Kansas

Born in McPherson, Kansas, in 1933, Conner grew up in Wichita; working in San Francisco from 1957, he had many simultaneous careers in motion by 1976: collagist, assemblage artist, painter, prankster, psychedelic light-show prestidigitator, photographer, and, from 1958, filmmaker. Made from an always-growing archive of found, scavenged, borrowed, pilfered, and even shot footage, there was, first, A Movie, a hilarious compendium of disaster clips. Then Cosmic Ray (1961), with a soundtrack of Ray Charles's "What'd I Say"—and, after that, among others, Report (1963–67), on the first Kennedy assassination; Breakaway (1966), which set out the vocabulary plundered by the first generation of music-video makers; the luminous The White Rose (1967), on the removal, or eviction, of Jay DeFeo's huge painting The Rose from her San Francisco apartment; Permian Strata (1969), Bob Dylan's "Rainy Day Women #12 & 35" scored to four minutes of a forgotten Bible picture; and Crossroads (1976), U.S. government film of the detonation of an atom bomb over Bikini Atoll in 1946, the birth, death, and afterlife of a mushroom cloud, over and over again, from many different angles, until the event seemed like nature, like a whale spouting. Though there was never any dialogue, Conner spoke in many different tongues in these and other pictures; Take the 5:10 to Dreamland and Valse Triste altogether changed the language. From the start, they were visionary works, the ordinary flooded with the uncanny— except that there was nothing uncanny about the images you saw, the music you heard, or the presentation of either. The ordinary was the uncanny.

In Lumberton, the town where Blue Velvet is set, there is no fixed sense of time: the 1986 film is set in its own present, but the Slow Club is a roadhouse out of a forties crime picture, the facade of an apartment house puts you in the twenties, the decor of an apartment inside is faded forties Deco, teenagers at a house party dance demurely to rockabilly and drape all over each other for a pop ballad recorded before they were born, drug dealers worship Roy Orbison, a nice teenage girl wears dresses straight out of 1961 and has a huge framed post-accident photo of Montgomery Clift in her room while her straight-arrow boyfriend wears a tiny gold earring. *Take the 5:10 to Dreamland* and *Valse Triste* too are enveloped in the aura of an earlier time, but while the aura remains as the films play, no sense of the past holds. As Conner assembles segments from educational and training shorts, promotional films, Chamber of Commerce footage, recruiting movies, and the like, all carrying the feel of the thirties, the forties, or the early fifties, you are sucked into a mute play about a vanished way of life, made up of certain rituals: the gestures and postures that portray a family farm, a homogeneous community, a public high school, the apprehension of nature, the acceptance of technological progress. Yet that way of life is so familiar—as it appears on the screen, not culturally but naturally American—that it seems not only still present but in the future, a promise that what is truly American will never change, that the future will most of all resemble the past.

A Common Memory

As *Take the 5:10 to Dreamland* opens, there is the comfortingly repeating sound of birds chirping, and then a single reverberating tone that plays foreboding against the comfort. In brief segments, each separated by black leader—no matter how short, each bit of film seems to tell a story, to unfold—a farmer with an ax in his hand squats to drink from a stream. Beneath barren mountains, there is a fenced-off area and an opening into a rock face below, suggesting missile storage, or a vault for radioactive waste. There is a culvert. A white rabbit sleeps, then sniffs itself awake. There is a split second of a woman's face with rounded, Semitic features. Ore is knocked into water. There is a white horse.

In a sequence that lasts under a minute, but in this five-minute movie feels like a feature film, a girl bounces a ball on a concrete

walkway. You see her only from the knees down, but you are struck
by her striped socks, and the suggestion of horizontal stripes on her
skirt. When the camera pulls back, you are already convinced that
to see the girl as she actually is, her face and her entire body, will
be a kind of pornography, but what you really take in, as the perspective widens, is the wealth of the neighborhood in which she
stands, bouncing her ball: the mansion shielded by tall trees in the
background, the canopy of protection, the spreading lawns.

After this, with the chirping constant and a movie theme
played on strings rising into the frame, a radiator in a genteel room,
and next to it a table with flowers, is already suspenseful. A girl approaches the radiator as if it is an altar; she seems about to place
something on it when the screen goes black. When the scene re-
sumes, the girl opens her hands, and a tiny feather floats into the
air; the girl vanishes as a body but remains on the wall as a shadow.
The footage Conner is using was made for a particular appliance
company, to demonstrate the flow of warm air from its new radiator; as Conner has set the footage, you feel yourself rise into the air.

There is what seems to be the filament of a lightbulb. Slowly,
the receding image reveals itself as the flame of an ascending rocket
ship. As it disappears into the sky, flickering as if it will never completely leave, as if you will never quite see the flame go out, it gut-
ters like a candle. There is a diagram of candle power and light
dispersal. And then, in a sequence lasting over a minute, a young
woman suits up for gym class. She faces a mirror; when she turns,
it reverses the 12 on her back, and the shot holds, but inside itself
it also begins to slip. The mirrored 12 can suggest a secret nu-
merology, as if the numbers on the girl's shirt are the mark of a cult.
You can't tell if this is Conner slowing the footage down, for it is
still barely moving, or a point the original director of *How to Suit
Up for Gym Class* was trying to make. Deep within the mirror is an
image of a blackboard on the other end of what is apparently a long
room; on it is an infinitely suggestive diagram, really a pictogram,
something that looks as if it were made by an imaginative student
or a crazy person, that you will never be able to read. A drop of milk

falls into a saucer, with the image so close and its focus so soft it looks as if a bomb has been dropped onto the whole of the earth. The ripple made by the drop makes a mushroom cloud, and then a spout. At the top of the spout the drop re-forms and separates from the spout; as the spout falls, the drop hovers in the air, then falls back, and the pool swallows it up. There is the sound of thunder; clouds gather; it rains. "Somewhere there's all the ideas, and they're sitting there and once in a while one will bob up and the idea is made known suddenly," Lynch said in 1997. "Something is seen and known and felt all at once."

In the six-minute *Valse Triste*, set to the waltz by Sibelius— theme music for the 1939–44 radio drama *I Love a Mystery*, featuring hard-nosed detective Jack Packard of Omaha, Nebraska—there is simply more of a story, more of the kind of progression that opens *Blue Velvet*. A young blond boy with a crew cut and striped pajamas crawls into a bed with heavy blankets and nice sheets; as he falls asleep, the camera moves in to signal his dream. There is an old locomotive, and a coal car pushed by railroad men. A world globe spins. There are sheep, and a shepherd and his dog. A pickup truck turns onto Kansas 4; on the highway sign, the 4 is framed by a sunflower. There is a barbed-wire fence and a windmill. Brooking no nonsense even from the weather, a stout woman in a floral dress and a go-to-town hat strides out of a farmhouse and climbs into the driver's seat of a pickup truck; her husband and a small boy burn brush. A hand fingers a piece of satin; a bud opens; in the same manner, a fashion model opens a fur coat to display its three-tone lining. An industrialist sits at his desk under a photo of a locomotive so modern it has still not been built. There is a very old locomotive, and an engineer, looking as if he might wave if you keep looking at him. A boy delivers papers; an older couple gets into a taxi; cars with the bud-like tail fins of the early fifties circulate in a Midwestern downtown. Girls do calisthenics on a field; a spraying garden hose is dropped to the ground. The farm family poses for a portrait; an old locomotive slows until the film stops it. Cars from the thirties move down a flooded road.

Despite the title of the first film and the opening sequence of the second, the movies don't move like dreams, and they don't stay in the mind like dreams. As with the discrete set of shots that opens *Blue Velvet*, or the motel doors that appear in both a house and a motel in *Lost Highway*, they play like memory, and they stay in the mind like a common memory laying itself over whatever personal memories a given person watching has—because what the films seem to be showing a viewer is a proof that the notion of personal memory is false. The details of *Take the 5:10 to Dreamland* and *Valse Triste* can be excavated to match specific details of Conner's own boyhood, but what is striking about these small, quiet, burningly intense pictures is that nothing in them is specific to anyone. They are specific—overwhelmingly specific—only as movies about the United States.

"Do you have a video camera?" says one of the *Lost Highway* cops Fred and Renee call about the tapes someone is sending them. "No," Renee says. "Fred hates them." "I like to remember things my own way," Fred says. "What do you mean by that?" the cop says, as if Fred has just confessed. "How I remembered them," Fred says distantly, as if contemplating a country erased from the map a century before, his eyes emptying out. "Not necessarily the way they happened." Rather than a clue to *Lost Highway's* inner depths, which may be how these lines were meant when Lynch and Gifford wrote them, they are a clue to what memory is, and how it might come off of a screen—or through one.

Anyone's memory is composed of both personal and common memories, and they are not separable. Memories of incidents that seem to have actually happened, once, in a particular time, to you, are colored and shaped, even determined, which is to say fixed in your memory, by the affinities your personal memories have to common memories: common memories as they are presented in textbooks and television programs, comic strips and movies, slang and clothes, and all the rituals of everyday life as they are performed in one country as opposed to the way they are performed somewhere else. "In America, we treasure shared things, as if we had a constant fear of being helplessly divided or scattered," the film historian David Thomson writes in *The Whole Equation*, a study of the impact of Hollywood on the country as such. "There is the constitution and the president; the one great highway that goes everywhere; the eternal filling station; the songs on the radio, the sky, the fast-food franchises. The movies? Lines of dialogue fifty years old are current still."

This is what Conner is playing with—and this is how, with a deep and sliding match in pace, reassurance, and suspense, Lynch follows his lead, which is to say takes the same train. Each image or sequence—the fireman waving, the young woman in her basketball uniform, the farm woman getting into her truck, the girl bouncing the ball, the hose on the ground—is something anyone watching a movie made in the U.S.A. can be presumed to have seen before, and to have remembered as if he or she waved back at the fireman or picked up the hose, as if whatever it is that makes the image significant was determined by the person remembering it, and no one else. I think that sense of a common memory—a whole country, all of its history, made and unmade, present in a single image—is what Lynch is after. That's what Bill Pullman's Fred Madison is chasing as he tries to remember what happened, what he did, who he is, and ends up with a line running straight down the middle of the road. This is the drama of the iconic: the killer's eyes in the bland face, trying to remember everything they've seen, the eyes fixed on the familiar line, blinking like mad; the way the simplest, least burdened object, gesture, or expression can lead instantly to the most complex, the most crushing.

I Love a Mystery

Sunday mornin' gonna wake up crazy
Kill my wife and slay my baby
Nobody's business if I do
                    —Riley Puckett, "Nobody's Business," 1940

The establishing shot of *Lost Highway* shows Pullman in extreme close-up, in dark red tones. Fred Madison is in his house, smoking, holding the cigarette right to his mouth, as if he's pressing it into his teeth. It's a picture of a man trying to think when his mind is empty. His hair is disheveled, his cheeks are puffy, his eyes are milky. He looks as if he's just killed someone, or failed to kill himself. He looks half-dead, and as if he's waiting for the other half to come knocking on the door.

His front door buzzes. "Dick Laurent is dead," Fred hears through his intercom. The name means nothing to him. He puts the incident as far out of his mind as he can, which is not that far. He's a man caught up in a depression so bitter he can barely see his hand in front of his face. The last thing he wants in his life is a mystery, but this is where the mystery begins. Barry Gifford says that the breach in the film—"the breakdown where you want to flee something in your mind"—takes place when Fred Madison is on death row: "Pullman takes on a fantasy," Gifford says, "which doesn't work out any better than real life."* But this breach—this

---

*"David had optioned for film my novel *Night People*," Gifford wrote in 1999, "and we had talked for a year or more about how that could be done, but nothing happened. (He told me his daughter, Jennifer, wanted to play the role of one of the two lesbian serial killers.) He fell in love with a couple of sentences in the book in particular, one of which was when one woman says to another, 'We're just a couple of Apaches ridin' wild on the lost highway.' What did it mean? he wanted to know. What was the *deeper* meaning of the phrase 'lost highway'?"—and the description of Lynch as a version of the what-does-it-all-mean interpreters of his own films is priceless. "He had an idea for a story. What if one day a person woke up and he was another person? An entirely different person from the person he had been the day before. OK, I said, that's Kafka, *The Metamorphosis*. But we did not want this person to turn into an insect. So that's what we had to start with: a title, *Lost Highway*; a sentence from close to the end of the book *Night People* ('You and me, mister, we can really out-ugly the sumbitches, can't we?'); the notion of irrefutable change; and a vision Dave had about someone receiving videotapes of his life from an unknown source, something he had thought of following the wrap of the shooting of *Twin Peaks: Fire Walk with Me*. Now all we had to do was make a coherent story out of this."

flight into a fantasy where one prison, the prison of one's own paranoia and jealousy, leads only to the next prison, and the one after that—is better understood as beginning right here, as the film's establishing shot opens into the film's first scene, with the film itself the story of both the unbreakable momentum the fantasy takes on and the capacity of Pullman's squinting eyes to enclose it. Right here, with Madison's face a mask of sweat, stubble, and doubt, everything that follows is present, foreseen, desired; only the details remain to be filled in. The intensity in Pullman's face is the intensity of a man trying to follow his fantasy where it leads, to make it do what he wants, and failing. It is as modern a confrontation with the world left behind by film noir as a shot of Patricia Arquette's Alice, speaking to Pete Dayton over the phone, her face entirely in shadow except for the light on her red lips, is classic.

"Wafting cigarette smoke, the dance of shadow and light, moody music played by a forlorn trumpet," the critic and novelist Steve Erickson wrote in 2004, "all have upstaged the moral and spiritual bleakness that originally engendered noir." By that time noir had so expanded as an idea, as a nihilist slouch or a cynical glance, that it could take in almost anything: F. W. Murnau's 1927 *Sunrise* or Fritz Lang's 1931 *M* as precursors, all Clint Eastwood movies where he kills someone, everything by Fassbinder, early Godard and Truffaut, the Steve Martin version of Dennis Potter's *Pennies from Heaven*, the 1950s TV show *Peter Gunn*, and the Nixon administration. "That the style of noir made moral and spiritual bleakness glamorous might have shocked the noir directors of the 1940s," Erickson wrote:

Coming to America as European refugees, in many cases Jewish, with fascism at their backs, Fritz Lang, Otto Preminger, Robert Siodmak, and Billy Wilder brought with them a sensibility forged out of the German expressionism that was itself forged out of the trauma of World War I. By the time World War II gave way to the revelation of the Holocaust in all its stupefying dimensions and the prospect of nuclear obliteration in all its mind-boggling possibilities, noir had distilled what seemed like the collapse of civilization into human interaction at its most debased. Murder was just another career move, double cross a legitimate survival strategy. The bed that a man and woman shared was a cage, the bedroom door a threshold of no return. There was no love; there was just obsession, which lovers would have chosen over love even if they had a choice.

This is the man Bill Pullman is playing in *Lost Highway*, as every time Fred and Renee speak or gesture to each other something is off, halting, fearful, probing, each trying to trick the other into revealing something the other will do anything to keep hidden, even from him or herself, an effort that turns into Fred's self-loathing and Renee's contempt; this is the territory David Lynch is opening up. "Sometimes you can walk into a room and you can sense that something's wrong," Lynch said to Kristine McKenna, and there is never a moment in Fred and Renee's house when that isn't true—when it isn't happening. The house seems simple enough—bedroom, bathroom, living room, presumably a kitchen—but in fact it feels as if it's made of corridors, not rooms, dead ends, not doors, hallways without any endings at all. You can't imagine going from one room to another just to get a glass of water.

Inside the house, the film could hardly be more silent. You begin to hear the ambient sounds of the rooms themselves, then a rumble; these walls do talk, but they don't tell. It's as if the house is taking its space back from its occupants, the way a forest takes its ground back from an abandoned building. This is a vaguely stylish married couple's house as a haunted house; it turns people into monsters, breaks them down. Fred Madison goes to his gig at the Luna Lounge alone, with Renee staying home to read; when he calls between sets, there's no answer, and when he returns and finds her asleep, he already has a killer's gaze. Back from the party where Fred met the man in the makeup, he tells Renee to wait outside: if the person who answered the phone when Fred called his own house is really there, he's going to find him. He vanishes into a passageway; shot to produce a receding perspective, the passageway makes a V like a woman's crotch. When Madison reappears, he emerges from in-

side the phantom woman. Everyone who will die in the movie is already dead in his eyes. It isn't clear whether he knows it or not.

With each word out of his mouth shaped as if anticipating a rebuke, Madison sleepwalks through his waking hours. He sleepwalks even when he's trying to make love to his wife—in one of the
creepiest sex scenes ever put on film, shot in super-slow motion,
with Renee's breasts bobbing as if floating underwater, and she herself as far away as the Lake of Dreams. "It's okay," she says, patting
her husband's back, his flesh now made of shame, as hers is made
of scorn. Then there is even more death in his eyes. "I had a dream
last night," he says finally. "You were inside the house. You were calling my name"—and he sees himself wandering the house as if he
doesn't know his way from one place to another, passing a fire in a
fireplace as if it were brush burning in a desert. "I couldn't find
you"—and smoke rises in huge billows. "And there you were. Lying
in bed. It wasn't you—it looked like you. It wasn't"—and he sees
himself approaching the bed, and the woman in it screaming. He
looks back at Renee, back in real time, out of the dream. At first her
face only seems hideously old; then it is not even female; then it is
the pancake face of the man at the party, which seems to turn to
stone. But the man at the party is a version of Madison, who doesn't
understand that he has replaced his wife's face with his own.

This is the man who takes *Lost Highway* over its first cliff, and
his disappearance from *Lost Highway* is a great relief. When Pete
Dayton replaces Fred Madison, the tone is that of a normal movie.
At least until elements of Madison begin to surface in the young
body that is hiding him, and Pete too begins to dissolve, there are no
more mystery characters, no more echoes of a forgotten past, nothing that can't be fitted into the everyday. Events proceed according
to a pace that does not have to be explained. People talk. They make
jokes. They get angry. Scenes of sex or violence are preceded by ordinary incidents that might lead to sex or violence. It's this section
of the film that allows the viewer to relax into it, to forget the apparently absurd premise that has led to this banality, to follow the

action as if it's taking place in a regular film, but this respite also dramatizes the motionlessness of the first part of the film, the slow dance of its lassitude and tension: how bizarre it all is.

The intolerability of Madison's life and his inability to change it will send him out of his life: in fantasy, he will try to preside over his own execution for his own imagined crimes. When that fails, he will try to live out his life in a different body, with a different name, with a different past, in a different world. But everyone Madison meets in this new world—Andy, Pete Dayton, Mr. Eddy, who appears by name in the first scene of the movie as Dick Laurent, Alice, the Renee who reappears in the Lost Highway motel—is, like Madison's doppelgänger, his alter ego, a projected creature made out of what Madison wants and what he fears. Whatever Fred Madison does to them he does to himself, and so when the man in the makeup kills Dick Laurent and Madison returns to his own house and, standing at his own front door, says into the intercom, "Dick Laurent is dead," he is trying to prove that he has killed himself.*

The key to Lost Highway is not to look beneath its surface for

---

*"Doppelgänger" is an easy enough word to use on the page; it's less easy to follow when it leaves the page. There is no way, now, to avoid the fact, which on the stage set by Lost Highway is a fantasy, not a news story, that four years after Robert Blake appeared in the film, in what to that point was his last movie role, he was arrested in Los Angeles for murdering his own wife. On 4 May 2001, Bonny Lee Bakley was shot while sitting in Blake's car; he had, he told police, returned to the restaurant where they had just finished dinner to retrieve a pistol he had accidentally left behind, and when he came back to the car, Bakley was dead. There were no eyewitnesses.

Born in 1956, Bakley was a con artist with a mail-order sex business and a reputation for preying on faded celebrities; after an involvement with Jerry Lee Lewis, Bakley had a daughter, whom she named Jeri Lee Lewis, though Lewis denied paternity and none was ever established. Born Michael Gubitosi in 1933, Blake began his career as an actor with MGM's Our Gang comedies in 1938; he came to prominence in 1967, with the film adaptation of Truman Capote's In Cold Blood, where he played Perry Smith, who in 1959, along with Richard Eugene Hickock, murdered four members of the Clutter family in Holcomb, Kansas. Both men were hanged in 1965. As told in 2002 in I Don't Know Jack, a documentary film about Jack Nance directed by Chris Leavens, for which David Lynch served as executive producer, the story is that in the final casting for the role of Perry Smith, the choice was between Blake and Nance. You have to imagine the look Nance would have given Blake had they passed each other on the Lost Highway set: a look that said, in Nance's cocked eye and loser's smile, I see any kind of secret, but to find its surface, which is almost impossible to do. It is almost impossible even if it is looking you in the face—that is, even if the purpose of the movie is to lead you to accept that Bill Pullman's face is looking into yours, or that he is looking out of your own eyes, asking you if you too have not betrayed all the promises you have made to yourself and everyone around you, if you, too, do not deserve the worst you can imagine. On its shifting

---

right through you, all the way to the other side. "You have to love the person you are going to play," Blake once said. "I have played a lot of people who killed. I have been on Death Row. You know, I have never met a murderer in my life. That's because there ain't any. There are people who crossed the line. Some of us don't cross the line."

Blake became a star with the 1975–78 TV cop show *Baretta*: "Don't do the crime if you can't do the time" was his catchphrase. Divorced from his first wife in 1983, he was known around Hollywood in the 1990s for prowling nightclubs in search of women and taking them into parking lots to have sex in his truck; Bakley had at least eight marriages behind her when in 1999 she met Blake at a Burbank jazz club and climbed in. A daughter was born in June 2000; Blake and Bakley married that November. According to testimony at Blake's three-month trial—which received almost no media attention—he repeatedly tried to hire men to kill her ("'The baby was real,'" one witness testified Blake told her, "'the marriage wasn't'") and, rebuffed, finally had no choice but to do the job himself. So argued the prosecution—but on 16 March 2005 a jury found Blake not guilty of murder, and not guilty of soliciting murder; the judge dismissed a second solicitation charge after the jury hung eleven-to-one in favor of acquittal. "If you have to commit a crime," Stephen Colbert of *The Daily Show* reported from Santa Maria, California, on 14 June 2005, on the occasion of Michael Jackson's acquittal on charges of child molestation, "California is the place to do it"—a statement he later amended to "Southern California." He ran through a litany that included police officers acquitted for the videotaped beating of Rodney King, thugs acquitted for the videotaped beating of a truck driver during the riots that followed the acquittal of the police officers, the acquittal of O. J. Simpson for the murder of his wife and a male friend despite "her blood on his glove," and Robert Blake. "'I went back to the restaurant to get my gun' was his *alibi*," Colbert said.

"Probably guilty is not enough," Blake's attorney M. Gerald Schwartzbach told the jury in his closing argument. Several days after the verdict, Los Angeles District Attorney Steve Cooley denounced the jurors as "incredibly stupid." "He is as guilty as sin," Cooley told reporters. "He is a miserable human being." "Shut up," Blake said immediately after the verdict, when asked about the identity of the real killer. "Anybody got a question that makes sense?" "Mr. Blake said he would strike out on the road," Charlie LeDuff reported in the New York *Times*, "searching for freedom." Eights months later, on 18 November 2005, a jury in Burbank, California, ruling 10–2 in a wrongful death suit brought by Bakley's adult children, found that Blake "intentionally caused" her death and set damages at $30 million. "Before the trial began," the Associated Press reported, "Blake tried to settle with the family for $250,000, which he said was the remainder of his once-large fortune. They rejected the offer."

sands, *Lost Highway* is the freest of David Lynch's movies, the least afraid of its audience, with Lynch himself least afraid of his own sensations, his own ideas. It is also Lynch's artiest film, the one that most calls attention to its own composition, its cleverness, its refusal to meet its audience where these days an audience expects to be met: in its lap. The artiness leaves a perfume of transcendence, the transcendence of reality and ordinary life; it also leaves a sense that the apparent insistence on a secret hiding inside both the movie and the American landscape, the physical landscape, the psychological landscape, is a con, and that is because it is. The con is that inside this movie there is not a secret but another movie, one that in its time would have been laughed out of town if it had ever claimed to be about anything more than sixty-seven minutes long.

Route 66

The day we met, I went astray
I started rolling down
That lost highway
> —Hank Williams, "Lost Highway," 1949

I'm not the only pawn on the lost highway
> —Daved Hild, *Mirror Man*, 1998

"Fear is in the driver's seat," Lynch said in 1997 of *Lost Highway*. *Lost Highway* is not a rewrite or a remake of *Detour*, a sub-sub-sub B movie made in 1945 by Edgar G. Ulmer for Producers Releasing Corporation, a factory on Hollywood's Poverty Row with a name like a front for organized crime.* *Lost Highway* is a reinhabiting of *Detour*; Lynch's movie emerges from Ulmer's, inside out, just as, when *Lost Highway* plays, Ulmer's movie emerges from Lynch's,

---

*To cash in on the cult the film had attracted since the late 1960s, *Detour* had already been remade, in 1992, with Tom Neal, Jr., son of the original male lead, as the lead— and, supposedly, with the car used in the original film as the car.

flattening it, exposing its surfaces, linking one broken line down the middle of a road to another.

Lynch says he wants to take people "into the very depths of their being"; he speaks the language of art, and others speak for him in the same vein. Lynch, Martha Nochimson writes, shows "ordinary reality as a cultural system continually breaking down yet remaining in place." His work demonstrates that in "the *ideal* of completeness we find the human capacity for form, but in the *real* incompleteness of human systems, in their actual breaks and discontinuities, we find our capacity for truth." Another way of saying the same thing is that Lynch can be seen as a maker of splatter films as readily as he can be seen as a maker of art films. In 1986 many honest critics protested the violations of *Blue Velvet*—the obscenity, the violence, the sex that was indistinguishable from violence—at least before the art cavalry rode over the hill to save the day; by 1990, with *Wild at Heart*, a dog running off with a hand in its mouth could be described as merely "Lynchian." Without the aura of art, of the artist struggling to glimpse the truth and tell it—as opposed to the entreaties of the entertainer, always eager to exchange good times, or for that matter anything else, for money—Lynch's sex crime films might be lumped in with *Natural Born Killers*, and Lynch like Oliver Stone named not just a fetishist but an enemy of the people. But what if Lynch had to become an artist, had to set himself the task of seeing his country whole and then telling his fellow citizens what it looked like, taking them into an America where, though they live there, they never go, not because he saw the stars reflected in the gutter, but because he found himself thrilled by the filth—or the fear of death when an automobile teeters above a canyon? Why else do you climax *Blue Velvet* with a cop standing up dead, fashioning a tableau where the blood dripping out of the cop's head is somehow less appalling than his canary yellow sport jacket?

Edgar G. Ulmer had an art background; in Hollywood he learned how to talk like a gangster, or a comedian. Born in Austria-

Hungary in 1904, he was working in Berlin as a designer and assistant director for F. W. Murnau, perhaps the greatest of all filmmakers, by the time he was twenty; in 1927 he followed Murnau to Hollywood to work on *Sunrise*—Dreiser's *An American Tragedy* as a German folktale—which may be the greatest movie ever made. By the 1930s he was shooting cheapie Westerns, horror pictures, films in Ukrainian and Yiddish. In 1934, while directing *The Black Cat*, he began a romance that offended the head of the studio; after that he was blackballed by every major film company for the rest of his life. He never stopped working. In 1960, at the Texas State Fairgrounds in Dallas, over the same eleven days he made both *Beyond the Time Barrier* and *The Amazing Transparent Man* for Roger Corman's American International Pictures.

"The title is very commercial," Peter Bogdanovich said while interviewing Ulmer in 1970, two years before Ulmer died; Bogdanovich was speaking of Ulmer's 1943 *Girls in Chains*. "Of course!" Ulmer said. "That's what made the goddamned thing. At the beginning of the season . . . we would invent forty-eight titles. We didn't have stories yet; they had to be written to fit the cockeyed titles. I am convinced when I look back that all this was a challenge. I knew that nothing was impossible. When *Double Indemnity* came out and was a huge success, I wrote a picture we called *Single Indemnity*. We were able to write that junk in about two weeks."

Here you cannot untangle the language of the artist, who believes that everything is possible, from the language of the hack, willing to throw anything on the screen if there's a chance it might sell. Opening with that broken line running down the middle of the road, *Detour* is just as indecipherable. "Were these actors, hoping for careers," David Thomson asks of Tom Neal and Ann Savage, the two hitchhikers in *Detour* who meet on Route 66 on their way to Los Angeles, "or derelicts resolved to treat the idea of a movie with contempt?" It's a story Ulmer almost tells: "I was always in love with the idea and with the main character, a boy who plays the piano in Greenwich Village and really wants to be a decent pianist . . . And then the idea to get involved on that long road into

Fate, where he's an absolute loser, fascinated me. The same thing, of course, with the boy who played the leading character, Tom Neal. He wound up in jail after he killed his own wife. He did practically the same thing he did in the picture."

As Al Roberts, Tom Neal stands by the side of the road with his thumb out. We've already met him as the absolute loser, playing wildly, incoherently in a New York bar after his girlfriend and singing partner has left him for Hollywood because his ambition doesn't match hers. But now he's heading out to meet her. In Arizona he gets a ride from a blowhard in a fancy convertible, Charles Haskell. As the car pulls out, Ulmer, shooting from behind, shows the two men as doubles: they're the same size, their suits are the same shade, even their hats are blocked in the same way.

Haskell keeps asking Roberts for pills he has in the glove compartment. He brags about how he picked up a woman and tried to rape her, about the gambling business he has in Florida, about the family in Los Angeles he hasn't seen for years but there's money there and he's going to get some. "Yeah," Roberts says in a scummy close-up, cutting off the word as if it ends in a hard consonant, as if he can hardly bear to speak it. "Right." "Yeah." It's a fabulous sequence. Roberts knows the wrong attitude could get him kicked out of the car, but he can't really say yes to what he's hearing. There's nothing in his face but sweat, stubble, shame, and anger. All the shared gestures of the Great Depression are present in the way Tom Neal sits in the car; in a mute affirmation of the Declaration of Independence, a man who has nothing tries to maintain some dignity and distance in the face of a man who acts like he has everything. More than half a century later, with Pete Dayton sitting frozen in Al Roberts's seat next to Mr. Eddy's Charles Haskell, the political dimension will have disappeared, but the feeling will be the same.

Haskell stops at a diner and buys the penniless Roberts dinner, then tells him to drive and falls asleep. It starts to rain; Roberts pulls over to put the top up, but when he tries to wake Haskell, the man falls out of the car dead. "You're going to tell me you don't believe my story," Roberts says in a voice-over, startlingly addressing who-

ever might have been expected to be present in whatever grind
house *Detour* was playing in 1945. "I can see that don't-make-me-
laugh expression on your smug faces." If we won't believe him—and
despite what we've seen on the screen, we don't—what chance is
there the cops will? Roberts explains how he had to hide the body,
how he realized he had to take the car ("I couldn't leave the car here
with him in the gully—that'd be like erecting a tombstone"), not to
mention Haskell's money, his papers, and his clothes. He dresses
Haskell's body in his own clothes and leaves his own identification
on the corpse. "Al Roberts is dead," he says in his voice-over; as
Fred Madison will become Pete Dayton, Roberts becomes Haskell.
As Fred Madison will again become himself, Roberts is only wearing different clothes; he cannot change.

Stopping for gas near the California border, he picks up the
hitchhiker played by Ann Savage: "You can call me Vera," she says.
Her hair is greasy; her skin has a film of grime.* Her face is
clenched, as if she needs to kill someone. She looks like a harder,
thinner Gladys Presley, with the heavily shadowed eyes Gladys
passed on to her Elvis. Puffy cheeks, a threatening hawk nose, her
big features shaped not by prettiness but by wariness and mistrust—
all speak for the bitter knowledge of the consumptive, which Vera
is. And she knows everything. She rode with Haskell all the way
from Louisiana; she's the woman he tried to rape. Seeing Roberts
in Haskell's car and Haskell's clothes, she draws the obvious conclusion: murder. Just as quickly, she settles on the obvious solution: blackmail. They'll sell the car; she'll take the money and the
cash Roberts took from Haskell's body. Then she'll let him go. Oth-
erwise she calls the cops.

---

*Savage appeared for the scene made up, with her hair in place; Ulmer had the crew
smear cold cream in her hair and rub dirt in her face. As she stood in front of a gas station, with Ulmer getting ready to shoot from the roof, a car pulled up and the man driving tried to wave her inside; in 1945 he could figure any woman standing alone on the
side of a highway was a prostitute, or simply too desperate to turn down anybody with
his own machine.

Savage's eyes shoot out of their own blackness. Her voice is shrill, harsh, punishing, a complete explosion of every notion the audience of her day would have had of what a leading lady in a feature film was supposed to sound like. Her head is a gun and each word is a bullet; each word is an accusation, and every accusation is a threat. "Edgar snapped his fingers," she told the film noir historian Eddie Muller: "*'Faster! Faster!'*" "Just remember who's boss around here," Vera says, the words curling around Roberts's throat like a rope—she has sensed the weakness and passivity that Roberts is made of, just as Renee and Alice will with Fred Madison and Pete Dayton. Roberts sinks into a slough of self-pity. "That Haskell wasn't dead yet," he says as the film moves under his voice-over. "He wasn't stretched out still and cold in any Arizona gully. He was sitting right next to me, laughing like mad while he haunted me." But it's Roberts who is now Haskell; it's Vera who is Roberts's haint.

In Los Angeles, Vera rents the two of them a cheap apartment, using the name Mr. and Mrs. Charles Haskell: if they're going to sell the car, they're going to need an address. In what might be the only direct reference *Lost Highway* makes to *Detour*, just as Pete Dayton can't listen to Fred Madison on the radio, here Roberts can't stand the sound of a neighbor's saxophone. He and Vera settle into a routine of backbiting and boredom. "We'll be discussing politics next," she says with disgust after Roberts has expounded his the-game-is-fixed philosophy of life. It's a way of saying that she knows the two of them are part of the trash heap of the American republic, a last acting out of the promise that every citizen is free: morally free, now that all promises of equality and the pursuit of happiness have collapsed into the economy—into the specter of the Depression, as present in *Detour* as in any film made in the 1930s—to keep whatever he or she can steal. Drunk, she wants to sleep with him; his flesh crawls not because she is repulsive but because he's afraid of her. Roberts can't sleep with Vera in the same way that Fred Madison is impotent with his wife: the greater his weakness, the greater her contempt. "If this were fiction," Roberts says in his

voice-over, "I would fall in love with her, marry her, and make a respectable woman of her—or else she'd make some supreme Class
A sacrifice for me, and *die.*" "You sap!" she snarls, pulling Roberts
back to earth. Except for the sex scene in the desert, which in 1945
could only have been shot for a porn movie, Patricia Arquette's Alice walks in the footsteps of Ann Savage's Vera, and falls behind.

As Vera's plans for Haskell's money grow more and more
grandiose, she and Roberts fight. Drinking hard, she threatens
once more to call the cops on him; she runs into the bedroom with
the telephone and locks the door, passing out on the bed with the
cord draped over her shoulders and the phone in her hand. In a
panic, Roberts pulls on the cord under the door, to break it, he
says; when he finally breaks into the room he finds Vera strangled
to death. He runs, heading back east; he soon learns that in Los
Angeles, Charles Haskell is wanted for murder. He is Al Roberts,
but Al Roberts is dead. He walks down the highway in the middle
of the night; a police van pulls up beside him.

As *Detour* ends, the beginning and the end of *Lost Highway* come
together—just as when Bill Pullman rises naked from the sand,
where, moments before, Pete Dayton shouted under Alice, he all but
calls Tom Neal back from the dead. In Pullman's earlier films his features were soft under sandy hair, unformed; in this moment they are,
like Neal's features, sharpened like weapons. "He had a really great
haircut!" Lynch says; with dyed-black hair Pullman now moves like
the killer Neal turned out to be, just as, in the first scene of *Lost
Highway*, Fred Madison, with his red face, trying to think and coming up with nothing, is *Detour* from beginning to end.*

---

*Fred Madison had his double in *Lost Highway*; as Ulmer said, Neal's double was Al
Roberts from *Detour*, killing the woman posing as his wife, if it wasn't that Al Roberts's
double was Neal.

Neal's career in Hollywood—he appeared in nearly a hundred low-budget or no-

Bill Pullman's Face

Bill Pullman's face is pushed down by a weight he's suddenly realized he's carrying. His eyes shade themselves, as if he's sighted something on the horizon and is trying to bring it into focus—a ship that only he can see. But what you are seeing is pure pressure, the weight coming down, the muscles in the face straining to hold it up. The face begins to close, then it stops, and Pullman pulls back to think it all over, caught up in the joke or the horror of it all, wondering if somehow there might be more to the story, even if he knows there isn't. In *Lost Highway*, but also in *Malice* (1993), *The*

---

budget pictures—came to an end in 1951 after a fight with the actor Franchot Tone over the actress Barbara Payton. Payton married Tone but soon left him for Neal; Tone survived the scandal, but Neal and Payton did not. Neal moved to Palm Springs and opened a gardening business; Payton became a notorious Hollywood streetwalker and drunk. In 1961, Neal married his third wife, Gail; by 1965 they were separated and she was demanding a divorce. On April 1, Neal walked into a local restaurant and told the owners he'd just shot his wife while she was sleeping. They thought he was kidding. "It's not an April Fool's joke," he said. Gail Neal was found shot behind the right ear with a .45; Neal was charged with first-degree murder. At the trial, with Payton in attendance every day, Neal finally won "in the courtroom what had escaped him in his film career—top billing," as the Hollywood chronicler Arthur Lyons put it in 1999 in *Palm Springs Life*. Neal told his story: He and his wife had begun to argue over men she'd slept with while they were separated. She pulled a .45, and in his attempt to get it away from her, it went off. A graduate of Harvard Law School, Neal was still in a B movie—but then he shifted ground, back to the Los Angeles evangelist Aimee Semple McPherson and the Spiritualist and Theosophical cults that have flourished in Southern California for more than a hundred years. "Did you do anything after that?" Neal's lawyer asked him. "I prayed," Neal said. "I took her hand, I called her name, 'Gail! God no! Gail!' Then I said aloud, 'There is no life, truth, intelligence or substance in mind, all in infinity and its manifestation, for God is all in all. Spirit is immortal truth, matter is mortal error. Spirit is the real and eternal, matter is the unreal and temporal.'" Cold comfort as this might have been to Gail Neal, she wasn't listening—but the script had one more line. "Did you say anything else?" said Neal's lawyer. "Yes," he said. "Talithucumi, which is interpreted as 'Fair maiden arise, for thou art whole.'" The jury came back with involuntary manslaughter. Neal's attorney asked for probation; the judge responded with an indeterminate sentence of up to fifteen years. Neal was paroled in 1971, and moved to a small apartment in Hollywood. He was found dead there in 1972; he was fifty-eight. The only Google reference for "talithucumi," which sounds less like a word denoting an Aztec sacrifice than something H. P. Lovecraft made up, is for Arthur Lyons's article in *Palm Springs Life*.

Last Seduction (1994), The End of Violence (1997), the version of
The Virginian in which he starred and directed (2000), The Guilty
(2000), in Rick (2004), a no-singing version of Rigoletto set in a
Manhattan consulting firm, most unsettlingly in his small role in
Igby Goes Down (2002), where he plays a man so fascinated by his
own depression his every expression is a rehearsal for the dissolution of the face itself, there are moments when Pullman's face and
the weight pressing on it—the weight of the collapse of a marriage,
the collapse of belief, the weight of a world that looks just as it did
yesterday but no longer makes any sense at all—become the whole
of the drama. His face concentrates motives and events so sugges-
tively that it becomes its own landscape: a window opening onto an
America defined not by hope but by fear, not by reason but by paranoia, not by mastery but by sin, crime, and error. At its root it's a
Puritan drama, played out in God's country—a country, the face
says, that God long ago left to its own devices, a judgment the face
doesn't question, doesn't doubt.

Richard Avedon once caught that face. In his show "Portraits" at
the Metropolitan Museum of Art in New York in 2002, overfamiliar
work made Avedon's overfamiliar white backgrounds and every-pore
focus oppressive, but in a room featuring pictures from his 1985
collection In the American West there was a breach. Some of Avedon's shots of highway bums are so lurid they're unforgettable, in
the worst, freak-show manner; Clarence Lippard, drifter, Interstate
80, Sparks, Nevada, August 29, 1983 was different. Instead of the
lantern jaws and thieves' postures of the other men on the walls,
Lippard held himself in reserve. The countless big, dark freckles—
or skin cancers—that covered his face and hands spoke for a life
lived out of doors; his dark blazer and bleached white shirt made it
seem as if he were a gentleman farmer out for a stroll. Fine-looking
in an old-money, East Coast way, with a full head of sandy hair, Lippard appeared in two photos. One—showing him from the waist
up, as if shot from below—softened his features, weakening his
chin and turning his nose bulbous. But Avedon's second picture,

shot head-on and cropped at mid-chest, was Lippard gazing straight out, his chin strong, his nose hard. In the way he carried himself, he offered no quarrel with God, but dared you to judge him. His face suggested Gregory Peck or Robert Ryan; the disease on his skin deepened his face, until you could see Lincoln along with the movie stars. And then behind all the other faces you saw Bill Pullman.

You saw a version. "Dave always had Bill in mind," Barry Gifford says. "David likes to have a kind of neutral character. It was hard to read his face." "It's the sign of a great actor," Lynch says. "To inhabit the character, so that it changes him." "He can play Fred Madison," Gifford says. "He can go out and play *President* Madison." Or for that matter President Thomas J. Whitmore in *Independence Day* in 1996, which amounts to the same thing. Most often Pullman has disappeared into his face, into a mask of bland, sexless handsomeness—as the sheepish grin in *While You Were Sleeping* (1995), the straight man in *Sleepless in Seattle* (1993), the rogue CIA agent in *Spy Games* (1999), in a score more roles (mistaken for Bill Paxton in one, for Jeff Daniels in another) where his vagueness is so complete it becomes its own kind of nihilism. Pullman's earnest, bumbling nice guy circling Sandra Bullock in *While You Were Sleeping* is only a few steps removed from his humiliated doctor in *The Last Seduction*, who peddles scripts and runs drug deals to keep his wife happy, who wanders their apartment looking in mirrors, marveling at her nerve after she takes off with the $700,000 he's gotten from selling pharmaceutical cocaine. The fighter-pilot president in *Independence Day*, always clear-thinking and resolute in the face of an attack on the planet by aliens from outer space—a combination of the World War II pilot George Bush and Bill Clinton (for whom, at the White House, which in the movie is blown up, Bill Pullman screened the film)—is a character almost mathematically reversed in *Lost Highway* and *Igby Goes Down*. The persona an actor develops is itself a landscape; the roles where Pullman gets lost in the scenery are a backdrop for the real action, a foundation for the house that's going to be pulled down.

That may be what Lynch saw in Pullman's eyes—the rage, the insanity, in the guy next door. Next door may be where Pullman usually finds himself, but there was another country to be discovered, to be felt out in the course of a role: a nation sick of its burden of stronger, better, purer, truer, but lacking any other bluff to run, even on itself. Pullman calls the bluff on his everymen in *Malice*, *The Last Seduction*, *The End of Violence*, *The Guilty*, *Rick*, *Igby Goes Down*, playing a college dean, a physician, a Hollywood producer, a lawyer, a businessman in his fifties whose only job is to flatter his thirty-year-old boss, a middle-aged man institutionalized after a breakdown. All of these men are cuckolds, but they appear less surprised by the betrayals of their wives than stunned, amused, or even thrilled to find how intertwined the lives they've led are with evil.

With his cards faceup and worthless, in each role Pullman traces the footsteps of a previous character, and the effect is a feeling of suspension, as Pullman's face seems to contemplate itself more than the world or his enemies, as he tries to read his own mind, and a thin, curling smile pulls against the twitch of murder or suicide in his eyes.

The Hero

There is the feeling of a will toward a finale as the character tries to reach its fate. It's there in *The Guilty*, when Pullman's attorney Callum Crane, having parlayed the cover-up of the murder of a woman he raped into a Federal judgeship, makes his smugness inseparable from his self-loathing, his self-contempt as nothing against his contempt for a world so corrupt it could grease the rails for a man like him. It's present in *Rick*, where Pullman humiliates himself in front of his boss and then, with the two of them in a bar, humiliates a waitress who, back in his office earlier the same day, he goaded into losing her temper and blowing a job. What was business in the office is now cruel, sadistic, a toady offering a perfor-

mance of domination and entitlement to his boss, who laughs, because he gets the joke: Pullman, who back in the boss's office was
crawling on his hands and knees as the boss threatened to kill him,
rape him, or fire him, is performing what the boss is and he isn't.
"Fuck you," says the waitress when Pullman sneers at her. "Fuck
you," he says—and as the scene breaks you can see Pullman bring
the roles from his past to bear on this one. All the anger, fear,
mastery, even defeat in his college dean, his movie producer, his
doctor, his jazz musician is emptied out. What's left is someone
without will or desire, someone who will do exactly as he's told if
only he can maintain a presentation of power, and the double behind the eyes of the guy next door is not a killer but a zombie.
What's left is the embodiment of what Lawrence, coming off the
Moby-Dick chapter in his book on "the old American art-speech,"
called "post-mortem effects": "When the *Pequod* went down, she
left many a rank and dirty steamboat still fussing in the seas. The
Pequod sinks with all her souls, but their bodies rise again to man
innumerable tramp steamers, and ocean-crossing liners . . . What
we mean is that people may go on, keep on, and rush on, without
souls."

The drama of the character feeling for its last role is there most
finally in *Igby Goes Down*, where in scenes scattered through the
film Pullman takes his character from his office to the asylum.
Pullman's Jason Slocumb is the Swede without that last measure
of self-control: "He did everything expected of him and in his forties he just flipped out." In Jason Slocumb's office there is an absolutely clean desk made of blond wood; inside the long, shallow
drawers are hundreds and hundreds of cigarettes, individually
placed in beautiful rows, as if the drawers had been designed precisely for them, and nothing else. It's an image of the only desire
left to a man who has blown his brains out merely by emptying
himself of every other desire, an infinitely repeating image of the
condemned man's last cigarette. His son Igby, who, it turns out, is
not his son at all, grows up with a father who walks heartily, smiles

cryptically, and after a time never bathes. At the dinner table, his wife asks whether he's taken a shower. He gets up, as if offended, and then returns to the table naked and delivers a homily about the importance of personal hygiene. There is a squint, but there is nothing in it but an attempt to get the world to come into focus; at the end, in the asylum, there is not even that, just a puffy-faced man sitting in a chair staring at nothing, though somehow you see a naive but deadened intelligence, a memory of questioning that's like the phantom pain of a missing limb.

The Western-hero face was still there, some years back in the story, but even in *Lost Highway* the silent man was silent because he had nothing to say. It's one long, bad step past the roles that came before: Slocumb's sardonic smile, when he still recognized his son, is a more deadly version of the look on the face of Pullman's momentarily victorious killer in *The Guilty* or his chump from *The Last Seduction*, the deadness in his eyes in the asylum a step past the flat panic in Fred Madison's eyes—as if in this movie, in the few moments he had, Pullman stepped out of those roles in order to complete them. There is a momentum, a trajectory, implicit in each of them, something that demands a resolution, a last word, even if the resolution is the disappearance of the personality that from film to film has been taking shape, and the last word is silence. It's in the way Pullman's smile points backward and forward at the same time, knowing that nothing could have turned out any differently, admitting that it couldn't, that it shouldn't have ended any other way. And it's a weird confusion. Are all these roles part of Bill Pullman's filmography or his biography? Do these roles make up the biography of a fictional character with a single body and a dozen aliases?

In no moment when this actor appears on the screen is there anything so pat as a frown, a grimace, a moan in anguish or a cry of pain that lasts long enough to define a character, or even make you feel for him—nothing so cut-and-dried as David Letterman's cynicism, the sallowness of a man in a Richard Ford novel, Tom Hanks's

firm-handshake-to-the-last, or even Ving Rhames's thousand-mile
stare. There is no thousand miles in the country Pullman is looking at. The smile changes: a sly, bitter, self-knowing look floats
across Pullman's eyes in the revelatory moments of these pictures,
followed by acceptance, satisfaction, or terror. Behind any expression is a rising surge of doubt—Pullman's character's doubt about
himself, about justice, about the next decision that will ruin his
life—and in *Lost Highway*, where America is a field not for self-
invention but for displacement, and the individual is not someone
who can grow up to be president but merely a host for infectious
disease, the doubt that the country has anything left to say to the
ordinary man or woman, to the citizen who wants only to be left
alone, is replaced by the certainty that it doesn't. The citizen, the
representative man as Pullman casts him, is thrown completely
back on himself, and in his face the country fades out.

"Before," Lynch says, speaking of *Malice* and *The Last Seduction*, where Pullman was overshadowed by Nicole Kidman or Alec
Baldwin or Linda Fiorentino, his name never billed first, as it
would be in *Lost Highway* and rarely afterward, "he needed to hold
back, to maintain the balance of the movie. He didn't have the
power. He needed a movie that revolved around him, where he had
the power." You can see this happen; in his house, as he and Renee
play the first two videos, as they talk to the police, as they try and
fail to make love, as they speak their halting speech after the party,
Pullman's face is soft, his hair without definition, his clothes loose
when they're more than a bathrobe or pajamas. When Madison
plays the third video, alone, he is dressed in dark clothes; as when
he rises out of Pete Dayton in the sand, his hair is close to his skull,
his nose and cheeks and chin hard and cruel. Now, having already
killed his wife, in the fantasy that begins in the film's first shot or
in the reality it almost portrays, he looks like a finished man, as the
self he was meant to be. But it is only prelude to self-destruction.
"He needed a movie that revolved around him, where he had the
power": it's an odd thing to say about a character who seems pow-

erless even at his most violent, but that may be the whole point. As an actor, Pullman seems to use no power. You don't think of him as an actor at all; he seems a figment of his own dream and a fragment of that of someone else. Throughout *Lost Highway*, Pullman appears not so much to inhabit Fred Madison's body as to merge his character into the spectral bodies of characters from all across the landscape of American film: Paul Muni confessing "I steal" in the last shot of *I Am a Fugitive from a Chain Gang*, Ralph Meeker's sadistic bravado melting like the ice in his drink in *Kiss Me Deadly*, Frank Sinatra with his hands shaking in the beginning of *The Manchurian Candidate* and cursing "Hell—hell" at the end of it. He is the anonymous, mild-mannered, all but unnoticeable all-American anybody, on any street, in any town, who can at any time find himself ambushed by all that he trusts—and capable of horrible crimes. He is a representative man in spite of himself: handsome, soft, weak, and somehow still capable of surprise, even if he believes in nothing but that the worst is yet to come. That might be the power Lynch speaks of, the way Pullman can push his way through a movie like someone determined not to listen to the voice in his head for another minute, a frontiersman driven insane by keeping company with no one but himself.

The Virginian

Shot in six days—on a budget, you can imagine, of pills for the crew and clothes the actors got to keep—*Detour* is as severe and displacing, as austere and thrilling, as any film Hollywood has ever turned up, fixing precisely those qualities, or values, that as self-conscious artists David Lynch and Barry Gifford realized in *Lost Highway*. There the cauldron of dissolution is veiled with art, but the revel in dissolution is hidden only from the pious. The art in Ann Savage's performance, caught on film but so intense it throws off its own reality, is like a scientific experiment that can be recorded but never duplicated. In the language of cinema it can only be explained as too real. The idea of acting cannot enclose it, just as there are demands in Bill Pullman's face as *Lost Highway* begins that America may have sparked but that the country can satisfy only at the price of its own dissolution: a demand that no matter how destroyed he may seem, the country must acknowledge that the man who wears this face is as good as anybody else, with as much of a right to kill to say who he is as anyone else might presume the right to speak.

The America in Bill Pullman's face as it travels across Lynch's highway is a nihilist kingdom where anything can happen and nothing can be said. That America was always present, waiting for the right moment to appear; it's there in the climactic scene of *The Virginian*, as Pullman's honest cowboy stands facing the rustler Trampas, who he will have to kill in a shoot-out in the Medicine Bow saloon.

"Your kin was Yankee," the Virginian says, opening a few lines that aren't in the book, or any of the other movies.

"My kin was from the Illinois Seventy-seventh," Trampas says. "Helped Ulysses S. Grant whip you Rebs."

The Virginian, to the piano player: "Play 'Battle Hymn of the Republic.' We fire when he sings, 'His truth.' We're all Americans now."

Trampas: "Suits me. I know the tune *and* the words. Mr. Piano?"

So wrote Larry Gross in 1999 in his adaptation of Owen Wister's novel. But he didn't write the broken, strangled voice with which the piano player opens the song. He wrote the stare Pullman's Virginian puts on as he waits for his truth, but not the flicker of doubt that passes over his eyes as the words "his truth" come up in the tune. It's all on the surface; yes, you've seen it all before.

AMERICAN PASTORAL:

SHERYL LEE AS LAURA PALMER

W ho was Laura Palmer? "She was totally corrupt and totally innocent, of course he saw it," as the professor says in *The Human Stain*: "The extreme innocence *was* the corruption." Innocence is the colorless stain on the national tapestry. It violates the landscape; the only way to kill it is to cut it out.

In 1978, in *The American Jeremiad*, the historian Sacvan Bercovitch described the American artist as pulled back and forth between the urge to defy the country as it is and the urge to embrace it "as it ought to be"; the result was retreat, the artist taking refuge in the creation of "a haven for what Thoreau called 'the only true America.'" That meant a place of concord and love where everybody knows everybody else: precisely what, in "The End of the Innocence," in 1989, Don Henley, unafraid of the wind he was blowing through fields of true American corn, so perfectly called "that same small town in each of us." For David Lynch, though, the same small town in each of us has no meaning as a haven; it has meaning only as a cauldron. "I sometimes think I see that civilizations originate in the disclosure of some mystery, some secret," the philosopher Norman O. Brown said in 1960, "and expand with the progressive publication of their secret; and end in exhaustion when there is no longer any secret, when the mystery has been divulged." For Lynch, America as it ought to be comes into being when the secret takes over the town that stands for the country, when the secret is revealed and then suppressed, reburied in the town cemetery, the new tombstone carrying the same Puritan death's-head-with-angel's-wings that was chiseled on the old one. As Lynch wrote in the booklet that accompanied the soundtrack album for *Twin Peaks: Fire Walk with Me*, in big letters filling an entire page, as if scribbling graffiti on his own movie poster, *"IN A TOWN LIKE TWIN PEAKS NO ONE IS INNOCENT."*

Twin Peaks

From 1990 to 1991 *Twin Peaks* was a hit television series. It began with the discovery of the body of seventeen-year-old Laura Palmer, wrapped in plastic, floating down the river that snaked below the Twin Peaks lumber mill. Laura's friends try to discover who killed her and their parents act as if they have something to hide; the twenty-two-year-old Seattle actress Sheryl Lee played the corpse. *Fire Walk with Me*, released in 1992 as an almost universally derided feature film, was a prequel. It began a year before Laura Palmer's murder, with the discovery of the body of another seventeen-year-old girl, wrapped as Laura Palmer's would be, floating as hers would. It climaxes the night Laura Palmer is killed; Sheryl Lee played Laura Palmer. Appearing while the TV show was still on the air, and before the identity of the killer was revealed, was *The Secret Diary of Laura Palmer*, a 1990 exploitation paperback by Jennifer Lynch, David Lynch's then twenty-two-year-old daughter. The Laura Palmer in those pages commits acts far more wretched than anything even hinted at on-screen, just as a Laura Palmer more spectral than the most faraway look in Sheryl Lee's eyes appears in the songs that Julee Cruise performs in *Twin Peaks* or *Fire Walk with Me*—primitive, foggy versions of 1950s doo-wop and early 1960s girl-group hits, with lyrics by Lynch and music by Angelo Badalamenti. But everything about the story is unstable. Sheryl Lee's Laura Palmer was unforgettable as a face in the first episode of the

TV series: a lifeless face as the fisherman played by Jack Nance removes the plastic sheeting, but pristine, unmarked, untroubled, gray-blue from its hours in the river, with dots of water clinging to the skin like beads. As you look you wait not for the story to begin but for the eyes to open. But in *Fire Walk with Me* Sheryl Lee's death is so awful that it is almost impossible to remember. "It's strange," a friend wrote of Lee in 2004. "I saw her in some Lifetime movie a little while ago while I was flipping channels, and now I can only see her as a dead woman. She must be one of the most famous dead women alive."

In the year before her death Laura Palmer was known and loved by all as the good girl who tutored a retarded man and brought meals to shut-ins, as the homecoming queen who wore her blond hair long to set off pastel sweater sets that suggested that the Twin Peaks department store hadn't reordered since 1959— and, as she wrote in her diary a year before her death, she was perhaps not completely unknown as someone "embarrassed about being alive. The girl who received this diary on her twelfth birthday has been dead for years, and I who took her place have done nothing but make a mockery of the dreams she once had. I'm sixteen years old, I'm a cocaine addict, a prostitute who fucks her father's employers, not to mention half the fucking town." "It felt like the school and the town and the world were mocking me by voting me Homecoming Queen," she told her diary in its last pages. "How dare they make me a spectacle like that and ask me to smile again and again and again!"

Twin Peaks made Laura Palmer famous as a corpse; *Fire Walk with Me*, which is about her discovery that the demon who has been raping her since she was twelve is her father, is the greatest teen-jeopardy movie ever made, and even as she dies at her father's hands Sheryl Lee is more alive than anyone else in the picture. The movie is driven by as heedless a performance as any in the history of film, but in its most desperate moment all that's in question is the expression on the face of a high-school girl sitting down to dinner in

her family's nice house, on their quiet, groomed street, as her father asks if she's washed her hands. But like a window blown off its
hinges in a storm, her face opens onto a national landscape, where
promises are made for the pleasure to be found in their betrayal,
where it is only the betrayal of a promise that proves the promise
was worth making, where innocence is killed because it is an af-
front to the rhythms of the nation's story and cannot be tolerated.

In the Woods

Located somewhere in the northeast corner of Washington state,
near the Canadian border, Lynch's Twin Peaks was a not-so-small
town: as he defined it, not so small that everyone knows everyone
else. It was a small town in a shadow. "In my mind," Lynch once
said, "this was a place surrounded by woods. That's important. For
as long as anybody can remember, woods have been mysterious
places. So they were a character in my mind." It was perhaps a conscious reach back to Dante: "Midway in our life's journey, I went
astray," begins *Inferno*,

from the straight road and woke to find myself
alone in a dark wood. How shall I say

what wood that was! I never saw so drear,
so rank, so arduous a wilderness!
Its very memory gives a shape to fear.

On American ground Lynch's fantasy was likely a blind but coded
reach back to the original American wilderness, to the woods the
Puritans found waiting for them: "A Brief Recognition of New-
Englands Errand into the Wilderness," as the Reverend Samuel
Danforth titled an Election Day sermon in Boston in March of
1670. Danforth himself reached back to the town the Puritans
founded, that place described by Winthrop forty years before,
where every man and woman would have need of every other, or

perish: "leaving your Country, Kindred and Fathers houses," Danforth said, "and transporting your selves with your Wives, Little Ones and Substance over the vast Ocean into this waste and howling Wilderness"—"a woody, retired and solitary place." Winthrop had drawn from Matthew 5:14: "A city that is set on a hill cannot be hid." Danforth was drawing on Matthew 11:7–9: "What went ye out into the wilderness to see?" Jesus says to "the multitudes" of John the Baptist. "A reed shaken with the wind?" Or a "man clothed in soft raiment?" No, Jesus said, John went into the wilderness to see a "prophet . . . and more than a prophet." But Danforth paused over the words *to see*, as if they held a forbidden allure. "The phrase agrees to Shows and Stage-playes," he explained. "*Theatrical* Hearers, *Spectators* rather than *Auditors*, they went not to *hear*, but to *see*; they went to gaze upon a new and strange Spectacle." The woods are where the reed is shaken in the wind; the woods are where one goes to clear the ground for settlement, or to find a world where all certainties are dashed, where the landscape goes blank and men and women forget who they are.

It's a legacy, and the legacy is passed down. Thus in *The Secret Diary of Laura Palmer*, Jennifer Lynch follows a fifteen-year-old Laura into the woods around Twin Peaks, where Laura goes at night to be blindfolded and tied to a chair. Music begins to play. There are "sounds of water"; someone begins to beat a drum. People dance around her in a circle as if she is a fire. The next day she tells her diary what happened, how she became that reed, how through others' eyes she could see herself shaking in the wind.

Each and every fantasy one might conjure late at night, with the exception of farm animals, was performed on, with, or for me . . . These people, all of various ages, spent evenings in the woods, forgetting names and histories, using only their most basic feelings and wishes to be held and touched, wanted, and completely accepted, no matter what they looked like, or who they were at work or school the following mornings. It was dark and strange and almost intoxicating at times. I would sway, my head heavy in this darkness. The energy was so thick, I almost felt the air separate, part slowly to let me move. Each and every nerve in my body had something to say . . . a scream beneath the skin, constant and much greater than usual because I could not sense it coming. I could swear there were times I was sensitive enough to feel the fingerprints of those who touched me.

Is this Winthrop's loving community, now pushed into the woods? Or is that where you could always find it, hidden from the commerce, envy, scheming, and false witness of even the earliest Puritan towns? The community is there in Hawthorne's 1835 story "Young Goodman Brown." In a tale set perhaps ten years after Danforth spoke—in the kind of spectacle he might have been hinting at, but in the years before the witch trials he would not have dared to describe—a pious young Puritan is moving through the woods outside of Salem, Massachusetts, "rushing onward with the instinct that guides mortal man to evil." He has left his new wife, Faith, at home, closing his ears to her pleas that he stay: "On he flew among the black pines, brandishing his staff with frenzied gestures, now giving vent to an inspiration of horrid blasphemy, and now shouting forth such laughter as set all the echoes of the forest laughing like demons around him." He reaches a clearing, lit by four burning trees, and there he finds church elders and drunks, whores and virgins, all those whom, in the light of the new day, he will see or greet or ignore as he did the day before, as he and they go about their ordinary lives of labor, instruction, or indulgence: "It was strange to see that the good shrank not from the wicked, nor were the sinners abashed by the saints."

Under the burning trees, a priest celebrates sin and crime. "Evil is the nature of mankind," he says, embracing greed, murder, blasphemy, and the sacrifice of newborns: "Evil must be your only happiness." The night's converts are brought forth, and Goodman Brown finds himself standing before the altar of a rock with Faith. How did she get there? How can this be happening? What he has not told her she has not told him:

And there they stood, the only pair, as it seemed, who were yet hesitating on the verge of wickedness in this dark world. A basin was hollowed, naturally, in the rock. Did it contain water, reddened by the lurid light? or was it blood? or, perchance, a liquid flame? Herein did the shape of evil dip his hand and prepare to lay the mark of baptism upon their foreheads, that they might be partakers of the mystery of sin, more conscious of the secret guilt of others, both in deed and thought, than they could now be of their own. The husband cast one look at his pale wife, and Faith at him. What polluted wretches would the next glance show them to each other, shuddering alike at what they disclosed and what they saw!

Hawthorne leaves Goodman Brown waking from a dream. The images dissolve; he is left "a stern, a sad, a darkly meditative, a distrustful, if not a desperate man," shrinking from his wife's touch as he wakes in the night for the rest of his life. You don't know if he has dreamed what happened, or if, in his dream, he has remembered a true event he has devoted his life to forgetting. The story is a shape-shifting marriage of ordinary narrative and dream logic: just as Goodman Brown thinks he sees his own dead mother and father among the crowd of worshippers in the woods, when Laura Palmer returns at dawn to her unpretentious two-story family home—more impressive from the outside, with its rolling lawn and heavy structure, than from the inside, where drooping ferns and faded couches in a dim living room suggest a parlor that's barely been disturbed, or dusted, since the 1930s—she has, she tells her diary, "a daydream as I made my way upstairs that Mom woke up . . . and asked how the orgy had been. I gave her all the details and she began reliving her own experiences of strange evenings in the woods." Laura Palmer is not only imagining that she is a witch; she is imagining that she was born a witch, that she is part of a long line of witches, stretching back to the night that Young Goodman Brown—whose name, one hundred and seventy years after Hawthorne wrote his story, would regularly pop up in the upper-right-hand corner of Internet porn sites, as if he were the host—went into the woods, with Laura Palmer reaching all the way back across the country to reenact one version of its founding.

You can't ask the Laura Palmer who emerges from Twin Peaks

in all its facets what didn't happen in the TV series or what did happen in the movie, or how the diary and the songs tie the whole together or break it apart. As flesh or spirit—moving back and forth between the attacks of the long-haired, snaggle-toothed monster Laura calls Bob when he is not plainly her father and comforting dreams of a red room, hidden behind a red curtain, where a grossly misshapen dwarf launches slurred incantations ("With this ring I thee wed," he'll say, or "Let's rock," with such distortion that his voice is subtitled), time has no boundaries, and the dead make peace with the dead—Sheryl Lee walks Laura Palmer through the terrain opened up by a kind of common art project. Behind that project may be a single, guiding intelligence—a director who is also a songwriter who is also the owner of Twin Peaks®—but inside the project, on the loose, are voices and a face. Together the book, the songs, the TV show, and the movie make the town where Sheryl Lee tells Laura Palmer's story, where she acts out the country that is enacted by the town.

The Sylvan Village and the Film Noir City

The music that opened every episode of *Twin Peaks*—very slow, the romantic quickly rising to the soapy, suggesting a place where any dream can come true, with a distinct synthesized bass undercurrent, a strong fatalistic pull, stating that the only truth of a dream is waking from it, that whatever it is there's nothing you can do about it, that the story will be over before it begins (which, given that the series opened with the appearance of Laura Palmer's body and continued as a search for her killer, it was)—locates the town on a map where Washington state can fade into the country as it imagined itself decades before. The not-so-small town of Twin Peaks—POPULATION 51,201, reads a sign after an opening montage of a robin, timber-mill smokestacks, mill machinery throwing off sparks, and a waterfall—is made of two archetypes of the American town: the sylvan village and the film noir city.

Starting in the 1820s, it was the sylvan glade that the Hudson River school of American painters caught so irresistibly, but no painter caught the village more fully than the Blue Sky Boys of West Hickory, North Carolina, in the records they made a hundred years later. Bill Bolick was born in 1917 and played mandolin, brother Earl (1919–98) played guitar, and from 1936 through 1950 they sang the ballads and hymns that everyone knew along with newly composed tunes that sounded as if they'd been handed down for generations. They sang about God, courtship, marriage, alcoholism, prison, and death—tragic or violent deaths, sometimes, but mostly the kind of death that seals a life, even if it leaves a void, as with, again and again in their repertoire, the death of a mother. The tone was quiet, restrained, humble, very nearly humorless, describing a passage through life accompanied by Jesus's love and the fellowship of others like oneself. The town that rose up out of their music was a community of piety, limits, and manners—modest houses, well-kept gardens, a backstreet bar, and, at the center of everyone's life, good or bad, a church. "Let us sing a song as we go along, let us banish care and strife," the Blue Sky Boys would sing, and you picture them less on a stage or even strolling the streets than sitting in somebody's parlor, staying all afternoon if the neighbors keep dropping by: "That the world may know as we onward go, there's a sunny side of life." People loved that one best, no one missing the undercurrent, which brought up not doubt so much as fear.

The Bolick brothers looked like the nicest insurance salesmen you could ever meet. When they started out Bill might have been a high-school linebacker posing in coat and tie; the old publicity photos show a welcoming smile. Earl had a higher forehead; he smiles too, but in his long, drinker's face, the expression looks forced, guilty, as if he knows you'll never get a dime out of the policy he's sold you. There was something just slightly queer about it all, in the way that, as the years went by and Bill's body thickened and Earl's hairline receded, their expressions never changed; in the way that, no matter what the tune—"Where the Soul (of Man) Never Dies," "No One to Welcome Me Home," "On Top of Old Smokey," "The House Where We Were Wed," "Take Up Thy Cross"—they never raised their voices, or almost never played faster than slow. Is that why their most convincing songs are murder ballads? Is that why the murders that occur in "Down on the Banks of the Ohio," "Fair Eyed Ellen," or "Story of the Knoxville Girl" are psychotic in their blandness, with none of the sadistic cruelties of the Virginia banjoist Dock Boggs, singing "Pretty Polly" or "Danville Girl" ten years or so before—not a violation at all, somehow, just a slightly misunderstood continuation of ordinary small-town courtesies, of everyday life?

Does the sylvan village feel familiar not because it's part of a cultural memory everyone shares—even if nobody actually experienced what everyone remembers—but because what happens in the village is no more archaic than the If-I-Can't-Have-You-Nobody-Can murders chronicled in our own daily news, and just as routine? "He dealt with this in the good old-fashioned American way," says Detective Lennie Briscoe to his partner Ed Green on a 2004 *Law & Order* episode. "What's that?" "A .38." "The essential American soul is hard, isolate, stoic, and a killer," D. H. Lawrence wrote, speaking of what he took to be the nation's founding crime, the extermination of the Indians—so that there was no step one could take in the United States without stepping on unmarked graves. What the old murder ballads say—voicing, one can imagine, a helpless or even patriotic instinct as, generations after the events supposedly passed into the history textbooks, the solitary in the big city or the small town reenacts the whole of the national drama, from the erasure of the Indians to the filling up of the country with slaves who could be put down like cattle—is that America is a country where anyone can be killed at any time, for any reason, or no reason at all. The ballads call the cops, but the sense that the killer is justified, that he is only doing what everyone yearns to do, that almost everyone will root for his escape, is almost never missing.

In the Blue Sky Boys' version of "Down on the Banks of the Ohio," from 1936, in the trough of the Great Depression, a young man describes for his beloved the pleasant life he sees for them. How happy they will be on their wedding day! What a lovely home they will have! Or, rather, because there is no shouting in Blue Sky, how happy they will be on their wedding day, and what a lovely home they will have. A few small, timidly bright notes from the mandolin hold the couple's hands for them as the Bolicks' thin, reedy voices let you know how many times the man has rehearsed his speech; when his girl refuses him he cuts her throat and pushes her body into the river. There's no scream in the performance; instead of a sense of violence there's a sense of rectitude. The stunned, almost catatonic reading the Bolicks give the song, singing in the killer's first person, makes the nineteenth-century ballad seem no more traditional than the investigations Agee and Evans were conducting in Alabama two months after the Bolicks cut the song at their first recording session—and far more modern, even modernist, than the country surrealism of the Frankie and Johnny or Jesse James paintings Thomas Hart Benton was making in Missouri at the same time. The way the boys—and they were boys, sixteen and eighteen—suck the third word of the song, the "lurrrve" in "Come my love," into their chests, freezing it there, suspending it; the way they hang "Just a Closer Walk with Thee" over the head of the doomed woman, as if it's a blasphemous joke they refuse to acknowledge as such, produces the sense that the killer has been planning this for a long time. Forget the plot of the story, the suitor and his would-be bride, and listen to the person inside the voice: there is a settled, peaceful, utterly bourgeois set of assumptions contained in the way the killer accounts for himself, and as the killer speaks, you see not a drifter passing through the town, a tramp from the hobo jungle on its outskirts, or even the secret child molester living with his mother three streets down, but a clerk. You see a calm, honest man, a reliable employee who is never a minute late and never leaves a minute early. His life is bounded by expectations as orderly as the grid of the streets of his town. If those expectations are not met, the world makes no sense, and so the man who speaks so calmly, without ever altering his tone, who will take care to note just when it was, "'tween twelve and one," that he returned home from the river, sets out to end the world, and life in the town goes on as before.

The film noir city seems to be Manhattan or Los Angeles. At the heart of the form, whether in the movies or in the crime novels inspired by them, just as the most emblematic noir story is that of the soldier back in his hometown after the war to find the place a swamp of corruption, in the forties and fifties the most emblematic noir location is a small, vaguely Midwestern city. It is Midwestern culturally even if not exactly geographically—"They say native Californians all come from Iowa," Walter Neff says in Raymond Chandler's script for *Double Indemnity*—as in Chandler's *The Little Sister*, where Los Angeles is at least half Manhattan, Kansas, a place Philip Marlowe finds far more terrifying than anything in Hollywood.

It's Dashiell Hammett's Poisonville, his barely disguised Butte, Montana; the grimy, striving spot where Jim Thompson liked to set his murder novels; the sort of town that in the movies appears in *The Big Heat* or *The Asphalt Jungle*. In the twenties you would have found it in the cities where the first, vagabond professional football leagues appeared and disappeared—Pottsville, Pennsylvania; Decatur, Illinois; Duluth, Minnesota; Green Bay, Wisconsin; Buffalo, New York; and, in Ohio, Canton, Akron, and Dayton—the vaudeville circuit, or, as the noir historian Eddie Muller once put it, each stop "a town trying to be bigger than it is in all the wrong ways." It was the pretentious, provincial city with its fancy nightclub and rough roadhouse, imitation mansions and true flophouses, where the most respectable citizen is always the most criminal, a town big enough to get murders written up as suicides and small enough that no one outside the place cares what happens there. Perfectly, this is where you are in Ross Macdonald's 1947 novel, *Blue City*, and with Barbara Stanwyck, Van Heflin, Lizabeth Scott, and Kirk

Douglas in the 1946 film *The Strange Love of Martha Ivers*: "four people," the critic Manny Farber wrote at the time, "who have lived cataclysmic, laughterless lives since they were babies."

In the course of twenty-four hours Heflin's knockabout gambler Sam Masterson, veteran of Anzio and a half-dozen other battles, falls in with Scott's down-and-out Toni Marachek and is drawn back into the web spun by Stanwyck's Ivers. As a scared but gutty orphan, she was Masterson's teenage soul mate. "I won't let you talk about my father," the young Martha Ivers says to her rich aunt, her guardian. "Your father was a nobody, a mill hand," says the aunt, played by a forbidding Judith Anderson, in Puritan black from head to toe. "The best thing he ever did for you was die." Martha picks up the cue and kills her aunt with her own cane; now she's an heiress who dresses like a cobra and runs Iverstown, "America's Fastest Growing Industrial City." "I don't like to get pushed around!" a bruised and bleeding Heflin shouts to Scott after Douglas, the sniveling drunk married to Ivers, and also the Iverstown district attorney, has had Heflin beaten up by goons and dumped twenty-five miles out of town. Heflin is speaking democratic speech in a city where everything is bought and paid for, reminding you of why he left the town in the first place, a freight-hopping runaway: "I don't like people I like to get pushed around! I don't like anybody to get pushed around!"* "It's quite a thing in a small city like this," Douglas says. "You get to feel like God." With Stanwyck

---

*A line Robert Rossen, the screenwriter, probably took from the motto of the left-wing afternoon tabloid *PM*, founded in 1940 by Ralph Ingersoll: "*PM* is against people who push other people around," he wrote in the first issue. In 1940 that meant fascists, at home or abroad, bearing the name or not, steel and automobile manufacturers, power companies and war profiteers, what used to be called "Big Business," and corrupt officials in statehouses and city halls across the land. The paper ran cartoons by Dr. Seuss satirizing American indifference over the war in Europe as well as copy by I. F. Stone, Ernest Hemingway, and Erskine Caldwell, and photos by Margaret Bourke-White and Weegee. (As Philip Roth remembered in 2004 in *The Plot Against America*, the paper's Daily Picture Magazine "claimed to run photographs that other papers suppressed—controversial photos of lynch mobs and chain gangs, of strikebreakers wielding clubs,

and Douglas in a pas de deux apparently meant to prove that a will to power and self-loathing are equally corrupting, and Heflin lining out a version of Kyle MacLachlan's Dale Cooper, the FBI agent sent to Twin Peaks to investigate Laura Palmer's death, Iverstown feels like a direct ancestor of Twin Peaks—and at least before the killer is revealed *Twin Peaks* could be an homage to *The Strange Love of Martha Ivers.*

In the twenty-four-hour first-person narration of Macdonald's *Blue City*, a young veteran named John Weather—you can picture Brando in the movie version, as he was in about 1953—hitches a ride into his unnamed Midwestern hometown in 1946 to find his father, whom he hasn't seen since his mother divorced the man and left the place when Weather was twelve. But his father was murdered two years before Weather's return, no one was ever charged, and everyone Weather meets seems part of the crime.

Blue City reads like the best noir films play; Macdonald's dialogue has the slow build-up and deadpan ricochet used by such lead actors as Dick Powell and Humphrey Bogart, and even more effectively by bit players like Thelma Ritter. "How well do you know Kerch?" says Carla Kaufman, a B-girl and prostitute (imagine Gloria Grahame in 1947), after Weather, following a lead, has bought her a drink in Kerch's Cathay Club, which features a nightclub with plumy singers and slot machines on the first floor and a whorehouse on the second—a generic ancestor of *Twin Peaks'* One-Eyed Jacks, the luxurious brothel the Twin Peaks developer

---

of inhuman conditions in America's penitentiaries.") Just as notably, it launched Crockett Johnson's unforgettable wartime comic strip *Barnaby*, which featured a beer-swilling, cigar-smoking Irish guardian angel as, one can now see clearly, a harbinger of the revolt against cultural pieties that with the emergence of Jack Kerouac, Allen Ginsberg, William Burroughs, Marlon Brando, Miles Davis, and James Dean first broke into the open in 1948, the year *PM* published its last issue. "*PM* accepts no advertising," Ingersoll's first-issue credo went on. "*PM* belongs to no political party. *PM* is absolutely free and uncensored. *PM's* sole source of income is its readers—to whom it alone is responsible. *PM* is one newspaper that can and does dare to tell the truth."

Benjamin Horne runs just over the Canadian border.* "Don't know him at all," Weather says. "That's funny," Carla says. "You were talking as if you knew him." "I don't have to know him not to like him, if that's what you mean." "Wait till you get to know him. Then you'll really not like him." "Did you ever read the fairy story about the frog king?" Carla says. "My mother used to read it to me when I was a kid. Anyway, it's about a man that got changed by magic into a frog, and then changed back into a man. That's the way Kerch looks, as if he didn't change all the way back into a man." "Kerch was sitting at the desk counting money," Weather says after gaining admittance to the back room of the city crime boss (J. T. Walsh, 1997, grossly overweight, just before he died). "His wrists bulged out thick above his hands, as if someone had bound his hands and blown air into the rest of him."

In this town, murders are not a rent in everyday reality; they are the currency, committed for reasons everyone understands: greed, revenge, greed, hate, greed, jealousy, greed, megalomania, and greed. As John Weather enters the *Blue City* roadhouse, this is the noir version of the murder ballad: "My throat was busy resisting the fierce pressure of nausea that clenched my stomach and squirted streams of saliva into my mouth. It may have been the slick of blood on the floor where my foot had slipped. It may have been the half-naked man in the corner with the discolored neck and dead, swollen face. It may have been the woman who lay on the table with her limp legs dangling over the end. The gasoline lamp had been moved to the stove and shone fully on the bloody towel which wrapped her face." Weather discovers that his father was the town's

---

*In a perverse stroke of casting, Benjamin Horne was played by Richard Beymer, who brought a desire for revenge—fostered by the nearly thirty years in the wilderness of summer stock and forgotten TV movies that followed his career-making, nearly career-ending starring role as Tony in *West Side Story*—to bear in Horne's every word and gesture. Beymer's Tony pegged him forever as a fruit; in *Twin Peaks* he was still a fruit, acting most of all with his toothpaste smile, which was now a mask, as if what Tony had wanted all along out of *West Side Story* was not Natalie Wood but a chance to kill everyone in the film.

original racketeer, and that his father's young widow is bankrolling the man who picked up where he left off; he discovers that the impotent reform mayor is his father's killer. The town they've made is a place where union organizers are beaten or killed, cops work for gangsters, taxes for the rich are kept low and wages for everyone else are kept lower, and where an atavism, a will to social destruction, runs through the town like a disease that Weather can feel and even name: "native fascism."

The noir town had festered on or just below the surface of cultural consciousness for fifty years by the time Lynch and his collaborator Mark Frost thought up Twin Peaks; what was shocking in *Blue City* would in *Twin Peaks* seem inevitable, natural, with any missing detail unnatural. *Of course* both the nameless Weatherville and Twin Peaks are dominated by criminal businessmen with impeccable fronts. *Of course* there's a mysterious heiress and a tragic whore. *Of course* webs of crime are also webs of sex, and sex a form of disguise, of sinking one identity into another—and both crime and sex are forms of hysteria born of the fact that both towns are Nowheresville, where nothing you will ever do will make the papers in Chicago or New York, San Francisco or L.A. Of course both towns are laid out like a board game, with everyone fighting over the big hotel, the factory, the brothel, and the roadhouse—fighting to get in or fighting to get out.

The Mayor

Thus Twin Peaks, with its lovely waterfall and polluting mill, its web of illicit business deals and secret love affairs, its clean streets and solid middle-class houses, its decency and terror—and what makes it different from Blue Sky, Iverstown, or Weatherville is that it is in the West. As a place at the far end of the American march it remains less fixed, less settled, than the places left behind. The town breathes corruption, but it also breathes freedom; people here are more daring than their ancestors, and care less what anyone else thinks about whatever it is they do. If no one is innocent, no one is considered strange or foreign, either. So the stock characters, the doctor and the businessman, the whoremaster and the pimp, the rebel daughter and the decent son, the striving father and the worried mother, the teenage drug dealer and the tired-eyed woman who runs the diner where Laura Palmer picks up Meals on Wheels,* are surrounded by hermits and eccentrics, the sort of people who elsewhere would have been weeded out or pushed into invisibility long before: the sheriff Harry S Truman, whose very name makes his every word and gesture a non sequitur, and his deputy Andy Brennan, who breaks into tears at the sight of violence. The bikers at the roadhouse, oddly dressed in what look like World War II–era British motorcycle gear and listening intently, as to a poetry reading or a philosophy lecture, as Julee Cruise sings "Falling," the *Twin Peaks* opening theme with words dropped into it ("See," Lynch says, "the idea was that the bikers in Twin Peaks were the intellectuals—the beatniks"). The acid-casualty psychiatrist and the woman with an eye patch who's obsessed with venetian blinds; the agoraphobic Harold, Laura Palmer's only confidant, and the Log Lady.

Played by Catherine Coulson, the Log Lady is a primly dressed middle-aged woman who cradles a log in her arms everywhere she goes. The log is an oracle; it makes her a medium. Founder of a religion of which she remains the only adherent, she is at once the symbolic mother of the town and its bad conscience. She's the crazy woman standing at the door; she is also the town's secret mayor. Her job is to make everyone else feel normal, so that the real business of the place—delivering babies, doing homework, cheating on spouses,

---

*The diner owner was played by Peggy Lipton, who acted as if she'd lived every year since her 1968 *Mod Squad* heyday twice when her mother blew into town as a fastidious rich woman newly married to a con artist she describes as a "financial adviser": noir goddess Jane Greer, so alluring in 1947 in *Out of the Past* that, as Steve Erickson puts it, Robert Mitchum "can practically see his future down to the last bullet hole" the first time he sets eyes on her.

selling dope, executing property swindles, serving meals at the diner, promoting development, and running girls from the perfume counter of Benjamin Horne's department store to his whorehouse—can go on as it always has. The log gives the Log Lady a secret language to speak, or a forgotten language, and with it she will deliver Laura Palmer a warning: "The tender boughs of innocence burn first."

The First Victim

The first victim is seventeen-year-old Teresa Banks, supposedly a drifter passing through Deer Meadow, Washington. As *Fire Walk with Me* begins, it's a year before the death of Laura Palmer. Banks is floating down Wind River, her body cinched in billowing white plastic bags. Anyone who had followed *Twin Peaks* on TV—the only sort of person likely to pay money a year after the show was canceled to see a movie called *Twin Peaks: Fire Walk with Me*— would have known that Leland Palmer, Laura Palmer's father, killed her. Fourteen episodes into the show, one would have seen Leland Palmer kill his niece Maddy Ferguson, played by Sheryl Lee in a dark wig; then he wrapped her body in plastic and threw it into the river, thus revealing that it was he who killed Laura Palmer in exactly the same way—he, or rather, as the character was allowed to insist in the TV series, the demon Bob who has possessed him, making him as much a victim as the girls he kills. He was only a child when he was initiated into the satanic cult he has served ever since, the television version of Leland Palmer says in a dying confession after smashing his head against a cell door. He was forced to recruit for them, "They wanted others they could use like they used me," but Laura refused, she said she'd die first: "They made me kill her." But as *Fire Walk with Me* opens, the premise is that nobody knows this, and when it ends, none of the excuses Leland Palmer was permitted on TV will be offered. The TV series closed the plot with a cover-up of its own horror: "I've lived in these old woods most of my life," Sheriff Truman says to Dale Cooper after Laura's father has confessed, and died. "I've seen some strange things, but this is way off the map. I'm having a hard time believing." "Harry," says the FBI agent, who in a dream where he inhabits Laura Palmer's red room has already heard the dead girl tell a dead version of himself, "My father killed me," but who is now changing before your eyes into Mr. Smooth-It-Away, "is it easier to believe that a man could rape and murder his own daughter?" Yes, answers *Fire Walk with Me*. "Any more comforting?" Cooper says on TV. *Comforting?* asks Sheryl Lee out of the film. *Is that why I made this movie? To comfort you?*

Teresa Banks was a part-time prostitute; Leland Palmer was one of her clients. He's been thinking about a party, he says to her in a flashback, but when he shows up at their regular motel he glimpses the two girls Banks has hired giggling to each other: Ronette Pulaski, from the perfume counter at Horne's department store, and her co-worker, his own daughter. He rushes away before they can see him, and begs off to Banks: "I chickened out." The next time he sees Banks he beats her to death.

Two FBI agents arrive in Deer Meadow to take over the Banks case—because the body drifted from one state to another, or because the story needed outsiders, people who would not take the territory of the story for granted, people who would look at everything with wonder and trust nothing they see. One, Chet Desmond, laconically hard-boiled and played by Chris Isaak in a Reagan pompadour rather than his usual Elvis, is pulled off a shockingly staged school-bus hijacking in Fargo, North Dakota: two punk teenagers are in handcuffs and the driver has a gun to his head, but the screaming children at the bus windows make it seem as if the crime is still going on. Kiefer Sutherland's earnest Sam Stanley, brought in from Portland in a bow tie, barely seems out of his teens.

After showing their badges to the Deer Meadow sheriff and his deputy—after Desmond has ripped the nose off the sniggering deputy and pushed his way into the office of the sneering sheriff—the agents stand over an autopsy table, looking down at Teresa

Banks. Her eyes and mouth are open in shock, frozen in the instant she realized she was about to be killed, even as the shovel that crushed her skull was in the air. Short platinum blond hair, blazing white teeth: her face is still beautiful, and already rotting. At four in the morning Desmond and Sutherland move on to Hap's, the all-night diner where Banks worked for a month. Any establishment called Hap's is inevitably named after the owner, or the dead man who started it in the first place: someone called Happy. Away from the person carrying the word, "haps" means luck, good or especially bad; it can mean devil's haunt. For the Deer Meadow Hap's there's a neon clown face on the roadside sign and three vagrants huddling by the door. "Ask Irene about that," one says, looking through the door at the counterwoman. "Irene right there." Then he ceases to make sense, or begins to speak a different language: "Irene's her name and it is night. Don't go any further with it. There's nothing good about it."

This will turn out to be a fine description of what's inside. Everyone in the dingy room—the waitress and two customers—is either stupid, threatening, or both. Sitting at the counter, Desmond notices Stanley holding his coffee cup in his left hand. Desmond asks him for the time, and as the greenhorn turns his wrist to look at his watch he dumps his coffee in his lap.

Desmond wants him gone; something about the death has sparked an affinity the older agent will have to pursue on his own. But not yet. Desmond and Stanley arrive at the Fat Trout Trailer Park, where Banks lived—though it might as well be called the Red Herring. Inside Banks's trailer, they find her picture: she's wearing a ring that was missing from the body. Played by a scrofulous Harry Dean Stanton, the trailer park operator appears in a bathrobe, looking as if he hasn't gotten dressed since the Ford administration; he offers the agents a cup of "Good Morning America!" A filthy, hunchbacked woman holding an ice bag to one eye hobbles into the trailer on a cane.

You begin to notice the state of the trailers. Except for Banks's, which has a white picket fence around it, they are decrepit, peeling, cracking, boarded up, abandoned. The residents are blind and crippled. This is the residential hotel as garbage dump, or the last frontier of what could be called a town, a place that deserves a California Gold Rush name: Rough and Ready or Confidence for irony, maybe, Hangtown or Sloughhouse for what it is.

Desmond sends Stanley and the body off to Portland. With dusk coming on, he returns to Fat Trout, to check out the trailer where the sheriff's deputy lives, he says, though the way he walks and talks says something else. This is a place he cannot stay away from. It has a kind of gravity that can't be found anywhere else. The fact that there's another trailer in the place belonging to someone at least formally connected to the case is if nothing else an excuse to go back.

The park operator banters with Desmond; then he walks a complaining woman with a stiff leg out of the frame, and for a moment Desmond occupies the center of a shot so perfect it becomes less a frame in a film than a painting on a wall, a painting that is also a door. Though the shot occupies a split second, in memory it can expand until it seems like an entire scene, as if everything the film has done with Desmond up to this point has been nothing but an excuse to get him here, standing exactly as he is. For its moment it is one of the most complete and uncanny images of America ever produced.

Desmond is standing in the center of the picture, in his trenchcoat, with his feet planted on muddy ground, framed off center by a line of smashed-together trailers and splintering shacks on his right, the line fading out in a receding perspective; the same sort of structures are on his left, but with less weight. The lanky FBI agent is himself the weight, the only anchor the shot has; the longer you look, freezing the frame, the more abstract it feels, the more everything in it feels as if it's floating off the ground. Earlier, showing Desmond around Fat Trout, the park operator had stopped, looking at a telephone pole as if it were alive, as if it were reminding him it will kill him if he tells what he knows. Now Desmond sees the telephone pole, though really the feeling is that it sees him. Behind Desmond is a desiccated fir tree; far beyond that are the purple mountains you know from "America the Beautiful."

In the instant, a scene from the country's founding plays itself out again, Fitzgerald imagining the first Dutch sailors to reach American shores: "For a transitory enchanted moment man must have held his breath in the presence of this continent, compelled into an aesthetic contemplation he neither understood nor desired, face to face for the last time in history with something commensurate to his capacity for wonder." It's that contemplation that now fills Desmond's face—and if a trailer park can stand for a country, and if Fat Trout is saying that the country has been abandoned, no one left but people who have reached its absolute dead end ("I've been places," the park operator has said a minute before, begging the agent to accept his cowardice, to not ask why he doesn't want to talk, about Teresa Banks's murder or anything else: "I just want to stay where I am"), the mountains that form the backdrop to the ruins around Desmond say what they have always said: there was no last time. The wonder that was there to be seen nearly four hundred years before, and two hundred years after that through the eyes of the Hudson River painters, is as visible now as it ever was; what has been used up is not the wonder, but the eyes of the people below the mountains, the country that set itself up in their shadow.

Desmond Vanishes

Desmond stands before the mountains alone, and then the wrecked trailers and shacks are just a scrap heap. No one has lived in them for years. Only the mountains are real. Under the eye of the mountains, Isaak's Desmond stands for a peculiarly American loneliness, for the way anyone can be swallowed up by the vast emptiness of the landscape, as if he or she had never been born. All this happens—or is shown, is composed—in an instant, but it's where *Fire Walk with Me* signals that it is playing for keeps.

Desmond moves off to look at the deputy's trailer; under the trailer is a pile of dirt, and on top of the pile is Teresa Banks's missing ring. He reaches for it and the screen goes black.

A Year Later

As Desmond vanishes, Laura Palmer appears on the screen; it's a year later. Walking out of her house with books in her arms, a dreamy smile in her eyes, she stops on her way to school to meet Donna Hayward, her best friend. At Twin Peaks High she skips into the girls' bathroom, goes into a stall, takes out her cocaine, and takes one small sniff.

Wearing a towel, sneaking off from the gym showers, she meets her boyfriend James in a storeroom. You look into her face as he does, and you see what he can't: a young woman going to pieces. "I'm gone, I'm gone, like a turkey in the corn," she says like a scarecrow come to life in *Scarecrow IV*, if not a statue of a Neolithic bird goddess dropped down into the late twentieth century with its spells but not its language. "You're not a turkey," James says, as if she's a normal student at a conventional post-Enlightenment high school, where you learn the scientific method in freshman year. "A turkey is one of the dumbest birds on earth." Her face becomes a field of abasement, with odd, birdlike features, the nose slightly hooked as if to dig in the ground, the mouth like a beak. "Gobble, gobble," she says blankly, will and desire dissolved by the words, as she drops the towel and pulls James's hands down onto her body. "Gobble, gobble." It's a drama of abandonment, where someone abandoned by her town is now abandoning herself. There is nothing sexual about it, unless it's that she's trying to tell the boy that sex is death; she could be walking into a wall.

After school, in her perfect fluffy teenage bedroom, nobody home, Laura takes her diary from its hiding place behind her dresser. There are pages ripped out: the fear that rises from her eyes swallows her face.

In the moment, in a moment that will reemerge throughout the picture, there's a dim sense of being transported into the past—the silent-movie past, where the camera moved in on a face and stayed there. The face spoke, and the eyes were the mouth. Sheryl Lee shakes in Laura Palmer's terror, and for an instant it seems like too much: the terror of a girl whose secrets have been stolen as the Perils of Pauline, the heroine tied to the railroad tracks. But the movie has put your ear to the rails: you catch the rush of the locomotive. The intensity in Sheryl Lee's face makes the scene into a vortex; you can't believe the girl in the room gets out of it. The story is beginning to tilt; from this point on Laura Palmer will be the locomotive, hardly able to keep up with herself. This is the first hint of what will be the most bottomless female film performance of the latter days of the twentieth century—the most extreme, the most dangerous. The most ludicrous, it can seem, because today the emotional nakedness of silent acting, its totality, can seem ludicrous. You can laugh, and get off the train. You can stay on the train until the train runs out of track.

Laura takes what's left of the diary to the hermit Harold; it's Bob who took the pages from her diary, she says, it's Bob. "Bob . . . is . . . not . . . real," Harold says calmly, each word alone. "Bob is real," Laura says just as deliberately—and then, in an effect that comes off the screen like blood, her eyes flash and grow larger, and her face is lit with an inner glow. She growls horribly, her teeth protrude and turn yellow in a red mouth as she repeats the curse Bob has put on her: "Fire . . . walk . . . with . . . me."

The garish colors in the distorted face don't seem like an effect. The emotional conviction behind the moment, the conviction the actress has brought to the character, is too great for that. *How did they do that?* isn't what you ask; you ask what happened, why it happened, what will come next.

Then she herself asks what happened. Back at her empty

house, Laura forces herself up the stairs, forces herself to open her bedroom door, forces herself to look into her room, turns and runs when she sees Bob hiding behind her bed, grinning like an extra in a third-rate ghoul movie. She dashes across her lawn and huddles in the dirt under the shrubs separating her house from the house next door. She sees her father stride out of her front door, looking as if he's ready to go off and be important. Her face shudders; it almost breaks. "Oh my God, oh my God, no no no no no no no no no no no, no it's not him, no no no it's NOT HIM"—but for all the words out of her mouth, it's still the face that sucks the air out of the scene. Again you could be in a theater in 1918, with just a piano playing, or not even that. The face collapses, the eyes widen, the words drop away.

Bob, Laura has written in her diary, is like "a religion." In the pages of her *Secret Diary* you can read the story: He has taken her into the woods. He has masturbated onto her hands, forced her to hold his semen in her hands and lick it off, told her that he wants to be her, that he wants to breathe through her mouth, told her she is dirty, that like the girl in "Down on the Banks of the Ohio" she "should be thrown into the river so that I will be clean." But her father walking out the front door is worse. She has imagined that her parents know everything: that Bob is somehow blackmailing them to let him rape her; that they would help her if they could; that they know and don't care. The fantasies come like fish; they could all be true. But her father walking out the front door is not a fantasy; it's the end of any chance she has to believe that Bob is real.

She knows it's her innocence that attracts her father, and so she tries to kill it. Donna walks into Laura's house to find her friend very dressed up, drinking and smoking. "Where are you going?" "Nowhere fast, and you're not coming." With Donna chasing after her, Laura drives to the roadhouse.

The Log Lady is standing at the roadhouse door, taking the place of the bums outside of Hap's. With one arm holding her log to her chest, she puts a hand on Laura's forehead. "The tender boughs of innocence burn first, and the flame rises, and then all goodness is in jeopardy. When this kind of fire starts," she says, "it's very hard to put out"—and she's not talking about teenage hormones, or teenage sex and teenage drugs, or even teenage sex to buy teenage drugs. She's talking about a girl lighting the fires of hell, a witch binding herself to her own stake and lighting her own pyre. She can't know what's just happened to the girl, in her own house, at her own dinner table—or as a medium maybe she can. She waits at the door of the roadhouse for whoever might come along; when Laura appears she reads her face.

It's all so ordinary in tone, in timing; the Log Lady could be just another small-town busybody, a do-gooder, handing out sensible advice to teenagers, or condoms if that's not going to work. Her hand is still on Laura's forehead; now she's blessing her. Laura walks into the roadhouse where Julee Cruise is singing.

Angel Baby

When Laura walks into the roadhouse she seems to be moving in slow motion. She sits at a table and looks up at Julee Cruise—and then it's Cruise who seems to be caught in slow motion, even though sounds come out of her mouth in real time. The song she is singing, Lynch and Badalamenti's "Questions in a World of Blue," is barely a song at all.

With her white blond hair, deathly white skin, and nearly blank eyes, Julee Cruise looks like a ruined Laura Palmer—Laura Palmer with all the physical details wrong, the features muddy and coarse. She looks as if she's recovering from a beating—and she looks like Teresa Banks, dead on the autopsy table, and like the woman who lives in the radiator in *Eraserhead*. With her little-girl voice, with an air of experience, ten years of waitressing and five years in jail, maybe former or present-day heroin addiction, she performs as someone who herself has no future, but who holds out the possibility of a future, of redemption, to whoever might really hear her.

There's a dimension of sweetness, of forgiveness—forgiveness of life. In Cruise's repertoire it's all put across with the softness of fifties doo-wop, there in the way her "I Remember" ends with a flurry of drums off the beat, an orchestrated atonal ceiling above the surge of a pipe organ, and then, rising against a few piano notes, a quiet "Shoo-bop, shooby-shoo-bop . . ." It's there in the way the Fleetwoods, two girls and a boy from Olympia High School in Olympia, Washington, just across the state so long before, are present in Cruise's "The World Spins," their "Come Softly to Me," from 1959, as undeniable in Cruise's throat as Rosie and the Originals' "Angel Baby," from 1960. As Cruise changes the old songs into her own, they communicate as unkept promises, promises you can believe will be kept, at least as long as Cruise's "Floating" or "Falling" or "Into the Night" lasts: four minutes, maybe five.

In *Twin Peaks* as it played on television, the roadhouse where Cruise sings was a secret public place, warm and inviting, a refuge and a hideout, the place where people married to other people met to sit at a table in full view of everyone else and disappear into each other's eyes, where friends went to say what they couldn't say in the light or the open air, where people went to hear Julee Cruise. There, against a backdrop of red curtains, she would appear with her band, a modest ensemble, almost genteel, with Cruise herself in clean black leather—cap, jacket, short skirt—as her audience of middle-aged townspeople, Laura Palmer's high-school friends trying to figure out who killed her, and bikers passing through on their way to Spokane let "Falling" fall all over them. In *Fire Walk with Me* the roadhouse is the same place; it's also a border joint, with one room in the United States, where Cruise performs, and another in Canada, which is to Twin Peaks as Tijuana is to San Diego. In this room a cowboy band is playing stripper blues, naked women in the crowd dance like zombies, and all around them people's eyes are pinned with dope. There's a shot of the floor as the music sleazes across it, the boards covered with thousands of cigarettes, beer bottles, a bottomless dirt. Over the borderline there is filth; America must be kept clean.

Cruise stands on her stage in a white taffeta gown; against her bloodless skin her lipstick is impossibly red, with just a hint of a smear. She might be some prom discard who was dumped here ten years ago with no way to get home, either because she wouldn't fuck her date or because she did—and after that all she was good for was a laugh to get his buddies off.

With her face in a puddle of blue light and only red behind her, Laura sits alone at a table as Cruise begins her song. She's singing in a high croon, but there's an anchor in the smoothness of her tone, just the slightest burr of misery, and lifetimes of misery in the way she holds the song back, refuses to let it move. Though a full band is visible in the shot, except for almost silent brushes on a drum skin, and then a soft saxophone solo, a synthesizer is the only instrumentation. It makes a sound that's like a curtain being raised, but the curtain is raised only halfway, and then it hangs in the air. Laura begins to weep, but whatever sound she might be making isn't on the soundtrack; there's no melodrama, no corn, no sense of an unhappy girl crying to a sad tune. She is shattering, and there seems to be nobody else in the room to hear the lovely song. Certainly nobody can hear her, or wants to.

Why did you go?
Why did you turn
Away from me?

When all the world
Seemed to sing
Why, why did you go?

Was it me?
Was it you?

As the lyricist, Lynch insists on the banality of his own words; Julee Cruise's challenge is to transform the banality, to make the song stop time. She does, and it's unbearable, the way she turns the motion of music into utter stillness. "The most significant historical event of the twentieth century?" Kristine McKenna once asked Lynch. "The birth of rock 'n' roll," he said. Here, going back to the Fleetwoods and "Angel Baby," but stripping the sound of any nostalgia, Lynch creates a setting where the music can appear as if for the first time, complete and finished. The music makes a hole in itself, a hole that is part of Lynch's sense of what rock 'n' roll is, something so perfect even its fans don't quite believe that it's real, that anything could be so right. "Do you remember when this passion for music started?" Chris Rodley once asked Lynch. "Oh, absolutely," he said. "The exact moment."

It gets dark, you know, very late in Boise, Idaho in the summer. It was not quite dark, so it must have been, like, maybe nine o'clock at night, I'm not sure. That nice twilight, and a beautiful night. Deep shadows were occurring. And it was sort of warm. And Willard Burns came running towards me from about three houses down the street, and he said, "You missed it!" and I said, "What?" and he said, "Elvis on *Ed Sullivan!*" And it just, like, set a fire in my head. How could I have missed that? And this was the night, you know. But I'm kind of glad I didn't see it; it was a bigger event in my head because I missed it.

For Lynch the passion began in absence, with a sense of what you're missing, what you can't have, and that was what Lynch would put into his own songs. In "Questions in a World of Blue"— just typing the title is embarrassing, until the song begins to play— Cruise's style is distilled into an essence so fine that, compared with this, the ethereal songs she sings on the *Twin Peaks* TV series, or "Mysteries of Love," the floating tune she sings at the end of *Blue Velvet*, are obvious and vulgar. As you watch her sing in *Fire Walk with Me*, you can barely credit the body behind the voice; Laura Palmer looks away.

Music can make a utopia that shames life with its beauty, and that could be what Laura Palmer is hearing: the singer on the stage or her own soul telling her what she isn't, what she could have been, what she could never have been, performing that absent self, a Laura Palmer that she can only see in someone else. That's what's missing; that is the hole the music makes in itself, the door it opens. Though in Laura's dreams and visions, the red curtains behind Julee Cruise are the same red curtains that open into the red room—if the red room is not in truth in Julee Cruise's red mouth— this night she can't go through the door. In her mind the music sings it shut. Finally the spell breaks. Sheryl Lee focuses her eyes as Laura Palmer lights a cigarette.

At the Bar

At the bar, Jacques, the fat, greasy French-Canadian who runs the roadhouse, is pimping her. With a look he asks Laura if she's ready; she nods, and he sends two men over. "So you want to fuck the homecoming queen," Laura says; it's not a question. "Let's go all around the world, babe," one man says. "That won't get you to Walla Walla," she says, fingering the money he's put on the table. But then Donna appears. Sizing up the situation in a glance, she moves in on the other man: as a testament to her friendship, she will try to catch her friend's disease. There is no one else. If John Winthrop's founding call for a town where all would "make others Condicions our owne" is to be made good, she'll have to answer it. That town is gone, even if the call hangs in the air. If the promise is to be kept, Donna will have to keep it.

Soon the four of them are through the door dividing one half of the roadhouse from the other—and all the symbolism loaded into the journey, from one country to another, from the conscious mind to the subconscious, from earth to the underworld, good to evil, Faith and Goodman Brown as they are in their town and as they are in the woods, is wiped away by squalor. As Jacques drugs the girls' beer, his features seem to slide off his bones.

Ronette Pulaski, who was with Laura for the party that Teresa Banks set up for Leland Palmer, is there; there's talk about how it's been a year since Banks's body was found. "She was going to get rich," Ronette says. "She was blackmailing somebody." "Right," Jacques says, "she called me. She even asked me what your fathers looked like." The girls are scared, but then the drugs kick in. Laura is stripping off her blouse and dropping it into the dirt at her feet, dancing naked from the waist up with her john, miles and miles past Walla Walla, drinking and laughing at a table, even more naked in the harsh light, ordering the john to crawl under the table and suck her off, her head rolling back with a smile as he does. She's worked One-Eyed Jacks; she's worked Jacques's roadhouse. But now, with the genie of Bob out of the bottle and her efforts to push it back in failing, she is falling into so many pieces she barely exists.

At the House

She needs coke; she calls her dope-dealing boyfriend, a high-school thug named Bobby. They go into the woods to meet his connection, the Deer Meadow sheriff's deputy. When he pulls a gun Bobby shoots him dead. Bobby panics; Laura breaks out in giggles. Crazy with fear, Bobby tries to cover the body with handfuls of dirt; with a superhuman effort, Laura composes her face into a mask of solemnity. Then she cracks up again. Bobby looks at her in terror; this isn't a disease he can understand, let alone one he's willing to catch.

At Laura's house, her father seems to have drugged her mother, Sarah Palmer, who passes out. He turns on the overhead fan, a sign to Laura to prepare herself for Bob. Laura arrives home, climbs the stairs under the whirling fan, goes into her bedroom, and gets into her bed. She tosses and turns; she strips off the sheets. She imagines Bob crawling through the window; he climbs onto the bed and onto Laura. She wakes up in horror, then seems swept up as he rapes her. She sees Bob's face. "Who ARE you?" she shouts, breaking the spell—and then, as her father's face appears, a horrible, grinning, self-satisfied face, infinitely more awful than the face she has dreamed up to blank out his, she screams her soul out. It's overwhelming, beyond human. The scream is so big, so all-consuming, that it's less that the scream is part of the girl you're watching than that she is part of the scream. It exists whether she does or not. It's a force that finds its host.

You don't understand how a body could contain such reservoirs of sound, even as the dam is breaking: watching, frozen, you are also running away from the sound like someone trying to outrun a flood, as if anyone could. But then, through the noise, you see the look in Sheryl Lee's face—and the look she has created is so strong, so piercing and vengeful, that again it seems to shut down its own sound.

But she has already played this scene, and with none of the sensationalism of her demon turning into her father as he rapes her: the scene around which the whole film turns, and the scene in which the town in which the movie is set for a moment stands in for the country. Laura Palmer has seen her father come out of her house just after finding Bob in her room; she has realized who and what he is. But she has forced herself to forget it, as much as she can; when she comes home for dinner that day, her mind has forgotten, but her skin remembers.

At the Table

Leland Palmer, with his swept-back hair, his wide, devouring mouth, his eager-beaver boy's eyes, is sitting at the dining room table, waiting. When Laura enters the house, he tells her to sit down; she seems surprised but does what she's told. At first it's as if he just wants to make conversation, a father who doesn't know how to talk to his teenage daughter trying. "Are you happy?" he asks. "Not really," she says, but it could just be a bad day; the scene is inert on the screen, with no sense that anything is about to happen. It's all a trick; she is being set up.

As if he's been planning this moment all day, if not for years, Leland stares across the table: "You didn't wash your hands before you sat down, did you?" Of course she didn't, he never gave her the chance, but this is his chance. He rushes to Laura's side of the table and grabs her hands. He inspects them: if he finds dirt, he finds wickedness. That's what he wants: it will prove that he is right to do everything he does, to teach her a lesson, to instruct her in the wages of sin.

Leland attacks his daughter as if there's dirt in her mouth, but in an odd, condescending, almost joking tone, as if at any moment both he and Laura will start laughing, as if this is just a game they've played forever, the singsongy "Laura *Hasa* Dirty *Handsa*" game: "Why, these hands are *filthy*! Look! There's dirt way under this fingernail!" And then there's no chance that this is a joke. This is a game that can only be played once.

What pulls you in, what makes the scene truly horrifying, is that it is pushed only a few degrees past ordinary parental sadism, any parent's assertion of blind authority, the *Because I said so* of everyday family life. The action makes the viewer into a participant: what parent hasn't felt this power, what child hasn't felt this terror, what parent hasn't felt a child's terror and realized that, yes, at this moment, *I can do anything*? But this isn't a five-year-old cowering in a corner. This is a nearly adult woman with no more defenses than a five-year-old, and a father who has worked for years to make that true.

He goes on. He sees a necklace around Laura's neck, with half a charm missing; he realizes a boyfriend must have the other half. He sucks in his lips: "Did you get it from a *lover*?" Sarah Palmer— who from the desiccation in her face appears to live on cigarettes and gall—comes in from the kitchen: "They don't call them *lovers*, Leland." He ignores her. He grabs the skin of Laura's cheek and twists it, trying to get her to say who gave her the necklace. "Leland, leave her alone," Sarah says. "Don't do that—she doesn't like that." The mildness of her attempt to make her husband stop what he's doing makes it plain she knows everything he does, and that she has never done anything to stop it. And his awful response pulls off every mask: "How do you know what she likes?"

Chris Isaak's Agent Desmond, standing between the rows of trailers, the mountains at his back, lurks in the background as the scene plays; the stillness in the room as Julee Cruise sings in the roadhouse in her white prom dress, with her white face and red lipstick, is there, too. The scene is a train rushing back into the past, roaring past every limit to retrieve something that was lost, and you can begin to understand what Mary Pickford meant when she said, "It would have been more logical if silent pictures had grown out of the talkie instead of the other way round." "What I really like about it," Lynch once said of Los Angeles, "is, from time to time, if you drive around—especially at night—you can get a little gust of wind from the great days of the silver screen. All there in, like, living memory. It just makes you *wish* that you'd lived in those times. I think that if you could go back, that's the one place that you want to go back to." And then you're there: as Leland and then Sarah Palmer have played the scene, those times are present in Sheryl Lee's face. Pulling her character all the way into herself, until it seems as if Laura Palmer has begun to eat her from the inside, Lee has turned 1992 into 1917.

Lee has turned a talkie into a silent picture. Leland Palmer stands over his daughter as she looks up at him in shock, a body of water against a body of death. Disbelief, belief, knowledge, refusal of knowledge, a person now possessed by memories that appear and disappear in instants too short to measure, a stuttering memory that dissolves events and stops time—all of this courses through Sheryl Lee's face as she looks up into Leland Palmer's face, her eyes widening, her mouth opening, not moving, a person now composed entirely of a silent scream that for one and a half minutes does not stop.

After this, until Leland Palmer finally beats his daughter to death, in some twenty shots so quick they are nearly subliminal— dark mouth, bright mouth, mouth in a long shot moving into shadow, mouth bright to dark, then the mouth and the right eye, both open and dead, the most visually clean and emotionally unbearable violence David Lynch has put on a screen ("Fat Tony" Lynch, they call him when he comes trolling for extras in junkie alleys)— the movie is simply holding its breath.

In These United States

One afternoon Laura tells her diary about the day's events: driving stoned, she ran over a cat. A girl came running out of her house. It was her cat, Laura says, but the girl tries to comfort *her*: "Please, stop crying." "Such a willingness to forgive," Laura writes. "This one girl could love all of these United States and leave no one feeling lonely."

The phrase is a small shock: along with a few FBI agents, perhaps the only reminder that Twin Peaks is part of a greater community— or that, as you have followed its stories, Twin Peaks has replaced it. *These United States*: the old-time phrase calls up the country. It calls up the Fourth of July speaker, the march of the states from the East to the West, the one following the next into the republic as it grew, the graceful elision of the three words bringing the many parts of the nation into one, into a community where all speak the same language, where everyone listens to everyone else, an echo of Winthrop's community in the wind of the phrase as well. But when a father is raping his daughter, no one is supposed to know, and those who know don't tell, because if they did, the community would shatter. So the community disappears into the woods, where as the whole town gathers priests fill bowls with babies' blood.

In Martina McBride's 1994 country hit "Independence Day," written by Gretchen Peters, a woman takes a stand; with the song's title ringing through its choruses, she raises the flag for herself and everyone else. The story is plain: the woman's husband is "a dangerous man," and in a "small, small town" "word gets around"— everyone knows this guy is beating his wife. But the woman performs an act—a single, solitary gesture, because no one would listen if she merely spoke—that everyone must pay attention to, that everyone must have an opinion about, even if one's real opinion is not what one might ever say in public. The woman draws a line, creating a real community by dividing a false one: on the Fourth of July, she burns down her house and kills her husband.

As McBride sings it out, the act draws on national ethics, on the history of the country, its promises of community, liberty, and justice and its failure to keep them, for motive, justification, explication—and in the process the act and the song that describes it become part of those ethics, and join that patriotic history. The singer is remembering what happened when she was eight years old; now she's grown. McBride sings the story full-throated, with a bitter, no-one-gave-a-damn snap at the end of almost every line, cutting it off, throwing the listener off; within the patriotic drama the song insists on, McBride is making the story singular, an event: the song was written by someone else, but no one else would sing it this way. "Well, she lit up the sky on the Fourth of July," McBride sings from deep in the chest. "Talk about your revolution / It's Independence Day."

There's no hint that Independence Day is celebrated in Twin Peaks. Even if it were, it would be a travesty, a kind of patriotic Black Mass, which is how Laura Palmer understands her school voting her homecoming queen, and the whole town taking satisfaction at the picture of the beautiful girl in the paper: everybody knows she's a drug addict, a whore, and to both expose her and conceal what they know, to take away any chance that she could speak or act in a language anyone would understand, they've forced her to appear in disguise, a smile on her face, her eyes bright, a tiara on her head.

In Real Time

No matter how spectral "these United States" might be in Laura Palmer's diary, or how what happens in Twin Peaks can play like what happened in Blue Sky or Iverstown but was never written down, the drama on Lynch's screens did not take place in the vacuum of art. It played itself out in real places, in real time. Sometimes that was the territory, with Twin Peaks the map; sometimes it was the other way around.

The Other Twin Peaks

Olympia, Washington—the capital of the state, home to the governor's mansion, the legislature, and the bohemian Evergreen State College, but a quiet, even dull town for all that—is somewhat smaller than Twin Peaks was supposed to be: as of the 2000 census, pop. 42,514. In the late 1980s and early '90s, as *Twin Peaks* unrolled across the nation's TV sets, and then when *Fire Walk with Me* passed almost unnoticed in and out of a few of the nation's movie theaters, the town showed strange new faces.

"The anti-war graffiti was terrible in January and February," read the Metro Watch column of the daily *Olympian* in 1991, referring to the first Iraqi-American war and George H.W. Bush's Operation Desert Storm. "So now that the war's over? Don't ask."

On the rise downtown is graffiti most charitably described as anti-male. Some use blunter language.

The most quoted slogan is: DEAD MEN DON'T RAPE. UMBILICAL NOOSE is another. Others: WOMEN FIGHT BACK. GOD IS GAY. ABORT CHRIST. WOMEN REVOLT. And there are lots more, many we can't print in a family newspaper.

For that matter, some of the graffiti doesn't even make sense. One slogan Hutchings says he ran into again and again is: BIKINI KILL. Bikini Kill? Curiouser and curiouser.

Bikini Kill, a three-woman, one-man Olympia punk band led by Kathleen Hanna, helped spark the riot grrrl movement that for a few years made the town the world center of fervor in pop music: "Olympia, birthplace of rock," read the slogan of the local Kill Rock Stars label, insisting that rock 'n' roll could be born as if for the first time at any time, and anywhere. The Metro Watch quotation, with its reference to the Olympia police officer John Hutchings, appeared in Bikini Kill's *Girl Power* fanzine—like the band's *A Color and Activity Book* fanzine, made up of lines and pages scissored from disparate publications, typed screeds, and carefully detailed deconstructions of antifeminist put-downs, social conditioning, white privilege, trivializations of rape, and gender stereotyping. There were song lyrics, scribbled messages, and collaged illustrations from girls' magazines and history books, one spread of which featured Wonder Woman, girls playing dollhouse, and a pom-pom girl with an Ⓐ on her chest where the name of her high school should have been. Alongside the rest there was a drawing of a woman in a Puritan bonnet, her head encased in a harness over her eyes and mouth and, around the lips, a metal strap secured with a lock: "a particularly vicious and painful bridle used for silencing 'talkative' women. A metal 'tongue' intrudes into the mouth."

"What are your influences?" Hanna was asked by a writer. "Fourteen women in Montreal," she answered, referring to the women who on 6 December 1989 were shot dead in the École Polytechnique at the University of Montreal by one Marc Lepine—who entered a classroom, separated the women from the men, ordered the men to leave, and, shouting "I hate feminists," opened fire. "We seek to create revolution in our own lives every day by envisioning and creating alternatives to the bullshit christian capitalist way of doing things," read one draft of the riot grrrl manifesto, which, along with calls for girls to "resist psychic death" and "cry in public," called for "all girls to be in bands" and imagined a world where "girls rule all towns." That meant every girl standing up to speak in the public square, even if she had to create it herself, seizing whatever space there was, wherever a speaker or a singer or a band might find a place to play and someone to listen, in a club, at a school, in Olympia in those days in an International Pop Underground Convention parade down Main Street. It meant everyone claiming a chance to be heard.

All these years later, the thrill of what Thomas Jefferson called "public happiness" still leaps off the pages—the thrill of discovering the infinite subtlety of the language of oppression, and creating the language of refusal. "Why're we always explaining ourselves and our projects to boys? I'm serious. I have wasted more time and emotional energy doing this than i even wanna admit," wrote the anonymous author of "LAME LAME" in *Girl Power*. "It is not our responsibility to explain how boys/men are being sexist anymore than it is our responsibility to 'prevent ourselves' from getting raped." "ROCK FOR CHOICE—For <u>whose</u> choice are we rocking . . . ?" you could have read in the fanzine *riot grrrl*.

For the boyband on stage's choice to continue playing even though girlfriends in the audience are being severely harassed? For this boy's choice to decide how serious this harassment is, and that nothing can really be done about it? For his choice to label this social reality just an "individual dispute"? For his choice to "not try to be political"?

A few pages on:

Pretty Please
LISTEN TO US WHEN WE SCREAM!
I'm really sick of going to punk rock shows and having sweaty boys slamming into me for a good time. Ha ha, its really funny when you slam into me and my girlfriends. Cause you know girls like that sort of thing. It's a good time. NOT!!

I understand that people slam in order to get out aggression. Well fuck that. Ive got just as much anger in myself as you, possibly more, But I don't have to slam into otherxpent people to prove it or to get it out. I dance in my own space, <u>In THE FRONT!</u> I can even hold my friends hand and at the same time we can both get out our agdx anger. I'd like to see some mosher try and do that some time. Let's see if your strong enough for that.

Love,
A riot grrrl.
T.S.

It was a small revolution in many hearts that was soon enough turned into GIRL POWER T-shirts sold by the Spice Girls; for a time it was the creation of a new social space to negate the man's-home-is-his-castle, hear-no-evil-see-no-evil private estates that ruled Twin Peaks—or for that matter everyday life in Olympia. When Kathleen Hanna opened her mouth, a scream Laura Palmer never got to scream came out. "FUCK TWIN PEAKS," reads a scrawled headline in *A Color and Activity Book*, leading into a clipping from a piece by the film critic Lisa Kennedy about the 1990 episode of *Twin Peaks* where Leland Palmer is exposed:

In the end Cooper asks lamely, "Would it be easier to believe that a man would rape and murder his own daughter?" Well, yeah. I heard recently that the guy who raped, tortured for three days, then killed a dear friend of mine, was finally remanded. Six years after that friend's skeleton was found in the Colorado foothills, Laura Palmer is hailed as this year's breakthrough dead girl. "My father killed me," she says, but Cooper still gets the last word. With an end like that, there's really no breakthrough.

The most striking songs on the first Bikini Kill collection—an eight-song homemade cassette titled with the riot grrrl slogan *Revolution Girl Style Now*—were about father-daughter incest. "Daddy's Li'l Girl" was the Laura Palmer story, told without effect: "For Daddy's love, didn't know I'd have to lose myself—for Daddy's touch." But then the father speaks: "Listen. Listen! Listen. Dad has something to say, he has something for you to do—and he wants it done right now—and he wants you to do it his way." The song "Suck My Left One" was sardonic in its description, in a younger sister's voice, of her father coming into the room she shares with her older sister—"My sister pulls the covers down, she reaches over flicks on the light, she says to him"—and then hideous, Hanna's voice coming out of Linda Blair's ruined head in *The Exorcist* for the older sister's shout, "SUCK MY LEFT ONE," her acquiescence her only way to protect her sister from the same fate.

In her early twenties in the early nineties, Hanna often came onstage with "SLUT" written in Magic Marker on her stomach. "During performance she might take off her top, while screaming, 'Suck my left one,'" the journalist Emily White wrote in 1992. "Such acts probably terrify and confuse the teenage boys in the audience who've been waiting for this moment, but they make more and more sense to a generation of young women who are coming to understand that contradiction might be the most powerful feminist tool yet, creating a kind of paralysis, or night blindness, in the man/boy imagination." But it was the ending of the song that killed, as the mother took over the story—"You have got to be polite, girl / Show a little respect for your father / Wait until your father gets home"—and then the daughter's response, shutting down, willing her mind blank and her memory dead: "Fine fine fine fine fine fine fine fine fine." "FUCK DAD OR DIE," read a line on a page of lyrics in *A Color and Activity Book*.

"I was eighteen," Corin Tucker said in 2000. By then she was part of the three-woman punk band Sleater-Kinney, which had formed in Olympia in 1994 and dissolved in 2006. Six years later it was plainly the best band in the country; it was introduced that night on the stage of the Fillmore Auditorium in San Francisco as "the best band in the world." Tucker was remembering a time when she was a student at Evergreen, and how, in seemingly secret places, the town was beginning to change. "I went to a show that Bratmobile and Bikini Kill played. It was February 14, 1991. And Kathleen Hanna was—terrifying. People were just freaking out. She was saying things that were really direct and really emotional at the same time. She was so powerful. People were crying. And some people were like, 'They're the worst band *ever.*'" Tucker went on:

It was the first time I'd ever seen feminism translated into an emotional language. That I saw those kinds of thoughts and ideas put into your personal life, that's not in a textbook or an academic discussion. For young women to be doing that, basically teenagers onstage, to be taking that kind of stance, that kind of power, was blowing people's minds. And it totally blew mine. I was like—Okay, that's it. That's it for me—I'm going in a band, right now. You had the feeling they had started the band the week before: you can do it too.

Olympia 1991

The first band Tucker started, along with her high-school friend Tracy Sawyer, the wonderfully named Heavens to Betsy, was even more primitive than Bikini Kill—and, from their first performances, in 1991, the oddest and strongest band to emerge from the cauldron under which Hanna and others lit their fire. Tucker sang and played guitar or drums, Sawyer played drums or bass. They sounded as if they hadn't quite gotten their instruments out of their boxes before playing them; they could not have been more crude, or more unforgiving. In Sleater-Kinney, Tucker's voice is huge, a force of nature, like an animal that doesn't belong to her; in Heavens to Betsy's "Monsters," from 1993, her voice comes from deep in the chest, but it's suppressed, tense, so that you can feel that every word had to fight to get out: "You will live out all the horror stories / They told you when you were young / Someday you might fight those monsters / Someday you might become one." Then the words are screamed, but like a nice, acceptable, well-modulated movie scream—and then in the background, awful, barely human screaming, Laura Palmer screaming in her bedroom with her father's face above her, right off the movie screen and into the song.

A stage announcement, from a show that same year in Portland, could have been the manifesto of the two-woman band: they were there to make the forbidden speak, to carry the debris of the forbidden to the public square and make everybody look, and the place they were playing that night had a fortuitous name. "Welcome to the X-Ray," Tucker says into the mike.

It's, uh, Thursday night. We're gonna rock you tonight. We're on the radio, by some strange event, so, please be aware that you are being recorded. You are being produced live, on the air, everything you say, they might be able to hear. So if you have any secrets you don't want to tell over the air, you might not want to say anything. At all. At all. At all. [Singing] *You-might-not-want-*

to-say-anything-at-all. Or you might want to scream FUCK YOU! I HATE YOU, YOU SUCK, MAN! Or you might want to say, *Hey baby, how much are you going to pay me for this one*—that's my question, that's my QUESTION.

Or you might fuck up a lot tonight. We haven't practiced much, we never practice, and we never get paid very much, and that's the way it goes. So—that's our band. I hope you like it.

"*Heavens to Bettttssssssyyyyy,*" Tucker sang over Sawyer's loose bass; there was applause. "I love it when you can say anything and people will clap," she said.

The band's first recording, "My Red Self," made in 1991, was barely music at all, a bass thump, simple drumbeats, an almost tuneless chant: someone naked in front of the full-length mirror in her bathroom, talking to herself about her period. There was a gravity in the singing that pulled you in, then made it impossible to turn away—a quality magnified many times over with Heavens to Betsy's second recording, "Baby's Gone." Big guitar chords shimmer and break like something out of Jimi Hendrix's blasted version of "The Star-Spangled Banner," but it's Tucker's clipped and certain diction that makes the song a kind of nihilist anthem, and also the cruelest, most self-immolating punk rant this side of the Mekons' "The Building." The instrumentation is atmosphere, setting, a house; the action is all in the voice, and the voice is that of a teenager dead of her own attempt at an abortion, speaking to her parents. She enters her old house, but it's empty; up a staircase, her footsteps make an echo each time she reaches for a landing. At each landing there is a greater nothingness, a sound carrying dead air and dead weight, an unbreakable stillness, and so every line of the song

I grew up in your
House
I grew up with your
Rules
I know sex is what I shouldn't do
I know what I can't tell you

begins the trek all over again. There's no progression in the music. There is a tremendous reach in Tucker's voice as she sings to herself, imagining her parents in front of her, shaking in front of them, imagining them opening the front door of their house, climbing the staircase in turn:

Baby's gone away
Baby won't be back
Your baby's gone
I did what you told me to do, now I'm dead

Across its first tracks on Olympia compilation albums, on a handful of singles and one album under its own name, Heavens to Betsy's music was about revealing secrets, tearing off masks, digging as far down as one had to dig to find the secrets one had hidden most of all from oneself. And it all exploded with "My Secret," the band's first 45, shared with another band, the sleeve of the disc picturing the bare midriffs of two girls, just above their Levi's, just below their tops, "bratmobile" written on the stomach of the girl on the right, "heavens to betsy" on the stomach of the girl on the left, with the *o* in "to" circling her belly button. The song was a firestorm—and as you listen, it's hard not to think it was written right off the *Twin Peaks* TV screen, to give Laura Palmer a better ending. There's light clicking on drumsticks, then a wham-wham-wham from the guitar, a staccato rhythm, a quick march. Tucker's voice is strained, caught, and only more violent for that; each word that makes its own space throws off the others around it, as if the word is the entire song, the word slamming down like a stamping foot:

My
secret
is coming out
and
each
word
I let it out

The breaks between words, turning each one into a victory for the singer, and a terror, because now she will have to go on to the next word, make the lines where words actually follow one from the other—"I'll tell again and again / What you did to us when we were only ten"—feel as if the pressure is lessening. And then it all comes back, like a speeding car:

My
secret
is coming out!
Each
word
I let them out!
The truth, the truth
will get YOU
In the end!
My
secret
Is that I want you dead
*   I want you dead*
*   I want you dead*
*   I want you dead*

The Witches in the Woods

That was one upheaval in Olympia. The other—which, if not an inspiration for the mystery of who killed Laura Palmer, was so similar one can imagine that it was, for the TV series, jimmied in to solve the mystery—began just a year before the debut of *Twin Peaks*, and two years before the emergence of riot grrrl.

On 28 November 1988, Paul R. Ingram of Olympia, forty-three, the father of five children and the chief civil deputy of the Thurston County sheriff's office—who was as well the chairman of the local division of the Republican Party and a member of the Pentecostal Church of the Living Water, which traced its beginnings to the 1920s West Coast revivals of Aimee Semple McPherson's International Church of the Foursquare Gospel—was arrested on charges that he had molested his two daughters, Ericka, twenty-two, and Julie, eighteen.

Ericka and Julie had attended a Christian camp where a charismatic healer had visions of child abuse; hysteria broke out. The healer had a vision that Ericka Ingram had been molested for years by her father; soon she and her sister remembered that, and years of sexual abuse by their brothers, too. Confronted with the accusations, Ingram could recall nothing—but in the same breath he said his girls would not lie. If he did what his daughters said he did, Ingram said, "there must be a dark side of me that I don't know about." So wrote Lawrence Wright in his book *Remembering Satan*, in 1994—by then echoing what Lynch had already shown in *Twin Peaks* and *Fire Walk with Me*.

Soon, as the stories Ingram's daughters told built upon themselves, the bowl of blood from Young Goodman Brown's Black Mass in the Puritan woods around Olympia was filled with the blood of Ericka's own babies. Ingram himself began to remember years and years of horror, in damning detail—always as "I must have," "I can see myself," "I would have." He would have raped his daughter Julie when she was fifteen and forced her to have an abortion. He would have begun raping Ericka when she was five. He spoke without affect, with complete detachment. "That wasn't my dad there," said one of Ingram's sons when he visited his father in jail, as if like so many before them they were characters out of *Invasion of the Body Snatchers*.

Ericka and Julie began to remember much more: a whole coven of witches, gathering in the Ingram house on the edge of the Olympia woods. Mass rapes by their father, his friends, other police officers, with their mother presiding, or ritually penetrating Ericka with a pole. Not even farm animals were missing; there was sex with dogs and goats, forced on the girls and performed willingly by their mother. She was impregnated when she was in high school, Ericka said, and aborted with a coat hanger: "The baby was cut up and rubbed all over her body." As with the girls who cast the first

stones in Salem three hundred years before, the charges soon flew
into the air, chasing witches who changed shape and flew like
birds. In Olympia, there were orgies in the woods. The girls were
taken from their house. As Wright reports, Ericka Ingram wrote it
out for the police:

There was a table inside the barn. There was also a fire. All the people
around the table including my mom & dad wore a gown & a hat resembling
a viking hat with horns. There was a lot of blood everywhere. There was
pitchforks in the ground . . . The sacrifice. They would lay it first on the
table then the high priestess would pick it up all the people would chant &
the women would say words then the baby would be put on the table & all
of the people including my mother & father circling the table would stab it
with knives until it died . . . Then they would all walk to the pit and chant
and the high priestess would carry the baby and put the baby in something
white then put it in the ground . . . They would tell me this is what would
happen to me also. They also would say you will not remember this. They
would say it over & over again like a chant.

Thus the satanic cult into which Leland Palmer was recruited
as a child, into which he tried to bring his daughter, but she fought
him, so he had to— But, the Thurston County sex crimes detective
Loreli Thompson told Wright, she had seen perhaps three hundred child victims of sexual abuse in no more than four years, and
not because of recovered memories of satanic cults. There was
nothing strange about it, nothing at all. What was strange was how,
just as in the woods Goodman Brown saw all the people he saw
every day in his town, as if everyone were completely different and
completely the same, the Ingrams came to believe, in Wright's
words, that they "had lived two opposing lives—one as prominent
Christians in their church and their community, the other as covert
practicing satanists—and also that the good and aboveboard public
life of the family was entirely unaware of its furtive, monstrous un-
derlife." Or that, in a land where anything is possible, where liberty
can mean the freedom to kill whoever might trouble your mind,

where, finally, as each individual traces the history and the legacy of these United States, anyone can be killed at any time, in any place, for any reason, many people would rather believe anything than nothing.

In the Town

In two towns, one on the map in the Washington woods, one imagined onto the map, the city that Winthrop invented in his sermon plays itself out. In both Olympia and Twin Peaks, freedom meant the right to be left alone, to draw one's blinds, to get what you need and take what you want; in Winthrop's town, it meant the freedom of the city, the freedom of leaving the pettiness of your small, frightened self and discovering who God meant you to be. It was what, nearly three hundred years after Winthrop spoke, D. H. Lawrence discovered in America by its absence:

Men are free when they belong to a living, organic, *believing* community, active in fulfilling some unfulfilled, perhaps unrealized purpose. Not when they are escaping to some wild west. The most unfree souls go west, and shout of freedom. Men are freest when they are most unconscious of freedom. The shout is a rattling of chains, always was.

Men are not free when they are doing just what they like. The moment you can do just what you like, there is nothing you care about doing.

Though for a time, in Olympia, a new kind of public life was created, where anyone with the courage to face his or her fellow citizens could speak and anything could be said, as the story the nation told itself unfolded from 1980 onward, private estates did not merely persist in the ruin of the public. They replaced the public—with private schools supplanting public schools, public lands sold off to private developers, public funds transferred from the many to the few, and the few proclaiming that they owed nothing to the community, that in truth it did not even exist—and the new speakers retreated to their secret spaces. In Twin Peaks, the closest you could come to a public space was a roadhouse, where people gathered to live secret lives in an open room, where teenage girls worked as prostitutes and a doo-wop torch singer could make you believe there was more to life than this, if you could find it—as if the town could remain just as it was, its buildings standing, the woods as beautiful and silent as they had always been, but the people different, their eyes not furtive, their tongues not crooked, their hearts not coal, but, as Winthrop said in 1630, before anyone had the chance to make his words into a town, "onely though wee were absent from eache other many miles, and had our imploymentes as farre distant, yet wee ought to account ourselves knitt together by this bond of love," "as members of the same body."

Ronald Reagan would take possession of Winthrop's image of the city on the hill, as if by adding a word to the phrase he could believe the vision had come to him and him alone: "a shining city on a hill," he always said. In Reagan's vision—as in John F. Kennedy's in his Inaugural Address, where Winthrop's city became a burning torch, with its glow "the glow from that fire" that could "truly light the world"—the hill on which the city stood was a hill from which the city looked down out on the rest of the world, the city to which the rest of the world was to look up, a beacon. "I've spoken of the shining city all my political life," Reagan said on 11 January 1989, in his farewell address as president. "But I don't know if I ever quite communicated what I saw when I said it."

In my mind, it was a tall, proud city, built on rocks, stronger than oceans, windswept, God-blessed, and teeming with people of all kinds, living in harmony and peace. A city with free ports, that hummed with commerce and creativity—and, if there had to be city walls, the walls had doors, and the doors were open to anyone with the will, and the heart, to get here. That's how I saw it, and see it still. And, how stands the city on this winter night? More prosperous, more secure, and happier than it was eight years ago. But more than that, after two hundred years, two centuries, she still stands strong and true on the granite ridge, and her glow has held steady no matter what storm.

At Reagan's funeral, it was not mentioned that the ruin of the public, and the return of all things public to private estates, had been his goal, or that he had gone further toward its realization than anyone but he himself might have believed possible. He had so changed the country that the idea of the public, of what used to be called the common good, now barely made sense. Rather, Winthrop's words about the city on a hill were brought out again, and in detail; for a moment, the public was not a ruin but again a promise, an obligation, an oath. "We must delight in each other; make others' conditions our own; rejoice together, mourn together, labor and suffer together, always having before our eyes our commission and community in the work, as members of the same body," read Supreme Court Justice Sandra Day O'Connor in the National Cathedral on 11 June 2004. Former U.S. Senator John C. Danforth of Missouri, who, though not a descendant of the Samuel Danforth who had preached his sermon on the American mission in Boston in 1670, was both ambassador to the United Nations and an Episcopal minister, took Winthrop's city back to Matthew 5:14–16, to the Sermon on the Mount: "Ye are the light of the world. A city that is set on a hill cannot be hid." That was what Winthrop meant: the promise has been made, the covenant has been struck. Fail your promise, break your covenant, and there will be nowhere to hide. But Danforth immediately turned the coin, drawing out the sense of divinity, of "You only have I known of all the families of the earth," but setting aside the warning, "therefore I will punish you for all your iniquities." "Winthrop," Danforth said, "believed that the eyes of the world would be on America because God had given us a special commission, so it was our duty to shine forth. The Winthrop message became the Reagan message. It rang of optimism, and we longed to hear it." At the Reagan Library in Simi Valley, California, you can see it on a postcard. "A SHINING CITY ON A HILL—RONALD REAGAN'S AMERICA," it's titled: a painting by the architect Harry Newman. Placed at the peak of an enormous mountain at the top of an enormous mountain range, green and blue, is a colossus formed somewhere between the Emerald City of Oz and the mother ship in *Independence Day*. A spire of white light reaching thousands of feet into the sky sends out lines of glory to every corner of the globe.

Twelve days after Reagan's funeral, at a fund-raising event in San Francisco, the Democratic presidential candidate John Kerry, descended from Winthrop through his maternal grandmother, Margaret Winthrop, took up the theme. "The idea of a city on a hill," Kerry said, "is not what the Republicans say it is." The first president to repeat Winthrop's words, he said, was indeed John F. Kennedy, in a farewell speech to the Massachusetts legislature on 9 January 1961, just before he set out for Washington, D.C., to take the presidential oath. "During the last sixty days," Kennedy said, "I have been engaged in the task of constructing an administration. I have been guided by the standard John Winthrop set before his shipmates on the flagship *Arabella* three-hundred-and-thirty-one years ago, as they too faced the task of building a government on a new and perilous frontier. 'We must always consider,' he said, 'that we shall be as a city upon a hill—the eyes of all people are upon us.' Today the eyes of all people are truly upon us—and our governments, in every branch, at every level, national, State, and local, must be as a city upon a hill—constructed and inhabited by men aware of their grave trust and their great responsibilities." "It's not about what kind of *glow* you can attach to it," Kerry said. "John Winthrop said, 'We shall be knit together in the work as one man.' It's a *compact*—the social compact. That means having and holding to a vision of the common good, where individual rights and freedoms are connected to our responsibility to others." Then Kerry quoted Langston Hughes's poem "Let America Be America Again," from 1938. *"Say, who are you that mumbles in the dark?"* some of it reads. *"And who are you that draws your veil across the stars?"* It could have been Dos Passos, hammering away at the colossus in *U.S.A.*:

I am the young man, full of strength and hope,
Tangled in that ancient endless chain
Of profit, power, gain, of grab the land!

Of grab the gold! Of grab the ways of satisfying need!
Of work the men! Of take the pay!
Of owning everything for one's own greed!

Kerry read:

O, let America be America again—
The land that never has been yet—
And yet must be—the land where every man is free.
The land that's mine—the poor man's, Indian's, Negro's, ME—
Who made America,
Whose sweat and blood, whose faith and pain,
Whose hand at the foundry, whose plow in the rain,
Must bring back our mighty dream again.

It wasn't a great poem, or even a good one. But in the United States in 2004, with its president riding his triumph against a false enemy, a triumph that hid the nation's failure to defeat or really even to engage a real enemy, the poem was barely in the English language. "The land that never has been yet"—what could that mean? That the work had hardly begun? That in a town like Twin Peaks, tangled in that endless chain, no one was innocent?

Half the High-School Girls in America

"Agent Desmond has disappeared!" Kyle MacLachlan's FBI agent Dale Cooper is in his home office in Philadelphia, the place marked by a shot of the Liberty Bell; he's yet to lay eyes on Twin Peaks, or even hear of it. It's thirty minutes into *Fire Walk with Me* and it feels like a violation. You don't need a pedantic announcement to make literal what can never be made clear. Desmond has disappeared, yes, but where did he go? In the Philadelphia office Cooper is a would-be psychic earnestly calling up spirits and summoning specters; he tells his impatient colleague Albert Rosenfield that he is sure the killer will strike again. He has seen it in a dream:

the victim will be a woman . . . she will have blond hair. "She's in high school. She's sexually active. She's using drugs. She's crying out for help." "Well, damn, Cooper, that really narrows it down!" Rosenfield says, a satisfied grin on his face. "You're talking about half the high-school girls in America!" But when Cooper arrives at the Fat Trout Trailer Park to follow up on Agent Desmond's disappearance, all he finds is Desmond's car and "Let's rock" scrawled on it in pink lipstick. In a vision, Cooper has already heard the words dragged out of the mouth of a dwarf, in the red room hidden behind the red curtains.

The suggestion is that Agent Desmond has been abducted by supernatural forces, just as the mystery of Laura Palmer's death was solved on television by pinning it on a demon, not a man, on a satanic cult rather than a father who rapes and kills his own daughter. There is mumbo jumbo all through *Fire Walk with Me*, just as there was when *Twin Peaks* was running through the woods on TV. But where on *Twin Peaks* the aliens and spirits and incorporeal villains finally turned the characters into fairy folk and the story into a shaggy dog, wagging its tail like a finger, in *Fire Walk with Me* the mystification draped over the story is repelled by the desperation of its subject and the woman who plays her, and Lynch fails to carry out the betrayal of his story that he himself has plotted.

There is no way for Lynch to explain away what he has put on the screen. There is no way for him to erase what he knows actually happens, or what he doesn't know: when it is that the true secret of a town is revealed, and how it is suppressed. "Agent Desmond has disappeared!"—but coming out of the expressions you have seen on Desmond's face, out of a cool, quiet contemplation of a malevolence he has never learned to track because it is hidden by the beauty at his back, the feeling is less that he has been abducted by supernatural forces than that he has been devoured by the story, or gone to live in the woods.

CRANK PROPHET BESTRIDE AMERICA, GRINNING: DAVID THOMAS

In 1953, in an essay that grew out of a seminar he was teaching at Princeton on the literature of the Civil War, Edmund Wilson seemed to argue that a prophet is someone who calls a people to their defining, truest, deepest, or most resistant values: that is, those values hardest, or least possible, to live up to. "It was as if he had not only foreseen the drama but had even seen all around it, with a kind of poetic objectivity, aware of the various points of view that the world must take toward its protagonist," Wilson wrote. "In the poem that Lincoln lived, Booth had been prepared for, too, and the tragic conclusion was necessary to justify all the rest. It was dramatically and morally inevitable that this prophet who had overruled opposition and sent thousands of men to their deaths should finally attest his good faith by laying down his own life with theirs."

The prophetic figure may seem to predict or call forth the future, because he or she embodies his or her place and time—his or her commonality, and all those who make it up. This prophet looks at the present and the past, at promises made and promises broken—or perhaps worse, forgotten—and asks what fate is appropriate for the commonality. More than that, the prophet may embody both the promise and the betrayal, embody the fate of his or her nation—"nation," because for better or for worse the idea of prophecy has been bound up with the idea of a nation, a commonality, a people who are not like everybody else, ever since prophecy emerged from the mouths of Isaiah and Jeremiah and Amos. "You only have I known of all the families of the earth"—when the prophet speaks to the nation, the nation speaks to itself. This is not the Christendom described in Norman Cohn's *The Pursuit of the Millennium*, not Nazism or Stalinism, or the Caliphate that hangs in the air of the twenty-first century, empires of the extermination of all other families: *All are welcomed into our Holy Family, or to death.**

The prophetic figure speaks not from the body of the commonality but as its body, finding the voice that all members of the commonality can hear, or should hear. And if the prophetic figure cannot find the voice in the land, he or she makes the voice up—because the prophet is sure that the voice exists, and because only with that voice can he or she, as Wilson suggests, not only call a people to judgment but embody that judgment, trying to lead the people to accept that by their betrayal of whatever promise it is that they are betraying, they will call down the wrath of God. It may not matter if the betrayal is that of the promise that all men are created equal, the promise that everyone has rights no government can take away, or the promise, implicit in the founding of the nation on the rock of life, liberty, and the pursuit of happiness, that I can get what I want and be left alone and you can get out of my way and to hell with anyone who tries to stop me. The nation speaks in many voices, some hard to understand, some not. "If you see me coming / Better step aside," Tennessee Ernie Ford sang in 1955. "A lot of men didn't / A lot of men died." Those are lines from a pop song dis-

---

*Sheikh Ibrahim Mudeiris, Palestinian Authority Television, 13 May 2005: "We have ruled the world before, and by Allah, the day will come when we will rule the entire world again. The day will come when we will rule America. The day will come when we will rule Britain and the entire world—except for the Jews. The Jews will not enjoy a life of tranquility under our rule, because they are treacherous by nature, as they have been throughout history. The day will come when everything will be relieved of the Jews—even the stones and trees which were harmed by them. Listen to the Prophet Muhammad, who tells you about the evil end that awaits Jews. The stones and trees will want the Muslims to finish off every Jew."

guised as a folk song; as American speech they were not made but found. There are nations where those words make no sense; the U.S.A. is not one of them. Find an American who claims not to understand what Ford was saying and you'll find a liar; find an American who claims not to understand the idea that the nation must judge itself and you'll find a fool. Find an American who does not believe that God's judgment will come in a form that no one can predict—even in a form that few if any will recognize if judgment comes—and you may have found a liar, a fool, or an optimist.

Take Lincoln's prophetic lines, as he spoke of the Civil War as a curse on the land: "Yet, if God wills that it continue, until all the wealth piled by the bond-man's two hundred and fifty years of unrequited toil shall be sunk, and until every drop of blood drawn with the lash, shall be paid by another drawn with the sword, as was said three thousand years ago, so still it must be said 'the judgments of the Lord are true and righteous altogether.'" Shocking words, for their time, as we look back—but what if the words really point us forward? What if Lincoln's curse is a prophecy for our time more than for his? What if this is a national fact that we must all of us act out in our own lives, as actors in our own national drama or spectators of our own history, until some unknowable day when the debt, compounded every day that racial injustice persists, is finally paid—or when the interest becomes so great it's clear the national debt can never be paid, and the nation must declare itself bankrupt?

Lincoln's words are finally so strange, so unknowable, that it seems less likely that they would issue from a platform erected in front of the Capitol than from an alleyway. After all, prophets can be found in the shadows, like the figure named "The Prophet" early on in *Moby-Dick*, warning Ishmael of the satanic quest he's signing up for. "Have ye shipped in her?" the man says, and it's not the sort of voice Ishmael or anyone wants to hear, not the sort of man you look in the face: "He was but shabbily apparelled in faded jacket and patched trowsers; a rag of a black handkerchief investing his neck. A confluent small-pox had in all directions flowed over his face, and left it like the complicated ribbed bed of a torrent, when the rushing waters have been dried up."

"We have just signed the articles," Ishmael replies politely.

"Anything down there about your souls?"

"About what?"

"Oh, perhaps you hav'n't got any . . . No matter though, I know many chaps that hav'n't got any,—good luck to 'em; and they are all the better off for it. A soul's a sort of a fifth wheel to a wagon."

Especially in America, in this place where it is presumed that everyone has a right to speak, to be heard, to do as they please— and where, as Lawrence wrote in his American book, joining Babe and Joe and Eddie in the Do Da Room, "if I say anything that displeases them, the free mob will lynch me . . . I have never been in any country where the individual has such an abject fear of his fellow countrymen. Because, as I say, they are free to lynch him the moment he shows he is not one of them"—especially in such a place, it may be, as the Princeton student Tanya Kalivas put it in 2000, that "the American voice can only be heard in the collective stories of those who are for some time, no matter how brief, pushed outside of the definition of 'American' . . . the American voice is how one responds when silenced because of who he or she is." This is where the prophet steps out of the alley, to become the person standing on the street telling you what you don't want to hear, the person you pretend you don't hear, didn't notice, never saw.

The Nightmare

This is the crank, the outsider, the loser—at his or her most splendidly absurd, the type forced into heroism in such 1940s Preston Sturges movies as *Hail the Conquering Hero* and *The Miracle of Morgan's Creek*, people "trapped in such ridiculous situations," as Manny Farber once wrote with the poet and critic W. S. Poster, it seems certain "that headlines will scream about them to a hooting nation for the rest of their lives," like "such nationally famous bone-heads as Wrong-Way Corrigan, Roy Riegels, who ran backward in a Rose Bowl game, or Fred Merkle, who forgot to touch second base in a crucial" pennant race, "living incarnations of the great American nightmare that some monstrous error can drive individuals clean out of society into a forlorn no man's land, to be lonely objects of an eternity of scorn, derision, and self-humiliation."

"This nightmare," Farber and Poster said—anyone's worst, naked-in-the-halls-of-my-old-high-school nightmare transposed into a national drama—"is of course the reverse side of the uncontrolled American success impulse, which would set individuals apart in an apparently different but really similar and equally frightening manner."

This is the sort of person whose name becomes forever after a warning of how utterly silenced one can become in America, how one's very presence can be an embarrassment to anyone forced to acknowledge it. Remember Jimmy Carter, who not only lost the presidency but, on election night in 1980, seemingly could not wait to give it up, as if to say to the country at large that he had never been worthy, almost offering himself for the sacrifice to which, over the next eight years, he was forced to submit, blamed by the man who replaced him for everything that went wrong? Remember how long it took this man who once led the nation—like the bum in Sturges's *The Great McGinty*, who thanks to the political machine becomes governor of his state and ends up running a bar in South America—to climb his way back to even a shadow of respectability, to the point where one could speak his name without shame, if that time has ever really come?

Tall-Tale Teller

"My name is David," David Thomas of the pre-punk, post-dada Cleveland band Pere Ubu sang in 1980, in a dashed-off ditty he called "Lonesome Cowboy Dave." "My name is David, and I've got a hat the size of Oklahoma / I've got shoes that look like Florida / I've got a coat that's like California / I've got spurs on my feet / Whoopie-ti-yi-yah."

Trying on the nation as if it were a wardrobe, Thomas was drawing on the oldest, richest strains of the tall tale. He was Pecos Bill or Paul Bunyan or Uncle Sam himself, dispatching his foes, crossing the continent in a dozen strides, kicking its mountains aside and drinking its rivers dry. He was Stagger Lee, shouting "rattlesnakes has bit me and crawled off and died." He was Goliath bragging in a minstrel show: "I kills my friends and makes hamburgers outer my enemies. Tornadoes and harrycanes follow me round like pet dogs, and lines and tigers is my playmates. I'm bad. I'm mean." With claims as big as Thomas's, "Lonesome Cowboy Dave" should have been a signature song, but Thomas didn't sing it when Pere Ubu appeared in the year 2000 at the Knitting Factory in New York City, one stop on the band's Twenty-fifth Anniversary Tour. Thomas didn't sing it as part of *Disastodrome!* the three-day, multi-act theatrical he staged at UCLA in 2003. He didn't sing it at a one-night solo stand, just himself and an accordion, in Seattle in 2005. He didn't have to. In Pere Ubu or out of it, Thomas has never made the charts; he's never had any hits, so he doesn't have to play them. "I know that the sacrifice of success breeds longevity," Neil Young once said of why he scatters terrible concept albums among dissonant masterpieces and craven, comfort-food crowd-pleasers. "Being willing to give up success in the short run ensures a long run. If you're really doing what you want to do." But it's unclear if David Thomas's story allows the words success or failure any meaning at all. Light and darkness, the riverside and the superhighway, the private eye's big city and the country singer's small town, the television screen and the all-night diner, are only a few of the warring territories that come into view when he opens his mouth to speak.

The band is still out there, turning up in Europe, in the United States, but whatever its travels always finding its way back to home base, making its records only in Cleveland, where the band's first members found each other. Place makes sound and sound makes place, Thomas has written again and again—and, he says, "I'm like Saddam Hussein. I only trust people from my own village." Those may be the only people he trusts, but that's not the only character he's like. Over time he has picked up many familiars. Treating a nation like a wardrobe may be the least of it.

The New World

More than thirty years ago, in 1975, emerging from what Thomas would call "the ruins of the industrial Midwest"—and with Pere Ubu founders Thomas and the guitarist Peter Laughner leaving behind a now-legendary band called Rocket from the Tombs—Pere Ubu thought it was the avatar of a new sound that would sweep the country, then the world. It was a sound the band tried, there in Cleveland, with nobody from anywhere else watching, to give the almost immediately meaningless name "New Wave." "We were drawn to art and in the early seventies rock music was the only valid art form," Thomas said in 2002. "If you were good you went into rock. If you were second string, if you were not quite good enough, then maybe you wrote or painted or made films."

The New Wave prophesies a new world—it says the new world is already present, and that a new art will reveal it. It says that a new world is waiting to be born, and that speech will call it into being. Such dreams can't be reduced to private riches and public fame, to private estates subsisting in the ruin of the public, to the definition of success that since the days when Ronald Reagan claimed the land has ruled the country: that new world, from the beginning, was what America promised itself it would be. America would be the new world or it would be nothing. But like any band Pere Ubu wanted it all: world conquest, with the rewards of the old world and the promise of a new world, the promise that like de Soto or Daniel Boone before it Pere Ubu could blaze a trail into the new territory. Despite the claims Thomas made from the first—"You have to bear in mind that I personally consider Pere Ubu to be a pop band," he said in 1978, "totally the same as Wings, or the Music Explosion or the Archies. It's just that we're doing more modern and therefore better pop music"—there was never a chance for the rewards of the old world, which today can seem all America promises anyone. The five or six or seven who passed through Pere Ubu in its first days believed far too deeply in self-destruction, disappearance, insult, confrontation, and the primacy of shadows over light for anything resembling financial security or commonplace renown.

Worshipping at the phonographic altars they had built to such mid-'60s avatars as the Southern California bandleader Captain Beefheart and the New York quartet the Velvet Underground, to the death-of-the-sixties Michigan drug punks the Stooges, Pere Ubu posited a sound it gave the ungainly name avant-garage. "David at one point drew a line across the stage and said, 'This is the intellectual side of the band and that is the tank side'—'tank' as in warfare," said Scott Krauss, the original Pere Ubu drummer. The band embraced the degraded trash momentum of the Seeds' 1966 L.A. grunge hit "Pushin' Too Hard"—a song so insistently simple that it seemed as it played to reduce itself almost to nothing, until for a brief instrumental break a melody emerged that pulled the song inside out, making you wonder where you were and how you got there. "Pushin' Too Hard" was Pere Ubu's "Louie Louie," the Rosetta stone scribbled in crayon on a supermarket bag. The displacement in its melody translated into many languages: rockabilly, rhythm & blues, the splayed, self-conscious voices of such pieces of mid-'60s Top 40 psychedelia as the 13th Floor Elevators' "You're Gonna Miss Me" and the Electric Prunes' "I Had Too Much to Dream (Last Night)"; traditional, even respectable European experiments with musique concrète and son trouvé; feedback and strangled cries from an abyss the band had dug for itself; vocals that faded out of words and into groans and squawks; horror-movie sound effects; heavy, fraying bass patterns sucking the air out of the room in which a song was recorded or in which it might be heard; odd comments from the side of the sound, as if from someone watching, not playing, as the band rehearsed for an audience yet to be, someone registering doubt against the self-justifying clatter, experience against adventures yet to be lived. "The bellhop in 'Heartbreak Hotel,'" Thomas says—the one whose "tears keep flowing," that's all you ever hear about him—"he is the key to everything I've ever wanted to achieve in the narrative voice. The observer who is part of the story and all the while the only question is whether he knows it or not."

You can hear this music on the band's first record, issued on the band's own Cleveland label: the single "30 Seconds Over Tokyo" / "Heart of Darkness," from 1975. The first side was a nearly literal summoning up of the Doolittle Raid of 18 April 1942, the first American assault on Japan after Pearl Harbor. A complaining guitar sound—one high, stretched, strident note that gave off the feel of someone trying to scrape dirt off his hand with a knife—rang through "30 Seconds Over Tokyo," growing more and less and more and less accepting as the drama took shape, nothing-you-can-do-about-it turning into I-can't-take-it-anymore and turning back. With fuzztones and a scrambled pilot's voice shouting through static, with drums and Thomas's words tumbling away from each other like cardboard boxes down the steps of the Capitol building, the sound was the last man standing, the witness, Ishmael after the *Pequod* disappeared: "And I only am escaped alone to tell thee." But up against its flip side "30 Seconds Over Tokyo" was contrived; for all of its drama it was just an idea. "Heart of Darkness" got inside the firestorm.

From its first beat, the tune had a pulse. As the band rushed forward on the single-stroke beat it probably picked up when the Velvet Underground blew through Cleveland in 1967 and their drummer, Maureen Tucker, kept "What Goes On" going for twenty minutes without changing her expression any more than she changed her count, dim, scratched-out guitar lines curled around the rhythm. There were holes in the music and there was room in the sound; it made its own gravity, and it pulled you in: "We want to make the listener feel as if he is the narrator," Thomas said years later. But there wasn't a single narrator. Singing against himself, out of one channel Thomas testified with a drawl, all stoic knowledge; from the other side he was confused, vague, then hysterical. Whatever the first voice knew, the second voice seemed to be saying, it didn't know enough; it didn't know enough to be scared. And then, in a story that despite its plain references to Conrad, the grisly 1933 horror movie *Island of Lost Souls*, and Raymond Chandler's *The Long Goodbye* seemed to call most of all on Ralph Ellison's *Invisible Man* for the nowhere it sought ("Maybe sanctuary is an electric light / I get so tired it's like I'm another man"), the first voice caught the second voice's disease. Now the first voice shoots out terror; the second, smaller voice begins to break up. The drummer and the guitarist play harder, noise pours through the story, and you begin to hear a second song: the song played by the bassist, made of small, scurrying notes, with no point to make, no goal to reach, no enemy to escape, merely Manny Farber's "termite-tapeworm-fungus-moss art," going "always forward eating its own boundaries." The feeling is calm, cool, someone saying he's seen it all before, someone saying he knows he'll see it all again whether he wants to or not.

Here, it doesn't matter why the building that's being eaten by termites was built in the first place, how much it cost, what the song wants to mean. From one bass note to another, what matters is to get from one side of the building to the other without being seen, to erase the distinction between the beginning of the song and its end without being heard, without anyone noticing that is what's being done. The first Pere Ubu record, Thomas wrote in 1996, was meant to be merely an "artifact," something that "would gain him entry into the Brotherhood of the Unknown that was gathering in used record bins everywhere." Thus the voices in

"Heart of Darkness" burned themselves up, but that wasn't the song the bass notes played. Pushing, running, doubling back, hearing no one else, not caring who raised the walls the notes are boring through, those notes are an enactment of the band as it would be ten, twenty, thirty years down the line, in for the duration.

The Old World

The people in Pere Ubu brought tornadoes to their Midwest; instead of hiding in storm cellars they walked around the deserted streets of their town, experimenting with the notion that their whispers could be heard through tunnels in the wind the tornadoes made. They could be, but Pere Ubu can also be heard in words written for the page. The best account of the band's call for a new world comes in a memoir by the synthesizer player Allen Ravenstine, a founding member. "In those days we'd play wherever they'd let us," he wrote some twenty years after the fact in "Music Lessons." "We had learned to speak, and we were certain that our voices were endowed with something to say. We lacked only opportunity, but its arrival was foretold. There was a certain current that ran through the air around us, something that seemed to be in the light that fell everywhere we went, a vibration that ran through all of our conversations . . . It was like putting your ear to the rail, and we could hear the rumble of the train any time we bothered to listen; our time would come. It was as tangible as the modern noise we made."

Summoning an oracular, nineteenth-century language—the language of politicians in the mid-1820s, who, the cultural historian Constance Rourke once said, spoke with such seductive majesty that "theatrical managers in Washington were complaining that plays failed in the national capital because gifts belonging to the stage were so freely employed by the national representatives and senators"—Ravenstine was leading up to an account of the avatars of the new world playing a high-school prom. It was 1975. Carrying their song "Final Solution" and "30 Seconds Over Tokyo," "Pushin'

Too Hard" and "Heart of Darkness," the Stooges' "I Wanna Be Your Dog" and Peter Laughner's "Life Stinks" ("I need a drink / I can't think / I like the Kinks / Life stinks"), walking down the high-school corridors they themselves had left behind only a few years before, the members of the band, Ravenstine said, knew their purpose: they were pioneers, the building was the forest, the students were the savages, and the music was the word. "We were missionaries, but we had not come to appeal to the ethereal, we were not there to make promises about a better tomorrow, we were not the bearers of good news," Ravenstine wrote. "We bore a darkness whose weight we foolishly felt was ours to wield, and we had come to share it."

As all avant-garde artists wish, the result was revolt—a revolt against the band, and inside that refusal, a second revolt against the first one:

We mounted the stage and the singer bowed. The crowd looked into each other's eyes, they were expecting people who looked like them . . .

Billy turned his hands loose and lit up his guitar, he released from its strings the things stored deep in the metal and wood. The things that were his alone to find. There were sounds that moved beyond the stroke and placement of his fingers, things that happened when he didn't seem to be moving. The guitar gave itself willingly, it bent itself to what he wanted. There was power and there was release.

We told the truth as we knew it, but we didn't sing about love.

The crowd didn't let themselves move, they were waiting for the real music to start. They waited and wondered if this might be some practical joke. Maybe there was a camera somewhere, perhaps there would be a picture of those incredulous looks in the yearbook. Sure, that was it, little black and white photos with captions: "James Oliver looks into the future and sees the tapes of his fumble at the Super Bowl," "Mary Campbell learns of her Pulitzer Prize nomination."

The music spilled from the stage and struggled to the floor. It danced alone there self-consciously like a gatecrasher at a country club. And then a few did hear it, they moved past the stunned and frozen and walked out to the floor. They danced and smiled and their bodies moved inside their clothes in a way that made you see how they didn't fit. These were the people we had come to play for, the ones whose parts didn't fit together in the prescribed way. The ones who look out a window and wonder if what they see is what their neighbor sees. The ones who aren't sure that Maybelline and General Motors have what they want.

The others were now certain that this was no joke, that the real music wasn't going to start and they'd be damned if they were going to be made fools of by these misfits. They booed and hooted, and some of the boys, feeling like they had to be men and defend the sensibilities of their womenfolk, approached the stage and swore at us.

"Turn that shit off!"

"Play something we can dance to!"

With that the singer pulled the mic from its stand and screamed, "Dance? You people don't know how to dance! I'll teach you how to dance!" He threw himself from the stage and with the true abandon of the insane he spun and tottered and writhed on the floor. He danced a reckless ballet befitting a man talking in tongues.

Then, as if following a script, the high-school administrator in charge of the dance pulled the plug. "We left that room as brothers," Ravenstine concluded, "bonded loosely by the trappings of renewed exile." The words ride on in perfect balance, and that balance conceals the rage behind the words—conceals but does not even begin to dim the rage of people born into a country they were sure had no use for them at all.

Cleveland

Exile was the territory. "The whole scene in 1974, even counting all the part-time musicians, sometime sound men, wives, girlfriends, hangers-on and friends of friends, amounted to not much more than 50 people," Thomas wrote in 1996. "It was a small, isolated society living in a space as isolated as any pioneer outpost on the plains of Kansas. And they identified with the land. Passionately. Except the land wasn't rural." They gravitated toward the Flats, the rotting industrial sections of Cleveland that fronted on the Cuyahoga River, so polluted that in 1969 an oil slick on the water caught fire. "Cleveland, city of light, city of magic," Randy Newman sang in 1972 from Los Angeles, as if to wipe the city off the American map, even though Newman knew that like Memphis or L.A., New Orleans or New York, Cleveland was one of the cities where rock 'n' roll began, in 1951, with Alan Freed's "Moondog Show" on WJW. "Cleveland, even now I can remember / 'Cause the Cuyahoga River / Goes smokin' through my dreams."*

As the critic Peter S. Scholtes put it long after, though, "The city emptied into suburbs at night, leaving behind cheap rent and cover bands." If exile was the territory, there were signposts if you knew how to read them. Cleveland, Thomas said in 2002, "was a nexus for all music. Record shops competed for the new and cutting, for the complete and final word. Almost everyone I can think of who was in a band was working in a record store. Not only the college stations but commercial FM stations played radical music." It was an artistic version of a floating crap game: "compact, informed, tough and protected from any threat of fame or acceptance." Four years after people smiled over Newman's joke, Pere Ubu set up in John D. Rockefeller's first warehouse, in 1976 housing a bar called Pirate's Cove—a "haunt for the sailors from off the lake freighters that dumped ballast in great stoney heaps just across the street," Thomas said. The band played there for a year: "Thursday nights in the Flats was like falling off the edge of the world. If you went there it's because you knew what you were doing. There was no chance of tourists stumbling in. Ubu was the

---

*"Now the Lord can make you tumble," Newman concluded in tones of somber wonder, like a preacher speaking of miracles. "The Lord can make you turn / The Lord can make you overflow / But the Lord can't make you burn." Nothing has changed; despite a trumpeted renovation of the Flats for Cleveland's 1996 bicentennial, in May 2005, with the then-retired professional basketball coach Phil Jackson considering several new coaching offers, including one from the Cleveland Cavaliers, the New York *Times* could report that the city "is routinely dismissed in the current Jackson sweepstakes as an intellectual washout and industrial wasteland." Jackson returned to the Los Angeles Lakers instead.

headliner so they got to go on first so you could go home early which was an important consideration if you had a job, and people had jobs." "It was a desperate, stubborn refusal of the world, a total rejection," Charlotte Pressler, part of the new world, wrote in 1978, as if she were recalling a story that had ended a lifetime before: "the kind of thing that once drove men into the desert, but our desert was the Flats. It should be remembered that we had all grown up with Civil Defense drills and air-raid shelters and dreams of the Bomb at night; we had been promised the end of the world as children, and we weren't getting it." "I used to take my Sony TC55 recorder down to the railroad yards in the flats along the Cuyahoga and record the steel wheels crossing a seam," Ravenstine says. "On stage I'd run the recording through my synthesizer along with other sounds I was making. I'd put it where I thought it fit. There was no plan."

The Ubu March

At the Knitting Factory twenty-four years later, in 2000, Thomas did not writhe on the floor. There was no room; the small space was packed. The end of the world was still present in the music, but no one even tried to mime the long-gone bohemian secret society. Across the last quarter of the twentieth century, enough who had heard the music had, year by year, stepped out of the larger crowd to give Pere Ubu an audience. There were calls for favorite songs.

Even in 1975, David Thomas took up enough space to make the notion of a hat the size of Oklahoma, shoes the size of Florida, and a coat the size of California credible. He called himself Crocus Behemoth in those days; on Pere Ubu's first singles he hid behind the name. The name of the band, as personified by its singer, was itself a clue. It was the century in a single body, and in Thomas's body it was the first New Wave. "Père Ubu" was a legend: the protean saint and unkillable demon of the avant-garde, arriving in

Paris in 1896 by means of Alfred Jarry's play *Ubu Roi*, his paean to a hated teacher, Père Ubu himself—fat, stupid, ugly, fascist, gross above all, the huge, clumsy monster embodying authority without intelligence, power without reason, respectability without honor. He was the King of Poland, the King of Nowhere, King of Everywhere, King of Europe first of all, lumbering like a two-legged maggot into the First World War, and then dragging millions of innocent American boys, the grandfathers of the young men now taking the name, along with him.

Jarry's Père Ubu waddled through the century, reemerging again and again as Rasputin, Warren Harding, as any businessman or military officer or priest in any painting by George Grosz, as Emil Jannings's Professor Rath in *The Blue Angel*, the Grand Wizard of the Ku Klux Klan in his white hood, Huey Long, Hermann Göring, V. M. Molotov, Kate Smith, Lyndon B. Johnson trumpeting that the true goal of the Vietnam War was to bring the Great Society to North Vietnam, Elvis Presley bursting out of his jumpsuit. Ubu was Zippy the Pinhead, Idi Amin, Imelda Marcos, Rush Limbaugh, Saddam Hussein, Bill Clinton at his most apologetic and obsequious, Newt Gingrich and his double Slobodan Milošević. Ubu crossed the bridge to the twenty-first century with the round, serene, unmarkable face of Karl Rove, always seeking new bodies to inhabit, always finding them.

This was the prophetic figure David Thomas named the band for, putting a redrawing of Jarry's grotesque Ubu woodcuts—a pointed hood over the head, the huge belly marked by a spiraling bull's-eye—on the sleeve of "30 Seconds Over Tokyo," where Ubu wore a long black coat, Lincoln's stovepipe hat, and sneakers two feet long. The physical resemblance between Thomas at twenty-two and Ubu as he, or it, was born was obvious. The love affair with the repulsive figure (a love affair that finally swallowed Jarry whole, the satirist taking on every aspect of the creature he'd invented as a field for satire: speech, dress, gesture, grooming, obnoxiousness) was only slightly less obvious. Ubu is what you latch onto as a teenager when you don't want to say "Holden Caulfield—is me!" "All the deepest, most unacceptable, most bestial and most banal impulses in the human being rolled into one" is how Charlotte Pressler would sum up Jarry's Ubu. "It was that character that [Thomas] wanted to impersonate."

It was a fantasy of total disappearance, total mastery, the kid everyone laughs at one day shooting his classmates down like animals, and everybody saying, "Him? Fatty David? Get out." "People out on the streets, they don't know who I am," Thomas was already singing in his band Rocket from the Tombs in 1974, the year before he formed Pere Ubu, pounding "Sonic Reducer" into the floor as Peter Laughner shot teenage self-pity out of his guitar as if it were a cannon. Thirty years later, Thomas and the other original members of Rocket from the Tombs temporarily put the band back together—minus Laughner, who was dead—and the song rang as true as it ever had. "I watch them from my room, they are just passing by," Thomas sang at fifty, his cranky old-codger voice affirming that if he had changed, the world hadn't, that it made no more room for him than it ever had. "But I'm not just anyone, I'm not just anyone / I got my dull machine, got my electronic dream / Sonic reducer, ain't no loser." He snapped the word off, *looser*; he dropped into a whisper, then rose up as his voice seemed to strangle on its own madness.

I'll be a pharaoh soon, rule from some golden tomb
Things will be different then, the sun will rise for me
Then I'll be ten feet tall, and you'll be nothing at all

"I went through high school as one does reading all the surrealist/ dada stuff I could get my hands on," Thomas says now. "That's the sort of age group that's suitable for the pursuit . . . I read all the Ubu plays. I was fascinated by the production ideas. The plays themselves were old hat but the idea of how to present theater linked in with my fascination for late-night talk radio and the Ghoulardi legacy"—the legacy of the late Ernie Anderson, in the seventies "The Voice of ABC Television," but from 1963 to 1966 Ghoulardi, host of a grade-Z Cleveland horror/sci-fi show featuring such wonders as *The Disembodied, Ghost Diver, World Without End, The Octopus, From Hell It Came*. The Ghoulardi show was where Thomas first found his idea that in culture, geography is destiny—manifest destiny.

In Seattle in 2005, at the Experience Music Project Pop Conference, Thomas explained. A greasy guitar instrumental from what sounded like a 1967 biker-movie soundtrack played behind him as, dressed all in black, he read his paper "Ghoulardi: Lessons in Mayhem from the 1st Age of Punk"; in the audience were professors, critics, musicians, the curious. "Driven by local circumstances, inspired by local characters, and fueled by the sort of unrefined exuberance to be expected in the last wild days of a technological frontier, isolated pockets of punk activity were capable of throwing up sometimes astonishing phenomena that blossomed and then withered unnoticed outside a limited geography," Thomas pronounced. "Where, in former times, mountains, deserts and rivers might have served to isolate communities, in the '50s and '60s, broadcast throw and reception range would act in a similar way. These were the days of regional radio hits—localized charts were the norm rather than the exception. These were the days of the wild child personality radio jocks . . . Less known, less appreciated and far rarer were the wild child TV punks."

That was Ghoulardi, "dressed in a lab coat with obviously fake goatee that was always slipping off, fright wig, sunglasses with one lens missing." In Seattle Thomas put dim TV footage on a screen: the man whose face appeared had Trotsky's eyes and Ho Chi Minh's beard. Slipping in and out of a Bela Lugosi imitation he clearly could hardly be bothered with, he sounded like an all-American Midwest hustler. "Run out of town eventually," Thomas said. "He viciously mocked local celebrities, newsmen and icons. Insulted sponsors so successfully they adopted his insults. 'Stay

Sick and Turn Blue' attack against a fast food restaurant led to them adding a Stay Sick and Turn Blue shake to their menu. Inserted himself into movies via blue screen and became part of the action or warned characters": *Don't open that door!*

"You really had to experience it," Thomas said, and from the stage he began to provide the experience himself, shifting in an instant from fond memory to assault, ranting, his body tipping, the tale rising: "Everyone who saw Ghoulardi will tell a favorite story."

Like the night he set off an egregiously large home-made explosive device sent in by a fan—he was always setting off fireworks and blowing things up in the studio—and quite clearly off-camera crew were telling Ghoulardi not to light it up and you could see people running across the studio, the camera abandoned to skew off balance, pointing at the floor, and then the entire room was stunned senseless for some minutes . . . live . . . smoke, curtains on fire, people stumbling around. Or the night he repeated the "What, me worry?" phrase for ten minutes progressing through the range of all possible inflections and dramatizations—or certainly enough of them. In a *Gunsmoke* parody he and supporting characters sat round a table not saying anything, not moving—stone-cold nothing—for a minute. "Let me think," he said and he sat there.

As Thomas seemed to hit his peak, he fell into a certain mode of American storytelling: the hysterical mode, Dennis Hopper's photographer running around Colonel Kurtz's compound in *Apocalypse Now* babbling such Kurtzian wisdom as IF YOU CAN KEEP YOUR HEAD WHILE ALL AROUND YOU ARE LOSING THEIRS like a cult member with his head cut off. You could understand that Thomas ranted for ideas—to dramatize them, but also to find them. As he pushed beyond vehemence, red-faced, his face soaked ("Oh," he said, "my eyes are sweating"), all but bursting out of his suspenders and his pants ballooning to the floor, you could almost see notions batting around his head like angels: notions of spontaneous generation and spontaneous combustion, Cleveland bands more than thirty years gone and their unrealized future, the future that still lay ahead. "Without Ghoulardi," Thomas insisted with such force people in the audience froze in anticipation of his eyes popping right out of his head, "would there have been an Electric Eels dressed in tin foil running a lawnmower over the stage? Or, a Rocket from the Tombs with a name that so obviously synthesizes sci-fi and horror B-movie-isms? The Mirrors sang about the people who live on the inside of the earth. Pere Ubu drew on a Ghoulardi-esque persona for its identity." He was shouting, and then in an instant he dropped into a tiny, patient, explanatory voice. Thomas was a performer, after all; meaning was in the timing, and now his timing made him into an anthropologist of his own story:

Consider the common characteristics of these bands. Foremost is a distinctive narrative voice which is an idiosyncratic mixture of the observational, the self-participatory, and the Intrusive Other, by which I mean the notion that the telling of a story should involve the incorporation of additional, intrusive POVs that might run in parallel or at some angle to the central narrative, crossing it, intruding, overlaying, contradicting, deprecating, or even ignoring it . . . These bands were fronted by guys with extreme personas, odd hosts

—and what an odd notion that is, a band's singer as a host, as for a talk show, or a dinner party, if not, as in other days, an army, or a sacrifice—

archly mediating a musical experience, each serving as a funhouse lens through which the musicians look outward at the audience and through whom, in turn, the audience receives context, perspective, and scale. The observer is himself watched. The narrator is generated by the story he tells.

Ghoulardi was a bomb; after it went off, you could see the world differently. What Thomas saw, as he wrote some years before the Seattle talk, was that "the media always lie, will always lie, can only lie, that to say something real you have to go sur-real—using the term the way the surrealists formulated it," above the real, "NOT the way they ended up pursuing it"—inside the real. "I remember being overwhelmed," he said, "by the rightness of the scene in *Ubu Roi* in which the Polish Army crosses some river and what happens on stage is that a placard announces the action while one person walks across the stage. This seemed to be the obvious way of engaging the audience's imagination . . . like radio plays in which you hear a creak or sigh and see immediately without verbal description Philip Marlowe's office with the dust motes frozen in venetian blind light.

"So it came time to come up with a name for a band," Thomas went on. "I chose 'Pere Ubu' because of the above—we were, remember, well down the path of using concrete/found sound to enhance the musical experience—and because the name looked good, sounded good, had three syllables and wasn't likely to mean anything to anyone in our audience and so would be neutral unless you had the knowledge in which case we were giving you a clue but the key to the clue was—and here is the vital point—the key to the clue was NOT the obvious one. And if all this sounds a bit pretentious for a bunch of kids in their early twenties remember that we were the ones who had taken the name of a French cinematic movement to apply to what we were doing. We were beyond pretentious. We were in the right place at the right time with the right tools . . . and we didn't care."

The Silver Jubilee

At the Knitting Factory in 2000, only Thomas and the guitarist Tom Herman remained of the Pere Ubu that had played that long-ago high-school dance; Peter Laughner, the guitarist Allen Ravenstine called "Billy" in his story of that night, was already out of the band in 1977 when he died from alcohol and methamphetamine use at the age of twenty-four. Thomas was an enormous, darkening presence in the mid-'70s—dressed in a long coat, his black hair tumbling out and down like a nest of snakes, an empowered vision of the pathetic outsider that Jack Nance was playing at the same time in *Eraserhead*—but in the year 2000, as in years to come, Thomas was if anything harder to read.

There was gleeful clowning in Thomas's palavers with the crowd. Seemingly as big as the other four people onstage put together—bald, with long sideburns, sweat pouring, wrapped in a bright red vinyl apron—Thomas seemed as much like Oliver Hardy as himself. It was a comic specter, belied by the frightening seriousness of songs introduced as jokes. "This is dedicated to the days when you could write songs about drinking and driving," Thomas said. "So I wrote this ode: '"I'm alive / Let's get drunk and drive."'" It took off on a zigzag rhythm. You couldn't keep up with it; you could barely follow it. An almost unfathomable amount of high, disconnected sounds flew through the air.

When Thomas let the wave of a tune carry him to the stack of amplifiers at the front of the stage, the microphone and transmitters secreted in his apron produced howls of feedback as he hugged the black boxes like a lover. He pulled two microphone stands together and sang into them both and two mikes didn't seem like enough. At another rise in the sound he held his arms wide, gesturing with a broad smile like a headwaiter happily waving the crowd back: *No tables! No tables!* The sound seemed to grow bigger with every song, but inside the rock 'n' roll sound was the high lonesome sound, the whine of a drunk wandering the streets of Leaksville, North Carolina, sometime in the 1920s, a sudden thinning in Thomas's voice, calling up the shade of the banjo player Charlie Poole, his reedy, grinning tone carrying him through his signature tune "If I Lose, Let Me Lose" as he bounced from lamppost to lamppost.

"This is a song written for men going through their midlife crises," the forty-seven-year-old Thomas announced, "who have punk roots. If there's ever a time for punk," he said, "it's when men have their midlife crises." Instead of driving out the demons, the band entered into a slow, languorous rhythm. "This is the pogo section," Thomas said, moving gingerly around a circumscribed area of the stage, and another Ubu came into view: Sydney Greenstreet in *The Maltese Falcon*.

Again and again the performance offered itself as a parody of a time that had passed—and then, with the sound turning fiercely elegant and Thomas hammering his voice and body against his words, the performance flew into the past as if it really were a rocket from the tombs, heading who knew where, toward what unimaginable future, a future that would look no different from what, in the moment, you were looking at.

Who knows where the past goes, in this case the past of the band David Thomas headed that night, or the past that shadowed that past, and which past was it that Thomas was conjuring up? Watching him, I thought about the last time I'd seen *1984*.

The Mistakes of the Past

George Orwell's *1984*, published in 1949, was first filmed as a live BBC television show in 1954; it was remade as a feature film in 1956. Both pictures had futuristic touches: faceless modernist buildings, blandly menacing uniforms. With John Hurt as the doubting Party member Smith, Suzanna Hamilton as Julia, and Richard Burton as the duplicitous Party leader and torturer O'Brien, it was remade again by Michael Radford in 1984—with the irresistible hook of the release date no doubt the main reason this version was made at all.

The most remarkable aspect of the 1984 *1984* was its ambience. Orwell dated his nightmare totalitarian future, his world of never-ending war and the complete replacement of knowledge with propaganda, simply by reversing the last two numerals of the year in which he actually wrote the book: 1948. In 1948, 1984 was impossibly far away; of course everything would look different in the future. Perhaps in the director's attempt to sabotage the hook his production had been hung on, the 1984 version of *1984* was set in streets and buildings, offices and rooms, that looked and felt like 1948. This was odd; this was the displacement, depicting the future as the past. The primary visual sensation was that of an overwhelming apprehension of griminess. Nothing—not furniture, clothes, walls, windows, office equipment—was clean, new, or cared for. Desks were scarred. The manual typewriters on the desks looked broken. No one seemed to value his or her environment, so no one noticed it; as no one noticed it, no one questioned it, and so from scene to scene the fundamental human posture seemed to be that of lassitude. Nothing was ever any different, the mind emptied by totalitarianism was telling itself in this posture, in this movie—and nothing will ever change. In other words, with the removal of all the gaudy pageantry of fascism and the Stalinist parade, the primary reality of totalitarianism in the 1984 film version of *1984* was that of cheapness. Totalitarian offices were cheap because they no longer needed grandeur; they no longer needed to affirm their own authority. They no longer needed to convince anybody of anything.

The picture was an argument against the very idea of the modern. What if totalitarianism could be what this *1984* said it would be: ordinary, dull, everyday, unremarkable? What if "modernity" is only a theory, or a construct—or a time that has passed, or an era to be overthrown? What if totalitarianism is the real modernity: the true future implied by technology and overpopulation, a modern experiment in politics and art, communication and philosophy, religion and science, power and justice, that merely has yet to find its proper form? Yes, those who do not remember the past may be condemned to repeat it, but those who do remember the past may be granted the privilege of repeating it—and without the mistakes of the past.

The mistakes of the past are sometimes filled with treasure; that is why the impulse to rediscover the past and then correct it is so strong. "We have to be absolutely modern," Rimbaud said. No one knows what that means—but to my mind, it means that to find the modern, you have to go back to the past.

A Memory of the Future

In the strange decor of the past, ordinary acts themselves seem strange. The attempts of artists to create a new world, to call it into being with a single, perfect act—or their discovery that they are already living in a new world, the existence of which remains a secret—seem stranger still. Such attempts to create, such discoveries, can flare up and flame out in an instant; even as they appear, they are suffused with the tragic, romantic power that surrounds those things that seem lost forever.

No sentence I know catches this sense of possibility and loss as well as a line from Steve Erickson's novel *The Sea Came in at Midnight*, from 1999: "A dream is a memory of the future." If you replace "a dream" with "art" you have some idea of how the phrase might work—but while I have held on to this line since I first encountered it, I don't think I began to understand it until a few years after that.

I was teaching an undergraduate seminar in cultural criticism at Princeton, in the fall of 2002. We were discussing David Thomson's *Suspects*, a novel published in 1985.

In that book, Thomson takes characters from all across the spectrum of film noir—defined as broadly as possible, so that film noir encompasses Natalie Wood's Judy Rogers in *Rebel Without a Cause* and Diane Keaton's Kay Corleone in *The Godfather* as well as Barbara Stanwyck's Phyllis Dietrichson in *Double Indemnity* and Humphrey Bogart's Roy Earle in *High Sierra*. Imagining that these characters are people, Thomson tells the stories of their lives as they were before and after we encounter them in their lives as circumscribed by their movies—"'after,'" he says, "if they survive the film." Thus Dietrichson was a cocaine connection for Mabel Normand and other silent film stars before combining with Fred

MacMurray's Walter Neff to kill her husband. After two failed marriages, the first to James Dean's Jim Stark, Judy Rogers moves into a commune in San Francisco and gets involved in the antiwar movement. "On October 11, 1968," Thomson writes, "she was killed, driving over the Bay Bridge when a homemade bomb she was carrying exploded."

At the seminar's next session, Thomson was a visitor. One student asked him why he chose film noir for such an experiment— why not the Western? Screwball comedy? Romantic melodrama?

"Because I know exactly when film noir began," Thomson said weirdly. And he went on to recount, for a class of students born in the early 1980s, the impact of the assassination of President John F. Kennedy on 22 November 1963.

He told the story as if it were a relic from another world. He described the shock and disbelief, grief and displacement, that the event produced in England, where Thomson, who is British, then was: "This man," he said, as if he did not quite understand what he was about to say, "this man was loved, you understand—*loved*, by people who were not even his own."

"But that," he said, "was not where film noir began." We were all of us in the seminar room beginning to wonder what in the world Thomson was getting at, but we were also nervous. "Film noir," he said, "began in the basement of a Dallas police station, two days later," when Jack Ruby shot Lee Harvey Oswald—when, to make history into genre, a nightclub owner shot and killed the man arrested for the crime.

But *wait*, everyone thought—and the question would have been asked out loud if Thomson had not been moving so fast—film noir goes back to the early 1940s; how could it begin in 1963?

"—and it was *then*," Thomson said of that moment in the police station, "that all the paranoia and fear that film noir had been prophesying for twenty years, the sense that our lives are not our own, that forces we cannot see or name are ruling our lives and our destinies—it was then that everything that film noir had prophesied in America exploded into real life."

The assassination of President Kennedy, and then the removal of that event from the realm of what could be known to the realm of mystery, to a realm where one felt what could not be known as a rebuke and an oppression, to a realm where to be a citizen was suddenly to be a party to a conspiracy you could not even be certain existed at all—all of this was the future film noir had, film by film, betrayal by betrayal, death by death, remembered.

Back to the Tomb

Look at art this way and all sorts of hidden, forgotten, ephemeral, seemingly meaningless experiments in culture, the mistakes of the past, loom up as something other than incidents in which people tried to discover a new world and failed—or even, in moments, succeeded. When such experiments are given the magic carpet of "a dream is a memory of the future" to ride, they come forth as well as warnings. They are warnings that to fail to imagine a different world, and act it out, is to abandon the very language of making a world one wants to live in, or refusing a world one does not want to live in.

Here, movies, records, concerts, novels, poems, paintings, can seem to vibrate with an energy repressed but not stolen by time. You begin to discover what it is you truly love. Like David Thomas with the walls of his skull decorated with pictures of Ghoulardi, Captain Beefheart, Sky Saxon of the Seeds, Alfred Jarry, and a hundred more, you begin to create a personal culture of maps and talismans, locks and keys, within the greater culture of which you are a part whether you want to be or not. When you approach the greater culture with a personal culture, you do so with the knowledge that the greater culture can never satisfy you, and the knowledge of what an earthquake it would be if it did: if the greater culture could, even for an instant, truly satisfy anyone, and then nearly everyone, as, on occasion, as with the emergence of Charlie Chaplin or the Beatles, it has. Look at it this way, and the music Rocket from the Tombs left behind might begin to speak.

In its time, in 1974 and 1975, Rocket from the Tombs never made any official recordings or released any records. In 2002, rehearsals and stray live recordings were collected on a disc called *The Day the Earth Met the . . . Rocket from the Tombs—Live from Punk Ground Zero, Cleveland 1975*—and while those who were there remain members of that vast secret society, meeting in every century on every continent, whose motto is *You'll never understand*, what you can hear now is only as cryptic as it has to be. The songs are easy to hear, now, because they truly did clear the ground so many occupied in the next decade, and ever since; they are hard to hear because public speech that tells those who have gathered to listen that the story was over before it began is always hard to hear.

The Day the Earth Met the . . . announces itself not merely as "an artifact of a specific time and place" but as "a tantalizing glimpse at one of the greatest albums never recorded." The modernist signposts are all planted: ground zero, beginning everything again from the beginning, the art of the dead rushing forward to attack the present in revenge for forgetting its dreams, the claim that art can change the world, self-destruction as a means to truth, the music that is reduced to silence as soon as it's heard, art with the life span of a fly, a heroic quest.

In his notes to that first Pere Ubu single, "30 Seconds Over Tokyo"/"Heart of Darkness," Peter Laughner offered a little film noir story. He and Thomas sit in a diner called the Kettle, smoking. It's four in the morning; it's Philip Marlowe in his early twenties, before he went to work for Raymond Chandler.

The big guy and myself had been huddled over bean soup and coffee long enough to watch two sets of customers come and go . . . He stubbed out Winstons in an ashtray that looked full of gray-white worms, sipped his double-cream coffee, bringing it to his lips with pale, nubbed fingers that shook a little in the transit; he glanced around from time to time in a way that you wouldn't call nervous or expectant, but you could tell that there was something just under the surface waiting to find an outlet . . . in fact, if you let the big guy's attitude get to you, you were liable to feel like maybe he wasn't such good company . . . making you edgy . . . acting like maybe the next customer to walk in the door of the Kettle would be the cue to get up and walk out. The big guy was facing the door, but I got this way of side-sitting in a booth that lets me keep a good view going if I want it, and all I saw come in were two overweight cops, Magnums hanging off their hips, looking for nothing more than a hot meal and a couple of stools to drape their fat rears on. They got their coffee and whatever while "Love Will Keep Us Together" scratched out of the jukebox, and the big guy lit another Winston.

Laughner takes a deep breath, then keeps going:

I swallowed some black coffee and gave up on the bean soup . . . it just wasn't riding right on a gut full of Jim Beam and beer, but I felt as wide awake as possible on an after-hours morning like this. The big guy's nerves were infectious . . . I was wired, all of a sudden, on some organic frequency that seemed to take hold of my motor responses and transmit "you are not fatigued but simply passive . . . use your muscles, your brain, your tissues NOW! MAKE A MOVE!" It was such a strong signal to my system that I reached for my wallet automatically, pulled out a five, and threw it on the table, gesturing frantically for the big guy to follow me up and out, which he did. The two cops at the counter didn't even notice as we moved through the door at a pretty good pace and hit the street, not speaking or acknowl-edging looks at all. We worked in silence, our breath misting, scraping the freeze-up from the windows with a plastic tool and the edge of a grade school ruler. With a few sober belches the machine started, and we were headed east on 90, into a vaporous dawn.

Don't you want to know what happened next?

In his songs "So Cold," "Transfusion," "Life Stinks," "Never Gonna Kill Myself Again," "Amphetamine," and especially "Ain't It Fun," Laughner strung chaos and harmony on the same wire and made it quiver; he made you want to touch it. Suddenly nothing worked as it was supposed to. Life is moving too fast, your mind too slowly; then it's the other way around. Anything was possible—especially nothing. There were things in the guitar "that were his alone to find," and that's what his playing sounds like, as if what makes an artist is his or her access to a secret language, and the will to make it public—as Laughner wrote in 1977 about music he loved, "like a memory of a thing that has never been before."

"This song is called 'Ain't It Fun, You're Gonna Die Young,'" Laughner said as Rocket from the Tombs prepared to make a demo of the number in 1975, a version neither he nor anyone else ever bettered. "It's dedicated to Jane Scott," he said, speaking of the woman who, born in 1919, had been the rock critic for the Cleveland *Plain Dealer* since 1966, and who would keep the job for twenty-seven years after Laughner spoke. "She'll stay *forever young*," Laughner said. "Forever sixteen. She won't die young."* The measured, suicidal cadence of the tune is terrifying—and more beautiful than it is terrifying. There is no way out of the room the music makes, but you don't want to leave. "Ain't it fun, when your friends despise—what you've become," Laughner sings, making his voice tear. "Such fun, such fun, such fun," and he is screaming, but the elegance of the guitar lines that lift every word to the ceiling calls the screams into doubt.

Singing about dissolution, self-hate, impotence, buying a gun to use on whoever gets in your way or on yourself—acting out each emotion, each situation, in words, tones of voice, notes on the guitar—Laughner sets the claims of nihilism against the guard of form: if anything in life can be so beautiful, how can life be meaningless? It's not an interpretation; it's the argument the song is having with itself. But if the cry that jerks a chorus out of the realm of creation and straight into life is real—and it's a shock, the way a moment of ordinary, unmediated speech can lay waste to anything constructed in its path—how can art be anything but a lie?

Laughner comes off the well-written, facile legacy of ain't-it-fun horrors—*ain't it fun when you've thrown away everything you've*

---

*"They are not studio songs with hours of recording expertise behind them," Scott wrote in 1982 of the first collection of Laughner's tapes. "You can see where better apparatus would have helped. But the feeling and the sincerity come across and remind you again of how much we have lost."

ever loved, destroyed everything you ever made, and finally gotten that sly, sardonic smile you've been working on for years just right—into a little middle-eight story that's worse, and then suddenly it's as if the art has fallen away and all the cool, bohemian things he's been saying are the floor rising up to hit him in the face. The voice begins to shred—even as it knows where its words are in every instant, stretching them out, snapping them off—and then it breaks.

Somebody came to me they spit right in my face
But I didn't even feel it it was such a disgrace
I broke the window smashed my fist right through the glass
But I couldn't even feel it it just happened too fast
It was fun
Such fuuuuuuuuuunnnnn
Oh, such fun
Such fun
Such fuuuuuuuuuunnnnn
Ohhhhhhhhh—God!

"Oh, God"—it may be part of the song, written down, practiced until it perfectly balances the lines that have preceded it, but that's not what it sounds like; that's not how it feels. You hear the singer shocked by himself; you can't see to the bottom of his disgust. You can run. You can wonder if the singer's attitude is covering up pain or if the pain is merely there to justify the attitude, until the guitarist—the same person, you understand, as the person who is singing, just as, listening, you know he must be someone else—underlines breaks between verses with what can seem like not two but four versions of himself, too many guitars speaking different languages and no translator needed. He pounds at his guitar, making noise that shoots in all directions, to escape this moment when life has doubled back on art and killed it. He hammers away at a fuzztone, again and again, convincing you he's said all he has to say, all there is to say. Then he steps into a gorgeous, stately solo, a

work of art within this small, chaotic incident, and you can picture
him holding his instrument like Errol Flynn held a sword.

Are You Now or Have You Ever Been?

"We did the first record not as a beginning, but as an ending,"
Thomas said in 1993, in likely the most interesting words ever
written for a record industry press release, in this case for the then-
new Pere Ubu album *Story of My Life*. "We wanted to leave an artifact that someone would discover. We were done—we were
about to move on to real life." But it didn't work out that way, he
said: "We had the misfortune to have a dream and vision at an early
age that was too powerful to shake in older life. If you're young
enough and if the vision is strong enough, you will never lose it—
like the people who became Communists in the '30s. They had no
alternative but to continue . . . We saw what rock music should be
and could be nothing less than that would ever do for us." When
the re-formed Rocket from the Tombs appeared on the third night
of Thomas's *Disastodrome!* theatrical at UCLA in 2003, Thomas did
not, as he had done for the previous many hours of the production,
wear a hat, presumably because he had not worn a hat twenty-nine
years before, when he was not bald. He wore a blue shirt. Everyone
else—original guitarist Gene O'Connor, a.k.a. Cheetah Chrome,
who looked like one of Dr. Moreau's mistakes in 1975 and still did;
original bassist Craig Bell, who looked like a high-school teacher;
Pere Ubu drummer Steve Mehlman, replacing Johnny Madansky,
a.k.a. Johnny Blitz, who was no longer interested; and the guest
guitarist, Richard Lloyd—wore black. What they did was typical
of what has happened to other punk bands twenty, twenty-five
years after their time has supposedly passed, whether it is Wire
in London or the Avengers in San Francisco. The music escapes
the restraints of time or age or circumstance; the vehemence is
immediately rediscovered; the difference is that everyone can play
better.

The band went into a huge song. Thomas pounded the floor with the cane he'd been leaning on for the previous two nights. The music was unstable. Somehow, all the armor fell from "Final Solution," its magnetic field was reversed, and you could hear the fearsomely named song for what it really was: Eddie Cochran's "Summertime Blues" crossed with Dion and the Belmonts' "Teenager in Love." But then Thomas took "Sonic Reducer" as fast as he could, which was very fast, into the realm where punk was not a fashion, which could go out of fashion, but a way of being in the world, a way of being that would lose its power of speech only when the world changed. The lines of the song were fired more than they were sung: "LISTEN TO ME!" Thomas ripped the mike away from his face after each phrase of the chorus, staring into space as if into the tense of future past. His head looked like an egg about to crack.

Cheetah Chrome sang "Ain't It Fun." He was never a singer; his voice was a gravelly smear. With Peter Laughner, the song emerged from the terrible way that each note, each word, is made to stand out separately, as if the nihilism in the song, the cruelty, the disgust, and even the majesty, is in the way each element of the music is banished by every other, and exile is the only story there is to tell. Here that receded in the face of the beauty of the song. You could relax into the loveliness of its construction, until Thomas came to the mike for the choruses, the nihilism he had left behind long before summoned for a moment like a prayer: *"Fun! Such fun! Such fun . . ."* It was scary, it was horrible, and you felt as if you were in the presence of something you understood completely and could never understand: something by the '30s blues singer Robert Johnson, but degenerating note by note, word by word, all with the grandeur of Cream's "Spoonful," the self-loathing of Mott the Hoople's "I Wish I Was Your Mother," and the rage of the Beatles' "Money." This was where Thomas's insistence that the people who gathered themselves into Rocket from the Tombs and Pere Ubu in 1974 and 1975 were like Communists in the '30s, that nothing less than what they found would ever satisfy them, paid off; this was it. "Your only reward," Thomas said in 2002, when the recordings brought together on *The Day the Earth Met the* . . . finally saw the light of day, "is a genuine shot at being the best. The caveat is that no one but your brothers will ever know it. That's the deal we agreed to."

Bad Conscience

Regret, shame, defiance, and most of all death are everywhere in Laughner's music. Today if he weren't dead he might be a clerk in a store selling vinyl LPs, barely able to talk, people sniggering, "Yeah, 'When you know you're gonna die young'—what a poseur!" He might be putting out an album every few years, waiting for the future he once remembered to come to pass, waiting for that moment when the whole world would understand, all at once. Instead he left a warning for Thomas and Pere Ubu to consider, after the band kicked him out, the gun he carried in his guitar case and sometimes fired too much to look at one more time. His music was the future the band remembered, on those nights when it failed to go as far as it could and no one could pretend it wasn't true.

The Shaggy Dog

All of that can be present whenever Pere Ubu takes the stage; in any given moment, none of it has to matter. For David Thomas, Laughner's music may be no kind of rebuke, but a lesson long since learned and made into Thomas's own music. Maybe Laughner's music was only part of the promise Thomas meant to keep; maybe the betrayal was not Pere Ubu leaving Laughner behind, but Laughner's betrayal of himself. "I don't think anyone should sit around in Omaha or Palo Alto or something and imagine Peter Laughner as some romantic figure who burned himself out for the *cause*, whatever that may be, or for *art*," Thomas said in 1978 to interviewers from the San Francisco punk magazine *Search & De-stroy.* "Peter was an extremely talented musician; he was also an extremely talented artist. He was also a fool, and the fool killed him! That's all you can say about it, that's all that *should* be said about it." At the Knitting Factory, as Thomas weighed himself down on the mere boards of the stage, opening his mouth as if waiting along with the audience to hear what sounds might issue from it, he was stirring. He was himself the flag he was unfurling: black flag, red flag, purple flag, anything but a white flag. He performed as a crank, even in the spotlight whispering bad news or just a drunken non sequitur from the alley; as a crank, he performed as one who knew the truth but would tell it only in bits and pieces, hints and warnings, jokes in their relation to the unconscious.

It was a thrill to watch, because hovering in the air was the promise that at any turn the truth of being in this place, at this time, in this moment, if only for an instant, would not only be told but summoned up, as if by a man casting a spell. Robert Wheeler, a great-great-grandnephew of Thomas Edison, who now runs the Edison Birthplace Association in Milan, Ohio, stood off to the side of the stage, waving his hands over two homemade theremins. The real thing, invented by Léon Thérémin in the Soviet Union in 1919, was a box with two antennas, one for pitch and one for volume, that varied the frequency of two oscillators; it generated its own magnetic field. It wasn't touched; when the musician's hands entered the field, pitch and volume would change—or rather, sound like spirits. It was a magic box that made weird sounds. Oooo-*weeee-ooooo*—when Wheeler made his first such device, in electronics school, his teacher denied him an A because he couldn't get the thing to play "America the Beautiful." These looked less like any sort of musical instruments than tiny UFOs; the faraway sound of creatures trapped within them sneaked through the room.

The theremin sound had been on Thomas's stage a few years before, in Rennes, France, in November 1996. Thomas's accompanists that night were his longtime lowercased collaborators, two pale boys—Keith Moliné on "midi-guitar" and Andy Diagram on "a Trumpet Machine Thing so each of them is generating two or three instrument voices at any one point," Thomas wrote in the notes to his disc *Meadville*, named for a town in Pennsylvania but recorded live in various European cities. The instrument voices were like the garbled soundtrack of a Ghoulardi movie when the swamp-gas tones the theremin makes were running—before Brian Wilson made the theremin the lead instrument in the Beach Boys' "Good Vibrations," in 1966, it was all over such 1950s science-fiction pictures as *The Day the Earth Stood Still*—and more like giants dropping large amounts of machinery on each other when they weren't. The little big band vamped through the Beach Boys' "Surfer Girl," which turned into Ben E. King's "Stand By Me"; then Thomas went back to "Surfer Girl" and started singing it. "Don't gather by the river," he crooned, letting a third song hang in the air and abandoning it in favor of a line from the Beach Boys' "Don't Worry Baby." "Don't worry about the blood—it rains like that every day," he warbled, seemingly singing to himself, his tones the aural equivalent of a grifter palming a ten for a twenty. "And don't worry about the frogs and worms—I've seen it rain like that before." High, swirling, wordless vocals—part of the two or three or ten or twenty voices two pale boys were churning up—floated over Thomas like Halloween ghosts, sheets on a laundry line, but lovely, inviting. In a voice that feels too small for his body, a flat Midwestern voice—"Gosh, mister," the voice says, as if that's the most remarkable thing anyone could say about anything—Thomas again assumed his hat the size of Oklahoma, his shoes the size of Florida, his coat the size of California, and began to tell a story. It was, perhaps, a new kind of tall tale, not about impossible obstacles and unthinkable triumphs, but about ontology, about the impossibility of being understood, about words as obstacles to thoughts, thoughts imagining their impossible triumphs over words, but the tale still part of the classic strain. "Half magnification, half sudden strange reversal," as Constance Rourke wrote, the tales "were likely to culminate in moments of 'sudden glory' that had a touch of the supernatural"; finally "the bottom fell wholly out of reality and the final episode rose like a balloon with the string cut"—like the one the minstrel Jim Crow Rice was telling in the 1830s about "the captain who was cut in two in a fight, joined himself together with glue, finished his enemy, lay down to sleep, only to find on awakening . . . that the glue had melted and that a thief had run away with his thighs."

"I want you to stand by—stand by," Thomas announced as the musicians behind him played the "Surfer Girl" bass line over and over, making it just slightly bigger each time. "You know," he said, "about twenty, twenty-five years ago, I heard a country song that changed the way I thought. It was called 'Stand By, Earth Man.' Now, I thought this was pretty amazing, because the *song* had nothing to do with a global perspective, aliens, or outer space. It seemed to be a standard man-woman tragedy, but it got to the chorus, it was 'Stand by, *earth man.*'" Two pale boys provided blips and robot squeaks. "I couldn't believe it!" Thomas shouted. "The rest of us were wasting our time with Captain Beefheart, Velvet Underground, all that stuff, while these *HILLBILLIES*, doin' country music!—were doing *post-modern*, before the rest of us had even gotten to *NEO-CLASSICAL MODERN!*" He came to a stop. "About a year later, maybe two," he said disdainfully, "I heard what was obviously a cover version. Except that they had changed the chorus, to be 'Stand by, your *man.*' And I thought, *Man! These people*, they're so far ahead of the rest of us. They done a double flip-around sort of thing here."

*Woo-woo-woo*s came out of the spectral instruments behind Thomas, and he went on, disappointed, the tall-tale teller who knows you already know the punch line, again in a Midwestern voice, the Midwestern voice that is completely devoid of attitude, con, or pose, thrown back into the America where one day promises only that it will be like the next, that its reality has no bottom and its string will never be cut: "It wasn't until many years later—not so long ago—I'se at a party, of, of many rock stars, selling millions of records"—there were underwater gulping sounds—"but I, I was the one everyone wanted to talk to." There were mocking sounds: "'Cause I'm David Thomas. *Legend.*"

There were high, lifting sounds from behind, somehow matched in tone by cheers from the crowd, and then the sound effects were lighter, the ghosts coming forward, circle-dancing in their diaphanous gowns. "So I'se hanging out in a corner"—Thomas suppressed a chuckle—"and there's many famous people, laughing at my every word." Two pale boys went Ghoulardi full bore. "Buying me drinks, and I'se, I'se telling 'em what it was like to be at the cutting edge . . . surfing the moment." There was a heavy, almost groaning reverb sound from the guitar, an echoing shudder.

And, things got around to country music, and—I'm really only able to deal with this embarrassment at this point. Because—in my moment of pride, and arrogance, I was brought low. I found out that the song had always been, "Stand By, Your Man." [From somewhere, almost a Bronx cheer.] It had never been, "Stand By, *Earth* Man." But I wasn't disappointed, *no-o-o* [and the bass line from "Surfer Girl" and "Stand By Me" only grew stronger, more precise, more sustaining]—'cause these hillbillies had done a *triple* switch-around sort of thing with me. And I was *proud*—

Okay, okay. Fine. I'll get to the point.

We *live*—in Fortean times. We *live*—in the beginning of a Voodoo Age, of magic, superstition, and ignorance. We are the last generation that will ever know what it was like to live in an enlightened world. Twenty years from now

—and Thomas's voice thinned, grew more brittle, became a voice more suited to saying "Yes, this is Mr. Anderson of Anderson Hardware" than anything else—

if we're all here, you'll dandle your grandchildren on your knees, and you'll tell them stories of the Golden Age of the Nineties. Ninteen ninety-six was a *good* year! You'll tell them, you'll tell them about how, in 1996, you didn't have to *wear*, Personal Laser-Guided Backpack Protection Systems. [The theremin sounds grew louder, more enveloping.] *Cows* were animals. And your grandchildren will look at you, and they'll think you're crazy. And in that moment, you'll think back to when you were a child, and your grandparents were telling you about the golden old days, and you looked at them and thought that *they* were crazy. That's the *heritage*, to be passed on, from generation to generation: an echo of *pain* . . . through time. It'll be too late, because your parents will be long dead, and no one will understand you. So

—Thomas seemed to wander out of the building of his story, into the woods, but with the addled confidence of a drunk who thinks he's walking a straight line—

I want to talk to the ladies in the audience now. Pere Ubu, Pere Ubu once opened for Kool and the Gang. Pere Ubu did a tour, opening for Kool and the Gang. And every night, Mr. Kool would come out, and say, "Ah want to talk to, the [the word was big, lubricious] LADIES in the audience." And we'd all be backstage goin', *"Man*—I wish we weren't serious underground rock avant-garde legends, I wish *we* could go out there onstage and say, 'I want to talk to the LADIES in the audience.'"

Ladies! Look at your man. I want you to *stand by. Stand by* . . . stand by . . . stand by

—and as the "Stand By Me" bass count slowed, Thomas began to sing, in a rising voice that grew bigger with every syllable—

. . . *stand by* . . . EARTH MAN.

Behind him, voices flew through the roof. The night was over.

Disastodrome

David Thomas first put on his *Disastodrome!* production in London in 1998 ("Disastodrome," in the words of an old Cleveland joke, "so nothing can go wrong"). Many voices shared the stage, singing odd songs in lovely voices, declaiming cryptic fables, but it was Daved Hild who went completely nuts, starting off a monologue reasonably enough with stories about geography and landmarks and odd formations of land and water he remembered from his youth in Florida and then speeding up, chasing his own words until like the tourist ranting at the travel agent in the Monty Python skit you just want him to shut up about "Now they tell you 'It's a Small World After All,' *IT IS NOT A SMALL WORLD!* It used to be a small world before Disney came, before Exxon came and took it all away from us, and took that smallness and made it BIG, *BIG IS GOOD, RIGHT?*" But despite the hysteria his voice was smooth, absolutely colorless, the real voice of Anytown, U.S.A., and you wonder how hysterical anyone with such a familiar voice can really get.

The answer given when Thomas mounted *Disastodrome!* at UCLA five years later was plain: not hysterical at all. The country won't hear you; it will swallow you up. You find your audience not by shouting but by whispering, not by haranguing a crowd but by speaking so quietly, or so queerly, that a crowd will gather out of a helpless curiosity, just to figure out what it is you're saying. One entered the Freud Playhouse through a Foyerdrome, filled with ads so old (for banks, appliances, real estate deals, or real estate scams) they seemed generic: whatever real life they once spoke for was lost. In the theater, above the stage or on it, was a washing machine, a neon Sinclair Oil dinosaur sign, telephone poles, a jukebox, a phone booth, a gas pump, a parking meter, a ventilator, signs reading, EAT ORANGES FOR LIFE, BE ALERT, and AVOID TRITE AND UNNECESSARY TALKING.

Over three nights, Thomas and the cast he'd gathered—the poet Bob Holman; Frank Black, the leader of the beloved 1980s band the Pixies; Robert and Jack Kidney of the Numbers Band, a.k.a 15-60-75, a combo from Kent, Ohio, that goes back beyond the last number in its name; the composer Van Dyke Parks; two pale boys plus the drummer Georgia Hubley of the New York band Yo La Tengo; the New York singer Syd Straw; the actor George Wendt, formerly one of the regulars at the bar on *Cheers*; the reformed Rocket from the Tombs and Pere Ubu itself—told stories

about bands forming and breaking apart, people meeting and separating, the way the whole country was connected through the Interstate Highway System, the towns the Interstate bypassed and
thus left behind, left out of the American story as if they had never
been. They told stories about how elements of speech, commerce,
and culture disappear, and how, after those things are gone, people
like those on Thomas's stage appear to reenact them. As the tale
unfolded, the cast grew even larger, populating itself with doubles
and familiars.

In the so-called improvisational opera *Mirror Man*—part sermon, part rant, part Chautauqua, part minstrel show—"lost highway" is the repeating theme, invoked so melodramatically it fell
somewhere between a prayer and a brand name, but the piece
could have been called "Route 66," if Route 66 could be reduced
to a single table in a café called Mom's. The screen behind the
stage flashed a shifting tableau that always told the same story: you
saw blue skies and open roads, historical scenes, a comic strip advertising an amusement park, old postcards of the Pacific Coast
Highway, but you felt like the action was taking place on a backstreet lined with boarded-up buildings. Wendt, Thomas, and Black
sat down together on a bench—"Mingle with the Stars," the ad on
it read: "Hollywood WAX MUSEUM." As the audience waited for
the bench to collapse under their collective seven or eight hundred
pounds, Wendt was Babe Ruth, Black was John McCain, and
Thomas was Fatty Arbuckle. But when Thomas took the mike—
leaning on the cane you couldn't tell if he used as a prop or to stay
on his feet—the character who came out of his body was, someone
in the crowd said, more like Orson Welles as Father Mapple in the
movie version of *Moby-Dick*. Or, someone else suggested, Welles
as Hank Quinlan in *Touch of Evil*. Or William Jennings Bryan at
the Scopes trial. As Thomas began to speak like a salesman—as
you caught the pitch along with the vague sense that you would
never know exactly what the product he was going to try to sell you
was for—he turned into Steve Martin's demonic traveling song-

salesman in *Pennies from Heaven*, the guy who believes every love
song he sells, the man who is evil because he can't believe he's capable of it. He makes your flesh crawl; you can't help but like him.

When the curtain came up that night, Syd Straw stood at the
café table, dressed in an aquamarine uniform, holding a pot of coffee, but she didn't seem to move. Black and Georgia Hubley sat
down and Straw took their orders. The stillness of the scene—as
off to one side Bob Holman recited a broken narrative, sounds
bounced off the walls, and songs were begun and sometimes finished—pushed the scene even further into the background than it
already was, into its own ordinariness, the way it has been repeated
countless times in every state in the Union every day since the automobile replaced the horse. Edward Hopper's *Nighthawks* drifted
into your mind as easily as it drifted out of it. You have no idea what
will happen to the characters in *Nighthawks*; you had no idea here.

"Elvis in our time will never be critiqued seriously, will never be
spoken of without condescension," Thomas once wrote. "And rock
music—the legacy of a lost generation of black & white poor
trash—will forever be officially relegated to the status of youth phe-
nomenon. Rock music is supposed to be the sort of disposable pop-
ulist nonsense you build a hall of fame for . . . the media priests like
it that way for the same reason David Lynch wants small town
America to be about weirdness and decay: it justifies their own life
choices." But as the night unfolded in Los Angeles, Lynch was the
missing actor, if he really was missing. On the first night of the production Robert Kidney of the Numbers Band held the stage like a
bad dream. "Look for me down at One-Eyed Jacks," he said, gesturing back at the whorehouse in *Twin Peaks*. He wore a dark suit,
dark shirt, dark tie, a dark fedora pulled down so far over his face it
was like watching the Mummy perform; all you could see of his
features was that they were creased and old. He sang in a melliflu-
ous, oddly unaged voice, his guitar stopping the rhythm inside
Robert Johnson's seventy-year-old "Last Fair Deal Gone Down"
and turning the tune into a fable: "Nobody really wants to hear the

blues because it's too slow, it's boring, it's tedious—like life, like my life." For an encore he and his brother Jack, on harmonica, played Bo Diddley's "Who Do You Love," and it was a spell, a threat, squirming the way Roy Orbison songs squirm in *Blue Velvet* and *Mulholland Dr.* As the song twisted in their hands, you could hear "Down on the Banks of the Ohio". "Arlene come and take a little walk with me tell me who do you love."

Moment to moment in *Mirror Man*, others stepped into Kidney's shoes: Syd Straw's waitress sitting at the café table alone, her head in her hands, the weight of her fatigue capsizing the theatrics of the men on the stage like Peggy Lipton's waitress at the end of her shift in *Twin Peaks*; Thomas sitting at a desk with a manual typewriter, crumbled paper, and what looked like a week-old sandwich as if he were Bill Pullman watching the third video in *Lost Highway*, clenching his teeth as if that would force thoughts out of his clotted brain; and everywhere, a sense of time as something already used up, somewhere in the past, by someone else.

The difference between Lynch's American towns and the decaying towns on and off Thomas's lost highway—the places, he said, where you think, this is how it must have been, "so you say aloud, 'We can renovate one of these old storefronts and move out here,' and, of course, you know you never will, but the vision has power because it answers a need"—was that in the most seemingly blank, dead-end actions Thomas orchestrated in Los Angeles, there was always the sense that his words and gestures were a setup. There was the feeling that all together they made a story which, when you heard the punch line, you would understand was just another tall tale, a story that rang true because, could you believe it, the country it described would brim with a sense of promise so full and unfinished the place would never die, would always be young, would never know the bitterness of defeat or the shame of betrayal. But the punch line never came, unless it was there in the beginning, back on the first night, with the last line of "Night Driving," two pale boys throwing a flurry of noise around Thomas as he opened a door to all the chanting voices, incantations, and reverberating guitars of the nights to come: "See ya 'round, sucker!"—the third word cracking like a whip, like a grin as big as the room.

The Other Side

The other side of the tall tale, which sweeps everybody up, is the story that nobody understands—or nobody wants to hear. That's the crank's rhythm: from words that sound like they were taken from folklore, or the portico of a museum, straight into a rant that could have been recorded in an asylum.

"This business of sexuality and adolescent rebellion has been *bolted on* to rock 'n' roll ex post facto," Thomas once declared in outrage and indignation; even over the phone I could feel his face turning red. "It's been grossly exaggerated. It's abstraction! That's why people are attracted to Elvis. People are attracted to the inarticulate voice . . . Abstract thought was his *big* thing. Elvis introduced abstract thought into hillbilly music and rural blues: he was going for the *sound* of the thing. He didn't even have to write his own words!"

If a critic were writing this no one would publish it; the ideas are too big and they come too fast, but the ranter slows down for nothing. "It was with Elvis," Thomas rushed on, "that the singer becomes the priest, the mediator between the secret Masonic cult and the public."

"The singer is the priest?" I said, more rattled than confused. "The secret Masonic cult is the band?" "Culture happens in secret, all art is secret," Thomas explained patiently, as if suddenly reclining in a wingback leather chair and lighting a pipe. "Ordinary people only see the ashes of art, or the failures, or frozen moments. Only rarely onstage do bands achieve reality; mostly it's in rehearsals, in lost moments. Nobody ever sees that, or knows anything about it"—but, he said, speaking of the great running back for the Cleveland Browns in the 1960s, "Jim Brown would understand."

So the crank rants on, and claims his true familiars: *you* may not understand, he screams or mutters to the few who have, for a

moment, gathered to see what the fuss on the street is all about
and who are now walking away as fast as they can, but Jim Brown
would! Never mind that most of the people walking away don't
know who Jim Brown is, or was.

The Shadow Knows

"Maybe I'm nothing but a shadow on the wall," Thomas sang in
"Heart of Darkness" in 1975; over the years he learned to sing like
one. He is an exemplar of the uncivilized, philosophically addled,
unshutuppable American, the Midwesterner who figured out that
just as you can always talk about the weather, you might as well talk
about what's actually on your mind. His Gnostic argument—that
art exists at once to reveal secrets and to preserve them—makes
sense of a particularly American form of storytelling, part yammer-
ing tall tale ("BUT DON'T TELL A SOUL!"), part muffled secret
("Pass it on").

In a big, multifaceted democracy, you're supposed to be able to
communicate directly with everyone, yet many despair of being
understood by anyone at all; the result is shame, rage, withdrawal,
or maybe shooting up a school. Pere Ubu's original recordings,
Thomas has written, caught the sound of "the inward turning, defiant stance of a beleaguered few who felt themselves to be outside
music, beneath media attention, and without hope of an audience." It's the voice of Ignatius J. Reilly, hero of John Kennedy
Toole's novel *A Confederacy of Dunces*, ranting madly against all
those things that keep America from achieving the greatness it has
promised itself, for example "Turkey in the Straw," the middle
class, romance movies, and *American Bandstand*.

"In a sense I have always felt something of a kinship with the
colored race because its position is the same as mine," the corpu-
lent, gaseous, thirty-year-old New Orleans hot dog cart operator Ignatius writes in his journal: "we both exist outside the inner realm
of American society." Not that he has had much occasion to join
hands with members of the colored race, he notes, "for I mingle

with my peers or no one, and since I have no peers, I mingle with no one." It's not a stance that works in America—in America, to feel yourself beneath media attention is to doubt that what you have to say is worth anyone's attention, including your own.

It's that dead end that may be the real source, or author, of Thomas's voice. He whispered in the beginning, and as time went on the whisper turned into a rasp, a bad telephone connection. The whisper turned into the sound of someone talking to himself—a sound heard through a glass held against the thin walls of the building that you and the speaker share. "Three Things," on Pere Ubu's *Ray Gun Suitcase*, an album from 1995, is no fun, it's utterly creepy, but you can't turn away any more than you can not look at a traffic accident. A chugging rhythm—like a needle sticking in the groove of a phonograph record, or a car trying to start on a cold morning—clatters behind a man whose singing is made of the cadences of a questionably literate man reading a letter out loud as he writes it in chalk.

"I find myself living in Heartbreak Efficiencies, at the corner of Governor and West 114th Street," he chants. Heartbreak Efficiencies—it's a long way down from Heartbreak Hotel, which at least had a bellhop. This place has "six units and no doorbells—but what do I need a doorbell for?"

The place couldn't be more familiar: the last-stop residential hotel. There's one in the Frederick R. Weisman Art Museum at the University of Minnesota in Minneapolis: *The Pedicord Apts.*, a permanent installation of a 1982–83 work by the assemblage artists Ed Kienholz and Nancy Reddin Kienholz. It's a single hallway: just walk in and you feel like you've stumbled into a hideout scene in *They Live by Night*. The longer you stay in the corridor, the more you find yourself imagining what crimes might have been committed behind the closed doors.

You can't think past a single drunken punch, though—the atmosphere is too dispirited, too enervated, for anything more. If anyone fired a gun in here, it'd be to shoot out a TV set. Of course there's always suicide. "The man in #2 hanged himself last month," Thomas reports in the voice of the man in Heartbreak Efficiencies, the sound of his voice like a flickering lightbulb: "tHe MaN iN number tWo HaNgEd HiMsElf LaSt MoNtH. I think I know why he chose the laundry room but I wonder what became of his two little girls."

In *The Pedicord Apts.*, the anteroom smells funny, even though the sand-filled ashtray stand is clean; it's the smell of dead air. You don't realize right away that the proportions of the anteroom have been reduced, so that the confinement will produce a keenly oppressive sense of claustrophobia you will feel as your own fault. In the dim corridor, lined with doors salvaged from the demolition of the Pedicord Hotel in Spokane, but planed down so that the hallway feels even more as if it's closing in on you than the anteroom does, there's nothing to see. Except for the letters on the doors—A, B, and so on— the doors are identical. The inclination is to look for detail, for the variation that speaks of human presence, for whatever crummy prize the artists must have hidden in this discarded Cracker Jack box of a hotel, so you lean into the doorways. Maybe, you think, there will be a peephole in one of them, and something to see. There aren't any peepholes, but when you put your head to a door, you break a laser beam, which activates a sound source behind each door.

You hear a dog barking behind B. There's a party in C. In E, a man and a woman are eating dinner or washing dishes, and arguing without any spirit. There's a mean, tired snarl from the man; the woman responds as if she's talking to someone else. "Do you know if Jean is coming over?" she says, and by this time you are so hungry for action, for proof that something could actually happen in this place, that for a moment you might consider waiting around to find out if Jean is coming over or not.

Ray's on the Phone

"Room 332 was at the back of the building near the door to the fire escape," Raymond Chandler wrote in 1949 in *The Little Sister*; an anonymous phone call has sent Philip Marlowe to the Van Nuys Hotel. "The corridor which led to it had a smell of old carpet and furniture oil and the drab anonymity of a thousand shabby lives. The sand bucket under the racked fire hose was full of cigarette and cigar stubs, an accumulation of several days. A radio pounded brassy music through an open transom. Through another transom people were laughing fit to kill themselves. Down at the end by Room 332 it was quieter."

Here the little drama opens up into a wider territory than the seemingly self-enclosed world of Heartbreak Efficiencies: Los Angeles, "a big hard-boiled city with no more personality than a paper cup"; a brother-and-sister team from Manhattan, Kansas, spouting Lutheran rectitude and practicing extortion and murder; a crew of mobsters from Cleveland living new lives under new names under the Hollywood sign. Thomas recorded a song called "Little Sister" with two pale boys in 2004, almost as a lullaby, or a distant memory. But under a different title—"Runaway"—the trio had cut the same number three years before, for an album called *Surf's Up!*, and there the tune is flying: running away from itself.

Written down, under either title the song is no more than a few lines from an offstage, off-the-page scene in Chandler's book, the whole plot reduced to a fantasy skipping from Marlowe to Orfamay Quest, the little sister, the scariest client he ever had: "a small, neat, rather prissy-looking girl with primly smooth brown hair and rimless glasses." She's come to Los Angeles to look for her brother, Orrin. "I've heard from Orrin," she'll tell Marlowe throughout the book, lying or not; in Thomas's lyrics the name is Ray, but the voice that never speaks in the novel, the brother's voice, is conjured up in the song. "Hey, yeah-yeah-yeah yeah, hey yeah-yeah yeah," Thomas sings slyly as the sound of a banjo kicks off a quick pace. Then suddenly it's no joke, a fanfare of suspense in a single chord sets the theme, and Thomas's thick, heavy tone alternates every few words with a higher, strangled, giggling voice, the voice of someone who started out torturing cats—"Little Sister / *Brother Ray is calling* / Little Sister / *From a phone booth in the desert* / Little Sister / *He says the stars are falling out here* / Little Sister / *He says the Greyhound's waiting"*—and you know, before you know anything else, before you hear that "he's gone to make a deal in heaven," that Ray is already dead. With the pace picking up, shifting from panic to reverie, warning to flight, a huge, fuzzing bass rocking notes down like pieces of a mountain, the music roars past the story, engines gunning and then cars rushing out into the desert to get the money Ray left behind.

A parade of Hollywood dead drift through the neon air of the song—Elizabeth Short, the Black Dahlia; Johnny Stompanato; Sal Mineo; Nicole Simpson—and you feel how far, in *The Little Sister*, Marlowe always was from the story, and how, with his strangled phone call, Thomas has gotten inside of it. The little sister, so clear-minded in her pursuit of the money she was promised in the Declaration of Independence, that stuff about the pursuit of happiness, you know, and Marlowe so confused by his faraway sense that in his sardonic refusal to give up on decency and right he remains a citizen of a lost republic—he's no match for a killer who talks like a Puritan. The republic speaks through him, but like a signal from a star that no longer exists, Thomas catching the drama in the sounds bouncing through his song, as if time doubled back and he was in the scene before Marlowe was. Marlowe sat in his office, counting the dead:

The play was over. I was sitting in the empty theatre. The curtain was down and projected on it dimly I could see the action. But already some of the actors were getting vague and unreal. The little sister above all. In a couple of days I would forget what she looked like. Because in a way she *was* so unreal. I thought of her tripping back to Manhattan, Kansas, and dear old Mom, with that fat little new little thousand dollars in her purse. A few people had been killed so she could get it, but I didn't think that would bother her for long. I thought of her getting down to the office in the morning—what was the man's name? Oh yes. Dr. Zugsmith—and dusting off his desk before he arrived and arranging the magazines in the waiting-room. She'd have her rimless cheaters on and a plain dress and her face would be without make-up and her manners to the patients would be most correct . . .

"Well, Dr. Zugsmith," I said out loud, just as if he was sitting there on the other side of the desk with a drink in his hand, "I don't know you very well and you don't know me at all. Ordinarily I don't believe in giving advice to strangers, but I've had a short intensive course of Miss Orfamay Quest and I'm breaking my rule. If ever that little girl wants anything from you, give it to her quick. Don't stall around or gobble about your income tax and your overhead. Just wrap yourself in a smile and shell out. Don't get involved in any discussions about what belongs to who. Keep the little girl happy, that's the main thing. Good luck to you, Doctor, and don't leave any harpoons lying around the office."

And that little wave to *Moby-Dick* really had to be there, didn't it?

One Nation Under the Sun

In Thomas's Heartbreak Efficiencies the man in the song is about to go out for a walk. On the street, he passes the man who walks through Bob Dylan's "Highlands," the nearly seventeen-minute song that ends Dylan's 1997 account of an emptied America, his album *Time Out of Mind*. Neither man has left his room or spoken to anyone for weeks, or months; they don't speak to each other, but something, maybe the same thing, the same street, opens up both men.

The man in "Highlands" is cramped, complaining, bitterly amused as he recounts his adventures, how a neighbor told him to turn down his Neil Young records—must be why he left—how he went into a café and talked to a waitress, how he saw a dog, how someone asked him if he was registered to vote—as if, the way he lets the word "vote" slip says, there were anything to vote for, as if voting is the way you say what you have to say, assuming you have something to say in the first place. But the man from Heartbreak Efficiencies is transformed by the air, soon talking on the street, talking to whoever throws him a glance as if he or she might actually listen and talk back. The horribly suppressed, ugly sound he made back in his room is now a voice seeking harmony, in every sense.

He begins to sing a version of "Down by the River"—which for at least a hundred and fifty years of American song has been lovers' lane as murderers' row, where the woman is killed and the body is dumped. There is no time in the song; as it plays, Neil Young's "Down by the River" (is that what the neighbor wanted the man in "Highlands" to turn down?) is as old as the Blue Sky Boys' "Down on the Banks of the Ohio." With each version of the fable, an essential American credo—a killer's certainty that a single act will solve every problem, will return him to the innocence the country promised him, and let him begin his life all over again—is set loose to roam the land once more. Every man in every "Down by the River" knows this—even if, in Dock Boggs's 1927 "Pretty Polly," the momentum of the lovers' walk to the riverbank, where the woman's grave is already waiting, has the buried tension of a man who can't bear to exchange anticipation for act.

The story in "Down by the River," as the man from Heartbreak Efficiencies sings it on *Ray Gun Suitcase*, is just as sadistic—if you only hear the words as if you're reading them off a page. But that's not the man's tone—telling a terrible story, he wants you to understand that life goes on, that no one can be absolutely sure what happened, that it's so good to be alive. "I mighta been fine if she'd never confessed," he confides, but the big power chords he hears in his head carry him forward, and now on the street the man and the person he's embarrassed into not turning away from him could be swapping ghost stories around a campfire, at sunrise running down an open road arm in arm to spread the news. Then the man goes back to his room, to kill himself or recharge his batteries.

The Other Side of the Ridge

He is an avatar of a certain American voice: you never know what he's going to say. When he opens his mouth, you're sure you don't want to hear whatever he's got in it, but it's easier to decide to turn away than do it. There is madness in his voice—the madness that gives off the odd feeling that it might be cultivated, that it might be a con, might be there to get you to buy something, even if you can't imagine what it is. There is authority in his voice—the authority of someone who really doesn't care if you listen, but knows that if you won't, the person behind you might, and you might be back. As a prophet he lays out the terms on which he, his audience, his city, and his country will be judged—by God, history, himself, ourselves, and that train of ever-present ancestors from Abraham Lincoln to W. C. Fields, Herman Melville to Myrna Loy. He embodies those terms: if we don't speak the truth as we know it, we will be forced into a life of self-hatred and self-denial, where suicide, fast or slow, is the only way out—and if you do tell the truth as you know it, you will be forced into the role of a crank, exiled in your own country. Your voice will become more and more strangled, more and more pinched, and you will have to struggle harder and harder to believe the sound of the noise you yourself are making. As for getting other people to believe it, Thomas has a story about that, too, called "Nowheresville."

As Thomas told the story in Rennes in 1996 with two pale boys, speaking in a flat, cornpone country voice, it was 1952. "Mexico— New Mexico. Outside of—oh, it doesn't matter what town." A web to knit the nation—or separate it—is about to be spun: "the America of the Interstates," as David Thomson wrote in *Suspects*. "This is a land like an airline map," Thomson said, "of major cities held in place by straight lines, a grid of business, population, and the certainty of being in the mainstream. Then there are the old back roads and places where no one would want to go except to live quietly in a small town . . . Imagine life there, with so many content to be unknown, and others who hope to get away and be recognized." As David Thomas has said again and again in the onstage story he uses to open at least a dozen songs, it's the half-abandoned town you pass through when circumstance takes you out of your way, the kind of place that fills you with fantasy—*We could renovate one of these old barns*—and you see yourself leaving your life behind, opening a store or a restaurant, smiling at the people who pull in, lost and found. "There's a diner out on Route 322 in western Pennsylvania," he will begin in Pere Ubu's "Woolie Bullie," from 1998. "I can't get that stretch of road out of my head. I hear it when I'm taking a shower or reading the paper. I'd look up and see it across the valley." "The America of the Interstates is where all the action is," wrote Yan Zhang, one of the students in the class David Thomson visited. "The other is the keeper of America's legends, feeding it with ambitious heroes with Manifest Destiny stamped on their foreheads. And at night, do the two Americas dream of each other?" They dream of nothing else, Thomas answers, back in New Mexico, back in his 1952, in Nowheresville.

There's a man—he had one fear, in his life. His wife, was the *one fear*, in his life. He was *afraid*, that *she* would *leave* him. As the story turns out, he was right.

This particular day, he sought, *refuge*, in a bar, where it was cool, and the voice in the back of his head was quiet. And he heard rumors going around town. He heard they were going to build a *superhighway* down the valley. And he thought to himself, I could build myself a gas station, where they're going to build the superhighway, and I'll be a rich man. And I can build a house on a hill—*and put my beloved light, my wife*, there. And I'll build her a swimming pool, and she will dangle her feet, in the cool water of the pool. She will look at her face, in the water, like a mirror, she is so wonderful.

This is the song he sings, later one starry evening, watching the lights, of the superhighway, that they built, on the other side of the ridge: "*People say, I wonder why, why do the stars, twinkle in the sky? Why do lovers, NEVER SAY GOODBYE? People say, I wonder why, people say—hey, I wonder how— HOW DO MEN AND WOMEN, EVER GET ALONG? HOW DO—MEN AND WOMEN—people say, I wonder where, where do brokenhearted people park their cars?*"

And he finished the tale in a voice so distant and distorted it made its own static: "*Down misery road—down misery road—down misery road—down misery road—again and again, again, again, again, 'gain, 'gain, misery road, mystery road.*"

Behind Thomas, the music sputtered out like a Dodge Dart throwing a rod. It was a story, but it was also a parable, with the superhighway the road the country took, and Thomas, trapped in the rumor he heard in Cleveland back in 1974, was it, 1975, "We saw what rock music should be and could be and nothing less than that would ever do for us," alone in his house on the top of the hill. But what if the superhighway is the dead end? "Pere Ubu exists in an alternate universe," Thomas said in Seattle in 2005. "When people ask what we do, I say, 'Mainstream pop'—unlike that experimental artist Britney Spears."

"Pere Ubu is not punk," Thomas wrote me in 2000, offended by the word as I'd used it to describe the band. He thought it associated the all-American Pere Ubu with the Sex Pistols, with Europeans, with *foreigners*. I said I meant "a dissident band with a sense of humor and a sense of doom," a definition I made up on the spot he put me on, and anyway, I said, what about all that business at the Knitting Factory about "if there's ever a time for punk, it's when men have their midlife crises"? "The demands of any joke allow for a certain latitude," Thomas said. "We are a rock band . . . in the mainstream . . . from a separate and lost evolutionary path if you must but still mainstream . . . we do not break with the past. We are in the direct line of descent of our esteemed forebears in rock music. We are our fathers' sons."

As a friend once said, "Everyone is the son of many fathers," and there may be no end to Thomas's. Just before Pere Ubu took the stage at the Knitting Factory, Thomas cued a little fanfare music. It was "Shape of Things to Come," a record not by Chuck Berry, or Little Richard, or Elvis Presley, or Martha and the Vandellas, but by a band that never existed: Max Frost and the Troopers, a concoction from the 1968 exploitation film *Wild in the Streets*, in which the voting age is lowered to fourteen, the pop star Max Frost is placed at the head of the Republican ticket and elected president, and everyone over thirty is put in concentration camps and fed LSD all day long. As a newly elected congresswoman, Diane Varsi gives her speeches with a tambourine; hovering in the background is a young Richard Pryor, playing Stanley X. A would-be James Dean named Christopher Jones played Max Frost, but he didn't even get to sing on the soundtrack. For that, the producer, Mike Curb, later lieutenant governor of California and for a time seriously discussed as a future Republican candidate for the presidency, hired one Paul Wybier, who hit No. 22 on the charts as Max Frost, but never touched them under his own name.

"Shape of Things to Come" was stupid, cheesy, phony, and inspiring in 1968, and it was inspiring in the year 2000. It made promises the rest of the night would keep, even if it was in an America that, for the night, might have comprised solely those who were present. "Nothing can change the shape of things to come," the phantom in the song sang, and you could believe it. You could believe the future was still to come.

"I chose it," Thomas said, "because of the uncompromised passion of the thing. I've always been a big fan of futures that never happened." He had put out a Pere Ubu album titled *The Shape of Things* earlier in the year, made from a cassette recording of a show the band played in Cleveland in 1976: "I gave the name to the CD because of the irony factor of THAT future that never happened. Convinced that we were destined to change the shape of music, that we represented the mainstream, we soldier on in futility— Japanese soldiers isolated on Pacific islands carrying on the war decades after defeat."

It's not that bad, you want to tell him. But who knows?

EPILOGUE

KANSAS

In 1997, an odd, two-issue comic book called *U.S.—Uncle Sam* appeared in comix stores around the nation. Written by Steve Darnall, "co-plotted" and illustrated by Alex Ross, it was presented in the language Americans have heard all their lives, in their schoolrooms, on the nightly news, coming out of the mouths of leaders and used to sell everything from wars to cars to books—now sounding out like a bugle call played on the soundtrack of a movie so old and the film stock so decayed that the voice you hear sounds as if it were recorded underwater.

The premise of *Uncle Sam* was a paradox. The country may have betrayed every promise on which it was founded; that means the promises remain to be kept. It was not the story of the U.S.A. as it was most eagerly received in that year. In those days, it was John Grisham's legal thrillers that most directly addressed the question of the nation as both ideal and fact.

Beginning with *The Firm* in 1991, Grisham's strongest novels all pointed toward escape. What made a typical Grisham hero was the willingness to flee, to leave it all behind: job, family, country most of all. At their most radical, as with *The Runaway Jury* and *The Partner*—published in 1996 and 1997, on either side of the two numbers of *Uncle Sam*—Grisham's books describe a national disease: an interlocking directorate of corruption that links public institutions, the law, corporations, and crime until none is distinguishable from the other and the only choice a decent man or woman can make is to steal from thieves and disappear.

The hero perpetrates a brilliant scam, reaps an unimaginable fortune, and abandons the United States for the gigantic fraud it has become or always was. The hero takes up residence in a sunny place with nice beaches and loose banking regulations; it may be just as corrupt as the U.S.A., but it doesn't pretend to be anything other than what it is. Its air may be as polluted as the air in Pittsburgh or Phoenix, but not with hypocrisy. There are no national fairy tales of innocence and good intentions, no comforting bedtime stories like the Declaration of Independence or the Gettysburg Address.

What the Grisham hero really leaves behind is illusion. In his or her place of refuge, the hero is at home in whatever racket it is that calls itself a nation; at least no one is fooled. Nothing—no ties of affection, familiarity, or nostalgia, no mystic chords of memory, no shared beliefs in liberty, equality, or the greatness of Chuck Berry's "Johnny B. Goode"—binds the Grisham hero to the land where he or she was born. And in truth, except as a plot device, as a hall of mirrors for the hero to smash, in Grisham's books the United States hardly exists at all. Leaving aside the revelations of corruption immediately preceding the Grisham era—the Nixon administration; the corporate state envisioned in Ronald Reagan's Grace Report; the coup Reagan staged against his own government with the Iran-contra conspiracy, in essence, as was said at the time, "selling off one half of his foreign policy," his insistence that the United States would never negotiate with terrorists, "to finance the other side," the overthrow of the Sandinista government in Nicaragua—in Grisham's pages the presence of the country as an absence created a weird kind of thrill. See everything you ever believed in thrown away like a Big Mac box!

That absence is the presence in *Uncle Sam*. The thrill is different: the books were an argument not that the country can be junked but that it can't be. Everything you ever believed in is going to go up in smoke ("The dream is under fire," read boxes floating across two panels, "burning down from the inside"), but in *Uncle Sam* that smoke is the air you breathe. It doesn't occur to the authors that there is anywhere else to go—or, given the enormous contradictions of the truths and lies that make up the U.S.A., that there is anywhere else worth going.

The Fly

An old man lies crumpled on a city sidewalk. He has thin white hair and a long white goatee; he's dressed in a black coat and red and white striped trousers. The star-spangled hat is missing. The panel puts your eye at street level, and from the concrete you see the legs of people passing: a man in a suit carrying a documents case, two young men in jeans. There's a fat, feeding fly on the old man's smudged forehead. His left arm is stretched out toward you; his curled fingers make a beggar's cup. He looks you right in the eye; his own eyes say he lies on the sidewalk not to ask for what you've got but to judge how you got it.

He's in an emergency room. "Walks right into the hotel restaurant and begins assaulting the . . . uh . . . the Savings and Loan guy," an orderly says. "There are 200 million stories in the naked village," says a box. "This is all of them," says another. A doctor tells the old man he has to leave. "There's nothing wrong wi—," the doctor starts to say, then thinks again: "There's nothing we can do for you." His pants ripped, the old man struggles, shouting: "No! I will never apologize for the United States! I don't care what the facts are!"

Soon he's back on the street. He shuffles past young men sleeping in doorways, a woman in a black-and-white dress talking to a transvestite in a brown shift. There's a wall of posters: for a space movie, "LOUIS CANNON for AMERICA," showing a fat-faced man running for the U.S. Senate, a ripped Cannon poster with the name "Ray Elliott" visible beneath it, an Elliott for Senator poster showing a thin man with a trimmed beard and "THE TIME IS

NOW" running at the bottom. "Top of the world, Ma!" Uncle Sam says out loud. "I don't know how long ago that was," he says to himself. "It's just one of those moments I sometimes remember. I sometimes remember a lot of things. The stench of Buffalo Bill's costume, the bloody blanket that carried Abe Lincoln out of Ford Theater . . . and a woman in a long gown. And the Alamo and Pearl Harbor. Pearl? Was that her name?" A man with a knife leaves the woman in the black-and-white dress on the sidewalk in a pool of red as the transvestite screams. The white-haired man doesn't notice. "Some of the voices in my head are muffled," he says. "They're wrapped up in the flag. But pull the flag away and the words don't make sense." It's a different language, this American, this U.S.A.-is-the-speech-of-the-people: "There are moments when everything happens at once. Then the whole nation comes into view."

In a page of crazy-quilt panels the whole nation is a vulture feeding on an outstretched arm, a crowd carrying "ADAM AND EVE NOT ADAM AND STEVE" placards, a longhorn sheep shot through the neck, a cop beating a man already down, dull-faced children in their school being frisked by police, a shut factory, a strip of casinos. "I want to say something magical and profound," Uncle Sam says; he finds himself singing "Life Is Just a Bowl of Cherries." He eats out of a Dumpster. Sitting in an alley, he dreams of his wife, about to make love to him before he leaves to fight with George Washington. She begins to pull his boots off. He wakes on the street: a man with his feet wrapped in bandages is pulling off his boots.

Barefoot, he goes back to the streets, but soon he is walking out of the city, and straight out of time. In the course of his travels, he will visit the battlefields of the Revolutionary War and the Confederacy's Andersonville prison camp, the site of the massacre of the Blackhawks by the U.S. Army in Illinois in 1832 and the site of the massacre of union workers by private police at the River Rouge Ford plant in Dearborn, Michigan, a hundred years after that. Under the cover of the nation's promises, evil is rampant everywhere.

"All is vanity"—and in America vanity means greed, selfishness, im-
poverishment, domination, hate, and death. All these sights and
many more—rendered in *Die Hard* scale, with big-budget, big-
screen drama, heroic perspective, panels squeezed for the intensity
of a tight close-up—leave the old man desperate and confused, except when his terror turns into comedy, which never holds for more
than a moment. In a hotel men's room, Uncle Sam encounters the
defeated senatorial candidate Ray Elliott—who suddenly turns into
Abraham Lincoln. Tarred as a liberal, Elliott speaks modestly about
the party regulars who crushed him, until words spoken in early
1865 are coming out of his mouth and Elliott's face is replaced by
that of the president who spoke them. "When the corporation becomes enthroned, an era of corruption in high places will follow,"
Uncle Sam sees Lincoln saying. "And the republic is destroyed." At
a rally for the victorious Louis Cannon, the old man breaks through
the crowd and tackles a version of himself on twenty-foot stilts;
taken to jail, he passes a cell full of young black men, which turns
into the hold of a slave ship.

In the countryside, on a muddy road, the grass is brown. "Texas?
Arkansas?" He's in the middle of nowhere; from the look of the Ford
parked in the dirt, it might be the 1930s. Up ahead of him is a junk
store, with rusting appliances on the porch, an icebox, a wood-burning
stove. ALL-AMERICAN ANTIQUES, reads the sign on top of the wooden
building; next to the words is a picture of Superman breaking a
chain with his bare hands. Inside, the man fingers a campaign button, "ANOTHER DEMOCRAT FOR NIXON"; there's a peace
button, too, and one for Alfred E. Neuman. There's a coonskin cap;
Uncle Sam puts it on and sings Fess Parker's 1955 "Ballad of Davy
Crockett." "Golly, there was no stopping us then," he says. "We were
a *powerhouse*. Was that the 1850's or the 1950's?" With the cap on
his head he argues with a wooden Indian. He picks up a windup
"Dancing Sambo" doll and turns the key. "Hey there, Mr. Bones!" he
says. "What did they always say at the start of those minstrel
shows?" "The crimes of the guilty land will never be purged except

with blood," says a black lawn jockey from a corner. "Actually, I think
it was 'Gentlemen, be seated,'" Uncle Sam says. "Actually," says the
lawn jockey through huge lips, "*John Brown* said that. Just before
they hanged him." And then with a turn of the page you are staring
into a panel so stark and luridly composed you can't immediately see
what it is. Uncle Sam and the black jockey are framed by the arms
and bloodied face of a black man, hanging upside down. The jockey
tells the man's story: He was a celebrated accordion player. One
night at a performance in Louisiana, a white woman passed him a
handkerchief so that he might wipe his face. White men ambushed
him after the show: "By the time they'd finished with him . . . he
couldn't remember who he was."

Same As It Ever Was

When Uncle Sam first appears, on the street, in the hospital, he has
no idea who he is. All that comes out of his mouth is babble, sound
bites of U.S.A.-is-the-speech-of-its-presidents, recent political memory vanishing into Uncle Sam's political unconscious. "People have
the right to know if their president's a crook. I'm not a crook."
"Message: I care." "I've signed legislation that will outlaw Russia
forever. We begin bombing in five minutes." The shape the voices
take is textbook schizophrenia, but somehow they escape their
sources. They go back into a pool of floating slogans, like the verses
that in the second half of the nineteenth century traveled from
song to song to song, "Ain't no one here to go my bail," "I'm a poor
boy, long way from home," "And my friends can have my room,"
"You gonna miss me when I'm gone," recombining into a shared,
national language, U.S.A. as the speech of all those with the
courage to open their mouths. The voices coursing in and out of
Uncle Sam's head bring fragments of cultural speech onto a historical stage, where they seize the nation's political story and tell it
as if it were new.

"This is not my beautiful house," Uncle Sam says as the man in the alley pulls off his boots, mouthing lines from Talking Heads' "Once in a Lifetime," written by David Byrne in 1980, though for Uncle Sam it could be 1880, or for that matter a hundred years before that. The song was itself quoting a sermon by the TV preacher Ernest Angley.* It was a great sermon. "You may find yourself behind the wheel of a large automobile," it began, as Byrne set it down for the group to play. He sang the words with surprise, not as if he were preaching, but as if the events he was describing were taking place as he sang. As the things of this world turn to ashes in his hands, a man finds God looking into his soul, and he too is forced to look.

And you may find yourself in a beautiful house, with a beautiful wife. And you may ask yourself—How did I get here? And you may ask yourself— How do I work this? And you may ask yourself—Where is that large automobile? And you may tell yourself—This is not my beautiful house! And you may tell yourself—This is not my beautiful wife!

Uncle Sam sits on the sidewalk, rubbing his bare feet. Young people in an open convertible wave at him; in an instant, he's in a

---

*If it was. That is how David Byrne remembered it in 2001, when he spoke to David Bowman, author of *This Must Be the Place: The Adventures of Talking Heads in the 20th Century* (*Fa Fa Fa Fa Fa Fa*, "the real title," in the U.K.). But four years later, twenty-five years after making "Once in a Lifetime," Byrne wasn't sure. "I have no idea what sermon inspired that song," he wrote over a picture of Angley holding his hand up to a television camera, his pink face sure, his toupee looking as if it weighed at least five pounds. "It may have been someone else, to be honest. He's known for the HEEAAAALL!! business on TV."

"It was long ago," Byrne went on. "I had religious stations on all the time on my boom box. You never knew what amazing thing you were about to witness, or have simulated over the airwaves. While I tended to look on all these men and women as inventors, creative poets and borderline sideshow artists, my feelings are changing. My landlord recently brought a prospective tenant into my office and saw some arty posters I'd done for my New Sins book, a fake tract. He was somewhat incensed, angry even. He suggested that if I wasn't an American citizen then I had no right to criticize American culture. I suspect he'll turn me in to Homeland Security or the US equivalent of the Taliban religious police.

"In other words, what I once thought was a bunch of creative freaks are now thinking they should run the whole world."

motorcade in Dallas. "I've ridden in that car so often, from every
point of view," he says, "and every time, I never see what's coming."
In the backseat, he turns to Jackie Kennedy. "This is not my beautiful wife," he says, and you may realize you are being pulled through
the looking glass of your own beautiful house, which is the house
Lincoln spoke of in Springfield, Illinois, in 1858: "A house divided
against itself cannot stand."

Uncle Sam climaxes with a clash of the titans: a battle in the sky
between Uncle Sam, the guilty ruminator, and a pseudo Uncle
Sam, whoever happens to embody the nation at the moment, which
in this moment is Bill Clinton. "Oh, it's *you*," Clinton says, casually
blowing smoke from his cigar into Uncle Sam's face as they tower
over the Capitol, their heads above the clouds, pseudo Sam's white
and blue top hat glowing in the sun. The back of his frock coat is
made of hundreds of TV screens showing every conceivable image,
so long as every image is predictable, a cliché: a baseball game,
giveaways, cheap jewelry on the Home Shopping Network, Saddam Hussein, O. J. Simpson, police arresting a suspect, a bathing
beauty, a newscast, what looks like a telethon to raise money for
the Pentecostal film *The Judas Project*, Beavis and Butt-head, Elvis
Presley, Geraldo Rivera. "Listen, this isn't a good time," pseudo
Sam says. "See, I'm ending welfare as we know it while building a
bridge to the twenty-first century. *Very* busy. So why don't you just
go back to your *cardboard box*, okay?"

"I-I came to get my hat," says the old man. Then he rallies, the
derelict throwing the whole country into the face of his official
doppelgänger. In a cascade of images to match the advertisements
on his rival's back, he reveals the real U.S.A., horror after horror,
crimes by government, crimes by citizens, blood on every street, in
every pasture. "You *are* the spirit of a nation," Uncle Sam says. "But
it's *not* America." The pseudo Sam knocks the old man on his back.
He mouths platitudes—"We've got to stay the course . . . Out of
these troubled times, a *New World Order* can emerge"—while lines
from the Declaration of Independence float in the air. Then the

true Uncle Sam blows on the false Uncle Sam, and he evaporates
like the Wicked Witch of the West.

Three Years Before

Three years before, in 1994, Allen Ginsberg, who in other days had
made a habit of appearing in public with an Uncle Sam hat on his
head, walked onto the stage in St. Mark's Church in New York City
to perform a patriotic poem, three decades old and forty-five minutes long. Born in Newark, New Jersey, in 1926, on this night he
had three years to live. He had led a scandalous life. From the time
he launched his long poem "Howl" at the Six Gallery in San Francisco in 1955 he courted obscenity squads; for some reason, despite
his travels around the world in search of new religions and new
drugs, narcotics squads mostly left him alone. As a left-wing noise-
maker attracted to every cause under the sun and always ready to
make a bad poem or even a good one out of any of them, he got in
trouble with Stalinist regimes from Czechoslovakia to Cuba. He
far outlived his comrades Jack Kerouac and Neal Cassady, dying
only months before William Burroughs, four years before his friend
Gregory Corso, and eight years before Lucien Carr, whose crime, a
killing, had brought them all together back in the forties. He grew old
but he never outgrew himself. For thirty years he cruised the whole
world of pop; he attached himself to Bob Dylan, the Beatles, the
Grateful Dead, the Clash. He was a wild-haired-bearded-commie-
homosexual-dope-fiend who was present, that night in New York, to
recite "Wichita Vortex Sutra," composed in 1966, in the middle of the
Vietnam War.

Ginsberg was always an uproarious performer, an entertainer,
trading in poetic card tricks and stand-up comedy. He had a sure
sense of timing; he liked the sound of his own voice. But he became a better reader as he got older. As he learned his own work
more fully, a new vehemence rose out of it; an insistence, maybe,
that it deserved to last. A year after his appearance at St. Mark's

Church, across town at the Knitting Factory, he closed a stanza of "Howl": "*Cast* on the pavement," he said, and you could feel the words cutting through the concrete and slithering into the earth.

Though his timing was stronger than ever, it seemed to come less from his own intentions than from the words as such; in places he slowed down, opened silences, not leading his words but following. Words traced too many times, from decade to decade, on this continent or that, slipped past their rote meanings, their tired dances, and began to glow, out of order, in a way he couldn't see coming. Which words would fall by the wayside, which would make it through? Ginsberg was reading to find the answers, and time was running out. The words beckoned: *Do you understand me?*

Ginsberg had made "Wichita Vortex Sutra" over a few days in February 1966. He was fresh from the San Francisco Bay Area, where he'd talked the Oakland Hells Angels out of attacking a Berkeley antiwar march, then led them down the aisle to front-row seats to hear Bob Dylan and the Hawks, setting the stage for a leftist romance with the murderous biker gang—"our outlaw brothers"—that would culminate four years later, almost to the day, when, at a Rolling Stones free concert, as the band played "Under My Thumb," Angels stabbed and beat to death a young black man from Berkeley. In February, Ginsberg was in Kansas for a series of readings, from Wichita to Lincoln, Nebraska, and back again. There were angry calls to the universities hosting him, threats to withdraw contributions or bring in the police, and sold-out halls everywhere. The Vietnam War was everywhere: Nancy Sinatra was about to lose the number one spot she'd claimed with "These Boots Are Made for Walkin'" to Staff Sgt. Barry Sadler's "The Ballad of the Green Berets." Riding in the back of a Volkswagen bus, composing into a Uher, a sophisticated, battery-powered tape recorder Ginsberg bought with six hundred dollars Dylan had given him, he found himself in the middle of a Dos Passos newsreel.

The radio was on; every time the van stopped for food there were headlines in the newspaper racks. In 1963, standing in the sun in Washington, D.C., Martin Luther King heard "My Country 'Tis of Thee" playing in the air of the Lincoln Memorial and in that very moment snatched it out of the sky and put it into his speech. For "Wichita Vortex Sutra," Ginsberg did the same with the Statler Brothers' "Flowers on the Wall," their happy-go-lucky ode to clinical depression; it was all over the radio, so that went into the poem like anything else. "Rusk Says Toughness Essential for Peace," read a banner in the Omaha *World-Herald*; that went in. Street signs, store names, billboard slogans, talk shows, advertisements for Pepsi—all that went in. Ginsberg was wrestling with what, halfway through the poem, as it broke through over the days, he would call Whitman's "Prophecy," "Our nation 'of the fabled damned'"— Whitman's prophecy that the nation would be called to judgment, and leave behind an irresistibly seductive image of perdition. SIN! SIN! SIN! Ginsberg shouted again and again, in scores of other words—single words, elaborate travelogues, sexual fantasies, the American pastoral as it passed by under his eye on the highway, unable to outrun the American berserk in Vietnam. He was there, "lone man from the void, riding a bus / hypnotized by red tail lights on the straight / space road ahead," to judge the country. And he was there to save it.

Twenty-eight Years After

In 1963 King brought the nation to the bar of justice; then, in his great peroration, as swept away by his own vision as anyone who heard him, he let the country believe that it might indeed escape judgment, that it might talk itself out of its fix one more time—or get away with King doing it for everybody else. But in 1963 the war was not on the map; now in 1966 the war was redrawing it. In a drama of continental drift, Vietnam was drawing the U.S.A. into itself. Vietnam was a vortex, from which nothing might escape; so was Kansas. The tornado that picked up Dorothy could sweep up anyone. That night in St. Mark's Church, before he began to pronounce his poem, Ginsberg explained: "Charlie Plymell, a poet who came from Wichita, and all the poets and painters of that time from the area"—Ginsberg's friends Michael McClure and Bruce Conner, in San Francisco in 1966, but in the late 1940s and early '50s high-school friends in Wichita—"used to refer to Wichita as a vortex, partially from the tornado, partially from the vortex of anxiety molecules that swirled through America during that period of war fever." Everyone knows Kansas is at the center of the U.S.A.; on a map it can be shocking to see how as a center Kansas is an absolute.

Twenty-eight years after Ginsberg composed "Wichita Vortex Sutra," as he stood on the stage in New York, King was twenty-six years dead. The Vietnam War had ended almost twenty years before. But all the sounds Ginsberg had heard in 1966 as the poem streamed out of his mouth, out of the radio, out of the Midwestern weather, were about to be re-created, dug out of the ground, set loose in the weather of the poem as if for the first time. There was an orchestra on the stage, led by Philip Glass on piano ("Mr. Boogie," David Thomas once called him): an array of a dozen of the most inventive musicians in New York, from the guitarists Arto Lindsay and Marc Ribot to the horn man Art Baron to the turntablist Christian Marclay. As Ginsberg stepped to the microphone, there was a high, lifting note, like a hand waving; traffic sounds swirled around the room, the rush of air as cars rolled down the highway, then horns honking as they pulled up in the towns. "In advance of the Cold Wave," read a weather report, "Snow is spreading eastward to / the Great Lakes"—as Ginsberg reads the words, they don't sound like a weather report; "Cold Wave" turns into "Cold War." "Kansas!" he says a moment later, pulling the word up the first flagpole of the poem. "Kansas!" It sounds a little phony, as if, back in 1966, Ginsberg is trying to pretend this is a bigger deal than he really thinks it is. But in 1994 a horn sounds a fanfare under the word. Da da da! It's thrilling; you can't wait to find out what's happening in Kansas.

Loan Me a Dime

Ginsberg came to Kansas with condescension and contempt. He was like "O. Wilde bringin' the Gospel of Beauty to the Midwest," he wrote to Lucien Carr, getting into that old-time Dodge City spirit, dropping his g's just like Chester on *Gunsmoke*. On Route 66 he was declaiming into the Uher, pounding old nails into old holes: "On Radio entering Texas / Please for Jesus / Grunts & Screams & Shouts / Shouts for the Poison Redeemer, / Shouts for the Venomous Jesus of Kansas, / Onward to Wichita! / Onward to the Vortex! / To the Birchite Hate Riddles, / cock-detesting, pussy-smearing / dry ladies and evil police / Of Central Plains State . . ." And yet, somehow, none of this found its way into "Wichita Vortex Sutra" when Ginsberg crossed the state line and began to take words and rhythms out of the Kansas air, and none of it was there in New York City all those years later. Plainly, the vortex was real; as Ginsberg reads, you can feel the whole country being sucked into it. It takes no time. "Telegraph wires strung from city to city O Melville!" Ginsberg said in his first minutes in 1966, because Melville had been there before him: "And now, concentric circles seized the lone boat itself, and all its crew, and each floating oar, and every lance-pole, and spinning, animate and inanimate, all round and round in one vortex, carried the smallest chip of the Pequod out of sight." The U.S.A. is a shower stall, Janet Leigh's body on the tiles is Vietnam, Kansas is the drain of the nation, the water swirls in concentric circles, and, if he can, Ginsberg will stop the drain with his bare hands and save the country.

"Prophecy," *prophecy*, PROPHECY! Ginsberg will say again and again as the poem goes on; he seizes on the word and won't let it loose. A curse, or a portent, has overshadowed the land. It's a peaceful farm state once called Bleeding Kansas, where the Civil War was fought out in miniature, in advance, and Indian raids and massacres of Indians went on for years after that. But a strange abstraction seizes the poem as it's made: for all the invocation of now-forgotten senators and presidential advisers, for all the naming of once-colossal magazines that have ceased to exist and a once-proud news service now owned by the Unification Church, Ginsberg could be speaking from inside the Peloponnesian War. He's pasting a mélange of Greek-Roman-Elizabethan-Victorian rhetoric—where poets are always commanded to *Sing!* and high drama attends every word and gesture—over everything popping up on Interstate 36, lines from Dylan songs tangled in the strings of Apollo's lyre. The poem meanders on, a cowboy walking a railroad track into the bedrooms of Wichita girls and boys, Ginsberg sneaking in behind him, a Peeping Tom who seems to think he can negate the war with desire. But as he goes from door to door, window to window, one thought leads to another, and to the first rip in the fabric of verses. "HOW BIG IS THE PRICK OF THE PRESIDENT?" Ginsberg shouted in New York, and suddenly Lyndon Johnson rose up, dead for more than twenty years but still fearsome, still six feet three and carrying himself as if he's at least three inches taller than that. Far more than with Ginsberg's dreamy bedroom visits, flesh comes into the words. And then, a stanza later, words take on flesh.

In Boz Scaggs's 1969 blues "Loan Me a Dime," there's a moment, several minutes into the long song, when a horn section begins to stiffen the rhythm with a hard, fast riff, a tiny fanfare pulling back against the tempo, repeated again and again—without that structure, the rhythm is going to sag and the band is going to lose the song. But then the guitarist Duane Allman locks into the new sound. He uses it as a staircase, climbing it, descending it, finally tearing it down and building it up again step by step, in a frenzy, so fast you can't follow his hands as they move. That is what happens now in "Wichita Vortex Sutra." The surge of energy brought on by Johnson's appearance fades. A glimpse of a high school in Salina, despite lines that try to call up "wreaths of naked bodies, thighs and faces," calls up no voice. But then the word "Language" appears, and the poem begins again. The word flits around Ginsberg's ear like a mosquito, buzzing four times, seemingly gone off elsewhere after that. The bus reaches Nebraska, "entering Lincoln's ear"—as

Ginsberg crosses into the town he finds himself whispering into the ear of the nation's guardian angel, Mount Rushmore looming up before him. In Lincoln, he passes Gold's Department Store on Tenth Street. The bus stops on "Zero Street"—"O" Street, "the longest, straightest main street in the world," says a city guide. "Once you find O Street, you will probably be able to find anything you need in Lincoln." Nothing is happening. The bus turns around, heading back to Wichita, but the fire in the poem has already been lit.

Face the Nation

As he's read through the first section of the poem, Ginsberg's voice is determined but sarcastic, sardonic, and you can't tell if his sardonicism is directed at the country or himself, the country betraying itself and Ginsberg fully aware of how ludicrous he is, playing the savior. The war is sending him a voice, but he hasn't caught it. But as the poem begins again he does. He picks up a terrific momentum, his words absorbing the panic people were beginning to feel in the face of the daily carnage of the war, the panic that in 1966 so many Americans, safe at home like Ginsberg, saw before their eyes when they walked into a store selling TV sets or turned on a favorite comedy or turned off the music on the radio. Very quickly, in 1994, the war is all-present, happening as you listen, no end in sight, no ending certain, no ending known, the real ending that people in the audience remember now erased from their memories. Names course through the poem, those forgotten, those remembered, some of them names some of those in the audience have never heard before: President Eisenhower, Secretary of State John Foster Dulles, General James Gavin, General Maxwell Taylor, J. Edgar Hoover, Harry Truman—not mentioned by name, "The Old Man," Ginsberg says with bitter wonder, *"still alive,"* Truman brooding, Ginsberg hopes, over the bombs he dropped, Truman brooding nearby in Independence, Missouri, as the ex-president waits for death, in 1966 still more than six years away. There is a crew of senators: Wayne Morse of Oregon, John Stennis of Mississippi, Stuart Symington of Missouri. The country comes into view, in all of its expanse and multiplicity. The radio is turned up: U.S. Senator George Aiken of Vermont, later famous for suggesting that as far as Vietnam went the best course was to "declare victory and leave," is on *Face the Nation* as the bus heads south. Ginsberg hears the voice of the war and swallows it like a man taking his first drink of water in a week. In a stroke of serendipity that disallows the disappearance of any of the poem's actors, that returns them from their retirements or their graves to the same stage Ginsberg is now walking, he seals the present tense of the poem as it is being recited three decades after it was written. On the radio, Aiken is saying that McNamara made a bad guess when in 1962 he said "eight thousand troops could handle the situation" in Vietnam. Anybody can make mistakes. Nevertheless— "'Bad guess?'" Ginsberg hears Ulysses S. Grant asking. "A civil war is not a 'situation,'" Ginsberg hears him say. He hears himself saying it. He tries it out. The poem finds the words that make its body.

"MacNAMARA MADE A BAD GUESS!" Ginsberg says, shouts, growls, brays. "'Bad Guess,' chorused the Reporters?" Ginsberg says, singing their chorus in a patient, reasonable, what's-your-problem-Ginsberg? tone. "Yes, no more than a Bad Guess"—yes, according to the best information available, the war was supposed to have ended years ago, but it's a *war*. SNAFU, you know, situationnormalall-fuckedup, whatever can go wrong will, war is nothing but a series of bad guesses, until you win. So the government promised the war will be over in, what was it, six months, a year, maybe two? Ten thousand advisers, twenty-five thousand troops, fifty thousand—as Ginsberg rattled his words into the tape recorder, two hundred thousand—there's no way the Vietcong can hold out against artillery, tanks, helicopters, B-52s. Ginsberg piles on statistics and historical events, the pseudo events that never took place ("Home by Christmas"), but the energy in his voice, the reach, the extended voice that he is naming prophecy, might even be coming from a future that, as he composed the poem in 1966, Ginsberg was already living out.

Only a year after Ginsberg pronounced his poem from the stage in St. Mark's Church, in 1995, Robert McNamara, secretary of defense under John F. Kennedy and Lyndon Johnson, the architect of the Vietnam War—or, if that title rightly belongs to McGeorge Bundy, the Contractor—will publish his memoirs. There will be headlines all across the country trumpeting McNamara's admission that, as it happens, he was wrong. The war was wrong, and unnecessary—and harder than it looked. Over many, many pages, and in many, many uncomfortable, my-soul-could-not-rest interviews, McNamara will now say that yes, perhaps not in so many words, but yes, as it happens, he made a bad guess. "Quietness, quietness," Ginsberg is saying, "over this countryside / except for unmistakable signals on radio / followed by the honkytonk tinkle of a city piano." "Put it *this* way / Declared MacNamara," he says. "Asserted Maxwell Taylor / General, Consultant to White House / Vietcong losses leveling up to three five zero zero / per month," the words spelled out to give them weight, and as a Duane Eddy guitar shudders a reverberating echo across the poem, the spelled-out numbers work as rhythm even more than weight, "three five zero zero . . . three five zero zero." But the quietness is only there to clear the ground. "O longhaired magician come home take care of your dumb helper," Ginsberg shouts, pounding down the words:

your magic errandboy's
   just made a bad guess again
that's lasted a whole decade!

Prophecy

Throughout the poem, though, Ginsberg is looking for more than atrocities to denounce, wrongs to protest, or butts for his jokes. He has had the nerve to say that he is here in Kansas, in New York, to "make prophecy," and so he will have to say what he means or act it out. "The awesome poem writ by the train" is almost prophecy, in a mode so corny the conceit dries up as it's spoken; "Passing thru Waterville, / Electronic machinery in the bus humming prophecy" carries fear. The prophecy of judgment is everywhere, and what is most threatening is that the judgment may be passed before you have time to learn its language. So stanza after stanza, Ginsberg raises his arms to that god. The mosquito that appeared ten minutes back is now an eagle. "Language," Ginsberg says again and again, every time, in 1994, pronouncing the word delicately, sensually, running his hands over the syllables, letting them run down his body like water and soap, like the hands of a whole city of imagined lovers: "The war is language." Soon the word is dancing, a saraband—

> *inside the church in Washington:*
> *Communion of bum magicians*
> *congress of failures from Kansas & Missouri*
> *working with the wrong equations*
> *Sorcerer's Apprentices who lost control*
> *of the simplest broomstick in the world:*
> *Language*

—and then a tango, the images the word calls up or collects out of the radio or off of the TV set wild and stomping, tumbling one on top of the other. "N-B-C-B-S-U-P-A-P-I-N-S-L-I-F-E," Ginsberg pronounces very slowly, as if deciphering each word from some media version of Babylonian graffiti.

> *Flashing pictures Senate Foreign Relations Committee room*
> *Generals faces flashing on and off screen*
> *mouthing language*
> *State Secretary speaking nothing but language*
> *MacNamara declining to speak public language*

—giving the word "public" a slight lift, raising the word to cock its ear at the words around it—

The President talking language,
    Senators reinterpreting language

When a word is used over and over, the way Ginsberg is using *language*, it loses its meaning. It begins to sound strange and foreign; it dissolves and goes blank. Here the opposite takes place. The word begins to expand, a magnet for all the words around it. It becomes the secret that, if the person speaking can get inside of it, might give up the magic words that would bring about the end of the war. And this is what happens—what, as Ginsberg wrote in 1966, but especially as he read in 1994, he can make you believe. "EMPTINESS!" he had chanted early in the poem, then spreading his arms wide: "Thy sins are forgiven, Wichita! / Thy lonesomeness annulled, O Kansas dear! / as the western Twang prophesied / thru banjo." It was too soon into Kansas to talk this way; he could have been a televangelist selling miracles on a sliding scale. But now, twenty minutes and hundreds of miles later, he has built up a head of steam sufficient to allow him to speak as expansively and get away with it. He looks over the Kansas plain to ask a question about the language that has made the war and that might end it. "Are these the towns," he says of Wichita and Salina, Beatrice and Lincoln, McPherson and Marysville, "where the language emerged?" And of course they are: the language once spoken in these towns by John Brown, William Quantrill, Wyatt Earp, Doc Holliday, Louise Brooks, Langston Hughes, Charlie Parker, L. Ron Hubbard, Charles Starkweather, and lawyers, gas station attendants, preachers, abortionists, bar dancers, and killers from their days to ours. This is the place, and so, with Philip Glass playing in the background—with what began as a striding parlor piece now rumbling and then rushing, the piano keys making a whole orchestra of echoing sound—Ginsberg calls on Kansas to make him King of the May, King for a Day, king of its language, in other words its prophet.

In words that ring with an audacity that, in the moment, is shrouded in modesty, in death, Ginsberg takes a deep breath. The country will not judge itself. Called to the bar, it calls for a drink. If the country is to judge itself, Ginsberg will have to be the country. "I search for the language / that is also yours," he says ("It's so American," says a friend—"an Old Testement prophet won't do, it has to be everyone"). "A lone man talking to myself," he says in New York as Glass pushes him on, "no house in the brown vastness to hear / imagining that throng of Selves"—all those whose voices he has taken, presidents, senators, war makers, orators, radio singers, shopkeepers, people honking at his bus as it makes a turn from the wrong lane—"that make this nation one body of Prophecy / languaged by Declaration as Happiness!" One body, one nation whole. As idea and fact, the nation is prophecy, in fulfillment or as "fabled damned." This is the purpose of American life: to enact judgment. For a moment, this, not the accumulation of wealth or even the spread of liberty, is the motor of American history.

I call all Powers of imagination
  to my side in this auto to make Prophecy

And, in a frightening voice, like a Merlin, calling on the gods of the East and the gods of the West—"Come to my lone presence / into this Vortex named Kansas"—he speaks deliberately, Glass hammering down for each word, separating one from the other, as if neither man can quite believe what he is saying: "I here   declare   the end of the War."

Bring the Past Forward

It's not the end of the poem. The states may tremble, the nation may weep, as Ginsberg proclaims, but he knows he's only Ozymandias: "Hear my words, ye Mighty, and despair!" The war goes on. In Florence the bus stops for gas. The news is back, noise in the poem, in 1994 noise in the room. Spinning turntables, Chris-

tian Marclay takes over the sound. The poem begins again in ordinary life. There is static, pops and blips, the feel of a hand impa-
tiently turning a radio dial as Ginsberg pits "The War is gone"
against "Wichita Eagle-Beacon headlines '*Kennedy Urges Cong Get
Chair in Negotiations*,'" neither more than a signal the hand passes
over, looking for a better song or better news. "I remember being
nervous having to follow Philip Glass, not an easy act to follow for
a collagist like me," Marclay said in 2005. "It was a challenge to be
heard while not alienating Ginsberg's voice, and also not being too
illustrative"—not, say, making the sound of gunfire when Ginsberg
said "they were struck with six or seven bullets before they fell."

"I started with the percussive sounds of a collaged record—two
different halves of a 12-inch glued together," Marclay said. "The needle jumps from one to the other, the joint is audible between the
beats. Some Western film music, then a military band, a record spins
and high tones emerge, revealing a slow popular tune. High pitch
flutes, skipping, looping." As Ginsberg wades on and on through the
war—"The war was over several hours ago!" he says in pure won-
derment, wondering why the radio hasn't changed stations on its
own, why corpses keep coming out of his mouth, "Marines killed
256 Vietcong captured 31"—Marclay eases the sound of the country itself over Ginsberg's voice, not drowning him out but baffling
the sound Ginsberg himself is making. As Ginsberg mouths words
Bob Dylan is singing on the radio, "Won't you come see me, Queen
Jane?" a marching band starts up, with the feeling of a memory
slipping away that comes when an old tape is slipping as it plays,
the notes smearing into each other. The band falls into "Ta-Ra-Ra
Boom De-Ay!" The music begins to get away from itself. There is
banging and gonging and the sound of roofs falling in; even out of
all this "Frankie and Johnny," played on a flute, flies out of the
noise like a sparrow. All the musicians on the stage are brought to
bear; excitement begins to build, as if they are all of them in the
same car on a roller coaster, cresting. "Slow beats into rattles,"
Marclay says. "Fifers become crazy electronic birds. Melancholy

folksy harmonicas. Then spinning furiously the record like a tornado, sucking in every sound and spitting it out. Speeding records like speeding wheels whistling by. The record becomes the vortex. Flutes spinning faster than 78 rpm." "ENOUGH!" Ginsberg said harshly. Marclay tore the needle across his broken record. It was like a runaway train hitting a wall.

Ginsberg stood on the stage, the sudden silence overwhelmingly loud. He took in the five, six, seven, eight, nine years the war spun on after he had, back in 1966, first pronounced the end of the war. He spoke the end of the work quietly, as if he had known, when he wrote it, that he would give voice to his work after almost all of those whose names he had spoken had fallen silent, and that, looking back, he would bring the past forward, as if his prophecy were not of the future but of the future shape of the past. When, for the last lines of the poem, Ginsberg says quietly, with fatigue and regret, as if the heart has been battered out of him as his prophecies have come true, "The war . . . is over now," the whole weight of what he has said comes crashing down on him, as it never really does with Winthrop, or Lincoln, or King, each of whom finally takes flight, all of whom, by the beauty and perfection of their language, somehow escape their own prophecies, relieve the nation of the reckoning they have prophesied, the judgment run down as waters, and righteousness as a mighty stream.

But here—perhaps because, in Ginsberg's pantheism, God is a heavenly reflection of the human face, because in "Wichita Vortex Sutra" the nation is left without a creator or a judge—prophecy has not summoned an absolute or a finality. Instead it has retrieved the prosaic, where each citizen has to take the same stand, struggle for the right words, convince others to listen. "A lone man talking to myself"—and what comes down is not promise or idea or miracle but fact. "The war . . . is over now," the old man says, and it's the strangest thing. Now, as you listen, really for the first time in the poem, in its last cadence, you understand that the war actually happened.

Public Men

Of all the public men named in "Wichita Vortex Sutra," Allen Ginsberg outlived all but one. In 1999, five years after Ginsberg sang
his poem in New York, two years after he died, I found myself sitting two seats away from Robert McNamara at the Aspen Music
Festival; Elgar's Violin Concerto in B Minor was about to begin.
"Do you remember Mr. McNamara?" said the woman next to me,
who'd come in with him. "He's had such a hard time lately, what
with all the criticism"—McNamara had just published his second
book on the folly of the war. The right had attacked him as a turn-
coat, betraying those he had sent to their deaths; the left attacked
him as a fraud, a man who could have saved those he'd sent to their
deaths, and all those who died at their hands. I glanced over. He
looked like a sea turtle, hard-shelled, pulled into himself: old, resolute, fastidious, like an executioner monk.

Five years after that, in February 2004, McNamara took a seat
on a stage at the University of California at Berkeley with Errol
Morris, who had made the documentary *The Fog of War* about
McNamara. Introducing the event, before the principals appeared,
a university dean asked the crowd for forbearance and respect; the
hall was full, with many of the seats occupied by people who once
fought McNamara with all they could muster. Some had been at
the Berkeley marches in 1965: the one the Hells Angels didn't attack, and the one they did. But there was no booing or angry shouts.
At eighty-seven, McNamara, who himself grew up just miles away
in Oakland, whose earliest memory, he said, was watching people in
the streets of San Francisco celebrating the end of the war in 1918,
a graduate of Berkeley ("1933 to 1937—four of the best years of my
life"), was in complete possession of his faculties. He sat down, un-
packed a pile of books from a sack, and stated that he would not
have agreed to appear if he had known only excerpts from *The Fog
of War* rather than the whole film were to be shown before the pro-
ceedings began. One might as well have tried to boo a building.

He didn't give an inch he hadn't already surrendered. Again and again, the moderator, the journalist Mark Danner, pressed McNamara to apply his damning conclusions about that time to this time. Again and again, McNamara—direct, lucid, at times monomaniacally focused—ignored the question, dodged it, refused it, denied it. Finally Danner announced he would read the "Eleven Lessons" from McNamara's 1995 *In Retrospect: The Tragedy and Lessons of Vietnam*, the book on which *The Fog of War* was based. "I'll ask you while I do so," Danner said, as if he hadn't already said the same thing at least a half-dozen times, "to keep the present situation in mind." One by one, the items went off like small bombs: "We failed to . . . We failed to . . . We failed to . . . We failed to draw Congress and the American people into the pros and cons of a large-scale military action before it got under way . . . We did not realize that neither our people nor our leaders are omniscient . . . We do not have the God-given right to shape other nations as we choose . . ." "When I read these lessons again, I felt a chill go through me," Danner said. "I was in Iraq. In October, reporting . . . they seemed to reflect with uncanny accuracy—it's for that that I've tried to push you, not only about—" McNamara cut him off. "What he has done," he said, referring to Danner but addressing the audience directly, seemingly looking everyone in the hall in the eye, "is extract those lessons from this book. Those lessons are in there . . . I put them forward not because of Vietnam, but because of the future." He turned to Danner: "You want me to apply them to Bush. I'm not going to do it." He turned back to the audience: "YOU APPLY THEM TO BUSH." Then he put his books back in his sack and waited for someone to announce that the evening was over. It was not "MacNamara [*sic*] declining to speak public language," it was the opposite.

"We drove and we listened," a friend wrote later that year of playing a CD of Ginsberg's 1994 performance of "Wichita Vortex Sutra" on the way from San Francisco to Santa Barbara—ten years after the fact, it had finally been released as an album. "Late in the recording we passed a billboard advertising tractors or feed or something like that. On its side, someone had tacked a small sign saying, 'The war is a lie.' What a strange and lonely incarnation of Ginsberg's thunderous words, 'the war is language.' Here, with this sign, the war was not something good or bad, but something spoken. And it was spoken here. The presence of the sign meant that the war had made it to this spot, on this nameless stretch of the I-5, and it was marked like an epitaph or a gravestone."

The Shape of Things

By the end of *Uncle Sam*, after all of the old man's adventures, taking him again and again to the edge of madness, always with the sense of the absurd, of the impossible, the idea of a nation founded on ideals as shining as those of the U.S.A. seems more absurd and impossible than anything else. With the great battle in the Capitol skies over, the tramp turns up muttering on the street again, bent over, choking on the dust left by the other Uncle Sam when he crumbled into nothingness.

A young couple asks the white-haired man if he's all right. "I'm okay. I'm fine," he says, looking at the ground. "We put a dollar in your hat," says the guy. Uncle Sam is confused again. He'd lost his hat, that was it, wasn't it, the whole story, down the rabbit hole, the white rabbit who lost his hat? Then the man sees a blue and white topper upside down on the sidewalk, pulls out the dollar, and puts the hat on his head. As he moves off, singing "Yankee Doodle," a bounce in his step, he passes under a hanging sign showing a pyramid topped by an eye. "Annuit Coeptis," it says on the top: "Providence Favors Our Undertakings." "Novus Ordo Seclorum," it says on the bottom: "New Order of the Ages." You might laugh; if you're lucky, you run your fingers over those words every day, every time you take out a dollar bill.

I laughed, when I reached the end of *Uncle Sam*, just as I sat staring at nothing when the last trump sounded in "Wichita Vortex

Sutra." I laughed, but I felt privileged and happy, as if I'd just been told a secret. That the true history of the country should be found in a junk shop, or its motto turn up as a come-on for . . . what?— The sort of occultist's parlor where you get your fortune told? A welfare office?—seemed like the perfect shaggy dog joke. "Was that the country I heard?" "Naw, it was just a shaggy dog."

Chase it—chase it back, Ginsberg chasing King chasing Lincoln chasing Winthrop chasing the right words to say what the town he was about to found was for, so many speakers along the way trying to say how people lived in the trap that had been set for them, caught between the promise and its betrayal, the betrayal itself the spark of the promise as time went on. Like all time travelers, we find that we can change nothing. We can only relive the prophecies, once made, as if they were never fully lived—except in those moments when the prophecies were made. After that, the dog barks. It runs down the street and out of sight. The nation appears in the sunset, and the day shrinks back to the borders of our everyday envies and vanities. You open a book, or put on a record, or turn on the TV to see what's on.

WORKS CITED

Films are listed by title. "Anthology" indicates a collection of recordings by more than one performer.

Avedon, Richard. *In the American West, 1979–1984.* New York: Harry N. Abrams, 1985.

Ayers, Bill. *Fugitive Days: A Memoir.* Boston: Beacon Press, 2001. Published, not fortuitously for Ayers's celebration of his years with the Weather Underground, on 11 September 2001. A profile of Ayers, subtitled "Life with the Weathermen: No Regrets for a Love of Explosives," appeared that day in the New York *Times.*

Badalamenti, Angelo. *Original Motion Picture Soundtrack: Blue Velvet* (Varese Sarabande, 1986).

———. *Soundtrack from Twin Peaks* (Warner Bros., 1990).

Bancroft, George. "Memorial Address on the Life and Character of Abraham Lincoln, Delivered at the Request of Both Houses of Congress of America, Before Them, in the House of Representatives at Washington on the 12th of February, 1866." Washington, D.C.: Government Printing Office, 1866. Courtesy Steve Perry.

Bercovitch, Sacvan. *The American Jeremiad.* Madison: University of Wisconsin Press, 1978. Pp. 181–82.

Bikini Kill. *A Color and Activity Book* (Olympia, WA, c. 1990).

———. *Girl Power* (Washington, D.C., 1991).

———. *Revolution Girl Style Now* (K Records cassette, 1991).

Blake, Robert. "Shut up." Quoted in Charlie LeDuff, "Baretta Star Acquitted of Murder in Wife's Death." New York *Times,* 17 March 2005. "I think psychologically it helps me get even with mankind," Blake's wife, Bonny Lee Bakley, wrote to him in October 2000 of her life as a grifter, just before signing a prenuptial agreement. "My father tried to get fresh with me when I was seven, while my mother was in the hospital having Joey [my brother]. He died before I could grow up and kill him" (New York *Daily News*, 9 May 2001; courtesy Chris Walters).

———. "You have to love the person you are going to play." Quoted in Richard Fausset, Michael Krikorian, and Kurt Streeter, "Wife of Actor Robert Blake Shot to Death." *Los Angeles Times*, 6 May 2001.

Blue Sky Boys. *The Sunny Side of Life* (Bear Family, 2003). Complete recordings, 1936–50. With a biography and song notes by Bill C. Malone.

Blue Velvet (MGM, 1986). Written and directed by David Lynch.

Bogdanovich, Peter. "Edgar G. Ulmer." In *Kings of the Bs: Working Within the Hollywood System*. Ed. Todd McCarthy and Charles Flynn. New York: Dutton, 1975. Pp. 399, 403.

Boggs, Dock. "Pretty Polly" (1927). On Boggs, *Country Blues* (Revenant, 1997).

Bremer, Francis J. *John Winthrop: America's Forgotten Founding Father*. New York: Oxford University Press, 2003. Pp. 174, 409 n 9. Details on the delivery and circulation of Winthrop's "A Modell of Christian Charity." Bremer considers it a commonplace sermon comprising entreaties, if not bromides, that would have been anything but exceptional for Winthrop's audience, whoever it was. Publication information on "Modell" courtesy Sean Wilentz.

Brown, Norman O. "Apocalypse: The Place of Mystery in the Life of the Mind" (1960). In *Apocalypse and/or Metamorphosis*. Berkeley: University of California Press, 1991. P. 4.

Bryan, William Jennings. "Imperialism." Originally delivered in Kansas City, Missouri, 6 July 1900. In *Speeches of William Jennings Bryan*. New York: Funk and Wagnalls, 1909. A later recording of Bryan reading the speech in his steady, rolling voice can be heard on TheHistoryChannel.com/speeches/archive/speech_30.html.

Byrne, David. E-mail to GM, 8 July 2005.

Cantwell, Robert. "Twigs of Folly." Unpublished, 1997.

Chandler, Raymond. *The Little Sister* (1949). London: Penguin, 1973. Pp. 48, 181, 7, 234, 235.

Chomsky, Noam. "On the Bombings" (11 Sept. 2001). Widely circulated, including on *Socialist Worker Online*.

Conner, Bruce. *Take the 5:10 to Dreamland* (Canyon Cinema, 1976). Included on *2002 B.C.—Eight 16MM Films by Bruce Conner, 1964–1981* (Michael Kohn Gallery, 2002).

———. *Valse Triste* (Canyon Cinema, 1977). Included on *2002 B.C.*

Cooley, Steve. "Incredibly stupid." Quoted in Richard Winton, "Blake Jurors 'Stupid,' D.A. Says." *Los Angeles Times*, 24 March 2005.

Corwin, Norman. *On a Note of Triumph* (Lodestone, 2005). First broadcast 8 May 1945. The Lodestone CD includes a complete transcript in booklet form.

Coughlin, Charles. "Probably the most disastrous doctrine Satan has disseminated." From Donald Warren, *Radio Priest: Charles Coughlin—The Father of Hate Radio*. New York: Free Press, 1996. P. 300.

Cruise, Julee. *Floating into the Night* (Warner Bros., 1989). Includes "The Nightingale" and "Falling" from *Twin Peaks* and "Mysteries of Love" from *Blue Velvet*.

———. "Questions in a World of Blue." On *Twin Peaks: Fire Walk with Me—Music from the Motion Picture Soundtrack*.

Crumley, James. *The Last Good Kiss*. New York: Random House, 1978.

Danforth, John. "Homily at Reagan Funeral." Associated Press, 11 June 2004.

Danforth, Samuel. "A Brief Recognition of New-Englands Errand into the Wilderness. Made in the Audience of the General Assembly of the Massachusetts Colony, at Boston in N.E. on the 11th of the third Moenth, 1670. being the Day of Election there." In *American Sermons*. Ed. Michael Warner. New York: Library of America, 1999.

Dante Alighieri. *Inferno*. Trans. John Ciardi (1954). New York: Modern Library, 1996. P. 3.

Darnall, Steve, and Alex Ross. *U.S.—Uncle Sam*, nos. 1 and 2. DC Comics/Vertigo, 1997. Collected as *U.S.—Uncle Sam*. New York: DC Comics, 1998.

Detour (Producers Releasing Corporation, 1945). Directed by Edgar G. Ulmer, written by Martin Goldsmith.

Dos Passos, John. *U.S.A.* (1938). New York: Library of America, 1996.

Douglas, William O. *Go East, Young Man—The Early Years: The Autobiography of William O. Douglas* (1974). New York: Delta, 1975. P. 82.

Douglass, Frederick. "The Meaning of July Fourth for the Negro," better known as "What to the Slave Is the Fourth of July?" (5 July 1852). In *Selected Speeches and Writings*, ed. Philip S. Foner, abridged and adapted by Yuval Taylor. Chicago: Lawrence Hill Books, 1999.

Dylan, Bob. "Highlands." On *Time Out of Mind* (Columbia, 1997).

———. "High Water (For Charley Patton)." On *"Love and Theft"* (Columbia, 2001).

The End of Violence (MGM, 1997). Directed by Wim Wenders, written by Wenders and Nicholas Klein.

Eraserhead (AFI, 1976). Written and directed by David Lynch.

Erickson, Steve. "Fade to Black." *Los Angeles Magazine*, Sept. 2004. P. 138.

———. *The Sea Came in at Midnight*. New York: Bard/Avon, 1999. P. 239.

Evans, Walker. "Robert Frank." *US Camera 1958*. Ed. Tom Mahoney (1957). P. 90.

Farber, Manny. Review of *The Strange Love of Martha Ivers*, *New Republic*, 9 Sept. 1946; quoted on the superb Web site celtoslavica.de/chiaroscuro/films/strangeloveivers/mivers.html.

Farber, Manny, and W. S. Poster. "Preston Sturges: Success in the Movies" (1954). In Farber, *Negative Space* (1971). Exp. ed. New York: Da Capo, 1998. P. 98.

Firesign Theatre. "How Can You Be in Two Places at Once When You're Not Anywhere at All." On *The Firesign Theatre Presents How Can You Be in Two Places at Once When You're Not Anywhere at All* (Columbia, 1969). From David Ossman's notes to the 1988 Mobile Fidelity Sound Lab reissue, on recording the album in the fall of 1968: "September. Three months since they got Bobby. That leaves Humphrey and Rockefeller and Nixon and Wallace . . . The album, which started out with Ralph Williams and L.A.'s obsession with vee-hickles, takes a left turn into the 'tropical paradise' of Viet Nam . . . In a parody of those half-forgotten Norman Corwin worldwartwotime radio pageants we paint new-car buyer Babe with blackface and draft him." A transcript of "How Can You Be in Two Places at Once" is included in *The Firesign Theatre's Big Book of Plays*. San Francisco: Straight Arrow Books, 1972.

Fleetwoods. See *Come Softly to Me: The Very Best of the Fleetwoods* (EMI, 1993).

Ford, Tennessee Ernie. "Sixteen Tons" (Capitol, 1955). Number one for eight weeks; the B-side of "The Ballad of Davy Crockett," which reached No. 5.

Garrison, William Lloyd. "Fifty-three years ago." "Address to the Colonization Society" (4 July 1829). Quoted in Bancroft.

Gifford, Barry. "The breakdown where you want to flee." Conversation with GM, August 1998.

——. "Dave always had Bill in mind." Conversation with GM, August 1998.

——. "Fuzzy Sandwiches; or, There Is No Speed Limit on the Lost Highway: Reflections on David Lynch" (1998). Foreword to David Hughes, *The Complete Lynch*. London: Virgin, 2001. P. ix.

——. "He can go out and play *President* Madison." Conversation with GM, August 1998.

Ginsberg, Allen. "Howl" (1956). On *The Allen Ginsberg Audio Collection* (Caedmon, 2004). Recorded live at the Knitting Factory, May 1995.

——. "On Radio entering Texas." Quoted in Barry Miles, *Ginsberg: A Biography*. New York: Simon and Schuster, 1989. P. 381.

——. "O. Wilde bringin' the Gospel of Beauty." Letter to Lucien Carr, quoted in Michael Schumacher, *Dharma Lion: A Biography of Allen Ginsberg*. New York: St. Martin's, 1992. P. 461.

——. "Wichita Vortex Sutra" (1966). In *Planet News*. San Francisco: City Lights Books, 1968. Ginsberg prepared reference notes for a section of part 1 and all of part 2 of the poem for his *Selected Poems, 1947–1995*. New York: HarperCollins, 1996.

———. "Wichita Vortex Sutra." Original composition tapes, 1966. Ginsberg composed the long poem, or first read it out for himself, in two sections, continually turning his tape recorder on and off, sometimes in the middle of a line. On 15 February 1966 he covered what appeared in print as "I" in eight minutes sixteen seconds; at thirty-two minutes fifty seconds, "II" came forth over the next days. There's none of the oratorical drama of the 1994 performance. Often Ginsberg speaks in a very low voice, as if talking right into the machine, worried someone might overhear what he's saying. His tone is flat, heavy, sometimes gravelly, often droning—again and again a striking, somehow insulated contrast to the frantic commercial announcements of the DJs or the pompous, clipped pronouncements of the news analysts you can hear on the radio in the background as the VW bus Ginsberg is riding in pushes down the highway or pulls up at a café. ("This is a *porous* individual," said Megan Pugh, in a class in Berkeley in 2006, measuring Ginsberg's 1966 tapes against the performance in New York in 1994. "The 'I' in 1994 is not the same as the 'I' in the bus in 1966, which can be changed by what filters in and out of the windows." Everyone present found Ginsberg's voice in the bus in 1966 infinitely more powerful than it was onstage in 1994—a "Creature Features" voice, a crank Frankenstein, unprotected by fame or an adoring audience, as if he has to be careful, as if anything he says might backfire.) Only well into the repetitions of McNamara's "bad guess" do Ginsberg's own words seem to engage him, as the vowel in "bad" stretches out as if of its own will, "*baaaaaad*," not quite into James Brown territory but close enough. As Ginsberg begins to recite the war news, he turns reactive, battering himself against the words.

In a diner, a cash register clangs; Ginsberg's voice drops. Sometimes he seems to be making the poem up as he goes; more often it's as if he's reading from notes, or a full draft ("Ah, we begin actually with the line—though there's a technical imperfection in the machine that didn't catch the language," he says at one point). He'll slot in bits of songs or the news as they catch his ear, but while Dylan is singing on the radio when Ginsberg quotes "Queen Jane Approximately," the Statler Brothers are not on the radio when he quotes "Flowers on the Wall." Parts of the poem as it was published are missing; words or phrases that go into the tape recorder ("Your *stupid* magic errand boy's just made a bad guess that's lasted a whole decade") don't always make it to the page.

If Ginsberg is reading, not composing spontaneously, he's doing so to discover how his words, lines, tumbling concatenations of accusations and invocations will sound in the open air, when, as he moves across Kansas and Nebraska from one speaking engagement to another, he will start to take the poem public, as a new Declaration of Independence, an act the Declaration itself demands from each citizen, the obligation to choose and speak: "What if I sang till Students knew I was free / of Viet Nam, trousers, free of my own meat / free to die in my thoughtful shivering Throne? / freer than Nebraska, freer than America?" He begins to play with cadence. "I here declare the end," he says, and seven seconds, a long time when you don't know what's coming next, perhaps long enough for you to stop wondering, go by before "of the war." But it's not until "Language, language" that the piece generates its own momentum, for a moment turning into an unstoppable stream of energy, a bus that's lost its brakes. Then again everything quiets, and you can't believe it isn't dusk. The tempo has slowed, there is fatigue, even defeat, but the particular quality of the light that so often comes when the sun is just barely hanging in the sky, its preternatural clarity, is present, too. The "Enough" that in 1994 would call down its own exclamation point like a thunderbolt is here a simple stop—or, really, a pause that rather than setting up the final lines of the poem detaches them, like a caboose. Courtesy Polly Armstrong and Bill O'Hanlon of the Department of Special Collections at Stanford University.

———. *Wichita Vortex Sutra: Recorded at the Poetry Project at St. Mark's Church—October 29, 1994* (Artemis Records, 2004). Hal Willner, who produced the event, provided an invaluable tape of the performance long before it was officially released.

Grant, Linda. "Being Jewish immigrants in Britain." Interviewed on *Fresh Air*, WHYY-FM, Philadelphia, NPR, 24 May 2000.

Grisham, John. *The Firm.* New York: Doubleday, 1991.

———. *The Partner.* New York: Doubleday, 1997.

———. *The Runaway Jury.* New York: Doubleday, 1996.

The Guilty (TriStar, 2000). Directed by Anthony Waller, written by William Davies.

Hall, Donald. "Prophecy." In *The One Day.* New York: Ticknor and Fields, 1988. Pp. 23, 27. Later, in "To Build a House," Hall, shifting from *Night of the Living Dead* to the terrain of *Swingers*, if not *Kiss Kiss Bang Bang*, follows the delegates to the Constitutional Convention as they leave Philadelphia and, unable to return home, begin to wander the land, until they turn up "to engage another Convention at the Hollywood–La Brea Motel—wearing their nametags, befuddled, unable to argue."

Hampton, Howard. "Chinese Radiation." *Artpaper*, Sept. 1989.

Hawthorne, Nathaniel. "The Minister's Black Veil" (1836). In *Twice-Told Tales* (1837).

———. "Young Goodman Brown" (1835). In *Mosses from an Old Manse* (1846).

Heavens to Betsy. "Baby's Gone." On the anthology *Throw: The Yoyo Studio Compilation* (YoYo, 1992).

————. "Monsters." On the EP *These Monsters Are Real* (Kill Rock Stars, 1993).

————. "My Red Self." On the anthology *Kill Rock Stars* (Kill Rock Stars, 1991).

————. "My Secret." On Heavens to Betsy, "My Secret"/Bratmobile, "Cool Schmool" (K Records, 1992).

————. X-Ray Café, live broadcast (KBOO, Portland, OR, 7 July 1993).

Henley, Don. "The End of the Innocence." On *The End of the Innocence* (Geffen, 1989).

Heylin, Clinton. *From the Velvets to the Voidoids: The Birth of American Punk Rock* (1993). New York: Da Capo, 2005.

Hild, Daved. "Don't get me started." On Thomas, *Mirror Man—Act 1*, "The Flying Dutchman of the Interstate."

————. "I'm not the only pawn on the lost highway." On Thomas, *Mirror Man—Act 1*, "Mirror Man Speaks."

Hitchens, Christopher. "So This Is War?" *Guardian* (London), 13 Sept. 2001. "In general, the motive and character of the perpetrators is shrouded by rhetoric about their 'cowardice' and their 'shadowy' character, almost as if they had not volunteered to immolate themselves in the broadest of broad blue daylight." The piece was dripping with condescension for "them"—for Americans, their government, and their "Maginot Line in the mind"—and described George W. Bush's naming of the terrorist attacks on New York and Washington "an act of war" as "crudely synthesised or plain confused." Hitchens went on to become one of the loudest and most self-congratulatory supporters of the second U.S. war on Iraq.

Homes, A. M. Speaking on *Forum with Michael Krasny*, KQED-FM, San Francisco, 28 Dec. 2004.

Hughes, Langston. "Let America Be America Again" (1938). See *Let America Be America Again and Other Poems*, with a preface by Senator John Kerry. New York: Vintage, 2004.

I Don't Know Jack (Next Step Studios, 2002). Directed by Chris Leavens; a documentary on the life and work of Jack Nance.

Igby Goes Down (MGM, 2002). Written and directed by Burr Steers.

I Married a Communist (RKO, 1949; also known as *The Woman on Pier 13*, 1950). Directed by Robert Stevenson, written by Robert Hardy Andrews. From Nathaniel Rich's *San Francisco Noir* (New York: Little Bookroom, 2005): "It premiered just several months after Joseph McCarthy publically launched his anti-Red campaign with a speech in Wheeling, West

Virginia, on February 9th, 1950, in which he accused more than 200 staff members of the State Department of being spies for the Communist Party. Although the film's propagandistic tone is chilling at times, it amusingly portrays the Communists not as Soviet apparatchiks or KGB spies but as your typical film noir gangsters. Thomas Gomez, who plays the character of Vanning, the leader of the Party's San Francisco cell [and based on Harry Bridges of San Francisco, in 1937 the founder of the International Longshore and Warehouse Union], is a Raymond Burr knockoff; Janis Carter [Rich: 'a beautiful blonde Communist agent who works as a journalist'] is a lanky, cut-rate Gloria Grahame . . . Ironically, besides noir gangsters, the other characters the Communists in the film resemble are the McCarthyites themselves. Vanning secretly follows his own Party members around the city, waiting for one of them to slip up or betray him. At one point, his men yank [Robert Ryan] out of a dinner party he is hosting and bring him to Party headquarters at the dock. When [Ryan] gets there he sees that he's at the back of a line of Party members being interrogated by Vanning. Vanning's men trust no one, especially those in their Party. They're haunted by the thought of American spies in their midst."

Kaye, John. *Stars Screaming*. New York: Atlantic Monthly Press, 1997. P. 19.

Kennedy, John F. Address to the Massachusetts Legislature, 9 Jan. 1961. *Congressional Record*, 10 Jan. 1961. Vol. 107, app. P. A169.

Kennedy, Lisa. "Only Women Bleed." *Village Voice*, 18 Dec. 1990.

Kerry, John. Speech at the St. Francis Hotel, San Francisco, 23 June 2004.

Kienholz, Ed, and Nancy Reddin Kienholz. *The Pedicord Apts.* Illustrations in *Kienholz: A Retrospective*. Ed. Walter Hopps. New York: Whitney Museum of American Art/D.A.P., 1996. Pp. 188–89.

King, Martin Luther, Jr. "The Great March to Freedom" (23 June 1963, Detroit). On *MLK: The Martin Luther King, Jr. Tapes, Featuring Speeches Given by the Rev. Martin Luther King, Jr.* (Jerden, 1995).

———. "The Great March to Washington," better known as the Address to the March on Washington for Jobs and Freedom (28 Aug. 1963, though misdated here to 18 Aug.). Included on *MLK*.

Krauss, Scott. Quoted in Simon Reynolds, *Rip It Up and Start Again: Postpunk, 1978–1984*. London: Faber and Faber, 2005. P. 33.

The Last Seduction (ITC, 1994). Directed by John Dahl, written by Steve Barancik.

Laughner, Peter. Notes to Pere Ubu, "30 Seconds Over Tokyo"/"Heart of Darkness" (Hearpan Records, 1975: "Written and Researched winter, spring and summer 1974–75"). David Thomas worked Laughner's piece into his *Mirror Man* theatrical, reading it himself at UCLA in 2003, but in 2000, at Queen Elizabeth Hall in London, the tale found its true form:

a hard-boiled detective story. With the poet Bob Holman speaking with a voice filter ("How does he make his voice *do* that?" as the Firesign Theatre put it in "The Further Adventures of Nick Danger") and Thomas orchestrating underwater organ music around him, the result is a perfect '40s radio play. Light jazz plays in the background; movie dialogue cuts in and out. "What's the trouble?" a long-gone actor says, sounding more present than Holman does; suspense builds. There's the sound of a door closing; Holman gets tougher, more bitter, by the word. "I killed a man back there," Bogart says out of *The Big Sleep* as the sound fades out. As Thomas put it in "Ghoulardi," the story was remade on the terms of the "Intrusive Other": "the notion that the telling of a story should involve the incorporation of additional, intrusive POVs that might run in parallel or at some angle to the central narrative, crossing it, intruding, overlaying, contradicting, deprecating, or even ignoring it."

——. *Take the Guitar Player for a Ride* (Tim/Kerr Records, 1993). Demos and live performances, with "Life Stinks" as if recorded on an open road with the top down, everybody shouting the song to the sky—and "Ain't It Fun" and "Amphetamine" as if recorded in the back rooms of the Madisons' house in *Lost Highway*. Compiled by Clinton Heylin.

Lawrence, D. H. *Studies in Classic American Literature* (1923). New York: Viking, 1964. Pp. 7, 1, 163, 6.

Lewis, Sinclair. *It Can't Happen Here* (1935). New York: Signet Classics, 2005. The inexpensive "What Will Happen to Your Family if America Gets a Dictator" reprint edition was published in 1939 by Triangle Books of New York City.

Lincoln, Abraham. "Address to the Young Men's Lyceum of Springfield" (27 Jan. 1838). In *Abraham Lincoln: Selected Speeches, Messages, and Letters*. Ed. T. Harry Williams (1957). New York: Holt, Rinehart and Winston, 1964.

——. "I expect [it] to wear as well." To Thurlow Weed (15 March 1865). In *The Collected Works of Abraham Lincoln*. Ed. Roy P. Basler. New Brunswick, NJ: Rutgers University Press, 1953. Vol. 8. P. 356.

——. "Meditation on the Divine Will" (2 Sept. 1862?). In Williams.

——. "Second Inaugural Address" (4 March 1865). In Williams.

Lost Highway (October Films, 1997). Directed by David Lynch, written by Lynch and Barry Gifford.

Lynch, David. "Before, he needed to hold back." Conversation with GM, August 1998.

——. "The birth of rock 'n' roll." See McKenna, p. 153.

——. "Fear is in the driver's seat." "Introduction—Funny How Secrets Travel" (interview with Chris Rodley). In Lynch and Barry Gifford, *Lost Highway*. London: Faber and Faber, 1997. P. xi.

——. "The fifties are still here." See Rodley, p. 4.

——. "His particular kind of hair." See *I Don't Know Jack*.

————. "I always saw something in his eyes." Conversation with GM, August 1998.

————. "I don't know what I want to say to people." See McKenna, p. 145.

————. "I like the nowhere part of America." See Rodley, p. 19.

————. "In my mind this was a place surrounded by woods." See Rodley, p. 167.

————. "It's like being locked in a building." See McKenna, p. 149.

————. "It's the sign of a great actor." Conversation with GM, 1998.

————. "It would be beautiful to have a great leader." See McKenna, p. 151.

————. "I used to think that the president." See McKenna, p. 148.

————. "I want to make films that occur in America." See Rodley, p. 114.

————. "Oh, absolutely." (On music.) See Rodley, pp. 126–27.

————. "One change of attitude would change everything." See McKenna, p. 149.

————. "See, the idea was that the bikers in Twin Peaks were the intellectuals." See Rodley, p. 170.

————. "Sometimes you can walk into a room." See McKenna, p. 141.

————. "We then get to know the secret lives of all the people in the town." See McKenna, p. 145.

————. "What I really like." (On Los Angeles.) See Rodley, p. 52.

Lynch, David, and John Neff. "Pink Western Range" ("A dog, a dog / Barking like Robert Johnson") on *BlueBob* (Solitude Records, 2003, recorded 1998–2000). Written by Lynch; vocals, bass, and guitarlekstra by Neff; guitars and machine and electricity percussion by Lynch and Neff.

Lynch, Jennifer ("As seen by"). *The Secret Diary of Laura Palmer.* New York: Pocket Books, 1990. Pp. 167, 179, 104, 105, 74, 58, 97. Written before David Lynch revealed, or decided, who Laura Palmer's killer would be, and all the more horrifying for that.

Lyons, Arthur. "Actor Tom Neal Wanted to Be Famous in the Worst Way. And That's Pretty Much How He Did It." *Palm Springs Life*, Aug. 1999. If Neal's story by itself isn't creepy enough, see also Robert Polito, "Barbara Payton: A Memoir," in *O.K. You Mugs: Writers on Movie Actors*, ed. Luc Sante and Melissa Holbrook Pierson. New York: Pantheon, 1999.

Macdonald, Ross. *Blue City* (1947). New York: Bantam, 1974. Originally published as by Kenneth Millar, Macdonald's real name.

Malice (Castle Rock, 1993). Directed by Harold Becker, written by Aaron Sorkin and Scott Frank.

Marclay, Christian. E-mail to GM, 6 July 2005.

Mason, George. "The laws of impartial Providence" (1774). Quoted in Bancroft.

Max Frost and the Troopers. "Shape of Things to Come" (Tower, 1968). Best heard on *Nuggets: Original Artyfacts from the First Psychedelic Era, 1965–1968*, first compiled by Lenny Kaye in 1972 (Rhino, 1998). Also includes the Seeds' "Pushin' Too Hard."

McBride, Martina. "Independence Day" (RCA, 1994). See *The Way That I Am* (RCA, 1993) or *Greatest Hits* (RCA, 2001). McBride on her number one country hit: "I don't think we realized how controversial it would be until after it was released and we had a hard time getting radio stations to play it. There were a handful of stations that never did play it!"

McKenna, Kristine. *Book of Changes*. Seattle: Fantagraphics, 2001. Includes interviews with David Lynch from 1986, 1989, and 1992.

McNamara, Robert. "The Fog of War. Robert McNamara and Errol Morris in Conversation." With Mark Danner. Zellerbach Auditorium, University of California at Berkeley, 4 Feb. 2004. Video at http//:journalism .berkeley.edu/events/details.php?ID=60. On 5 January 2006, McNamara was one of thirteen former secretaries of state and defense invited to the White House for "a bipartisan consultation" with President George W. Bush on foreign affairs and national security. "After an exceedingly upbeat 40-minute briefing on how well things are going in Iraq," as David E. Sanger put it in the New York *Times* the next day, five minutes was allotted for interchange between Mr. Bush and his guests. There was no report of any comment by McNamara, who perhaps, while willing to be used, knew there was no point in attempting to use the situation. "When he took the floor," Sanger reported, "Mr. Bush left no doubt that he believed his strategy to be the only path to victory, and he gave no hint, participants said, of self-doubt. 'It would be a stretch to say that he was really interested in many thoughts from around the table,' said one former official, who asked not to be identified so that he could speak frankly about a private meeting with the president."

Melville, Herman. "I would to God Shakspeare had lived later." To Evert Duyckinck (2 March 1849). In *The Portable Melville*. Ed. Jay Leyda. New York: Viking, 1952. Pp. 379–80.

———. *Moby-Dick* (1851). Ed. Charles Feidelson, Jr. Indianapolis: Bobbs-Merrill, 1964.

———. "There is the grand truth about Nathaniel Hawthorne." To Nathaniel Hawthorne (16 [?] April 1851). In Leyda, p. 428.

Moore, Rudy Ray, a.k.a. Dolemite. "Stack-A-Lee." On *Dolemite for President* (Kent/Comedian Enterprise, 1971). Rereleased on *Raw, Rude & Real: More Greatest Hits* (Capitol, 2001). Courtesy Ihsan Amanatullah.

Mudeiris, Ibrahim. Speech carried on Palestinian Authority Television, 13 May 2005. Quoted from David Brooks, "Bashing Newsweek," New York *Times*, 19 May 2005, p. A35.

Muller, Eddie. E-mail to GM, 13 October 2004.

Nance, Jack. "'You know, Jack.'" (On haircut.) See *I Don't Know Jack*.

Newman, Randy. "Burn On." On *Sail Away* (Reprise, 1972).

1984 (Virgin, 1984). Written and directed by Michael Radford.

Nochimson, Martha. *The Passion of David Lynch: Wild at Heart in Hollywood.* Austin: University of Texas Press, 1997. Pp. 175, 180, 200.

Patton, Charley. "High Water Everywhere Part II" (Paramount, 1929). Available on many collections; best heard on *"Screamin' and Hollerin' the Blues": The Worlds of Charley Patton* (Revenant, 2001), a seven-CD set, packaged in the form of an album of 78s, that is a world in itself.

Pere Ubu. *Datapanik in the Year Zero* (DGC, 1996). A five-CD career survey through 1982, including the 1975 singles "30 Seconds Over Tokyo"/"Heart of Darkness" (with, in the accompanying booklet, Peter Laughner's "The big man" notes, originally an insert to the 45) and "Final Solution"/"Cloud 149," live recordings, and numerous effusions from the band's original Cleveland milieu, among them "Amphetamine" and "30 Seconds Over Tokyo" by Rocket from the Tombs, "Heart of Darkness" by the so-called Proto Ubu, and a version of the Seeds' "Pushin' Too Hard" by Pere Ubu (all 1975).

———. "Down by the River." B-side, with "Like a Rolling Stone," of "Oh Catherine" (Fontana, 1991). A live recording (Washington, DC, 1995) is included on the EP *Beach Boys See Dee +* (Tim/Kerr, 1996).

———. "Down by the River II." On *Ray Gun Suitcase* (Tim/Kerr, 1995).

———. *The Hearpen Singles* (Tim/Kerr, 1995). A box collecting the band's first four singles, on their own label, in facsimile 7-inch format.

———. "Lonesome Cowboy Dave" (Rough Trade, 1980). On *Terminal Tower* (TwinTone, 1985).

———. *The Shape of Things* (Hearthan, 2000). "Recorded on cassette April 7 1976," at the Mistake, Cleveland. The band is Thomas; Laughner; Tom Herman and Tim Wright, bass and guitar; Dave Taylor, organ and synthesizer; and Scott Krauss, drums, playing both sides of Pere Ubu's first singles, "I Wanna Be Your Dog," "Life Stinks," "Heroin," and "Doris Day Sings Sentimental Journey." Onstage Thomas turns into at least a half dozen of himself for "Heart of Darkness," appearing both as lead singer and as his own chorus of harpies, but halfway through the set, after "Pushin' Too Hard," two guys in the audience know the night is up. Speaking of "Mr. Doinel—you know, Truffaut Doinel?" they practice French accents, then English accents: "Band seems to be lacking a bit of energy this evening." "Bit of *something*." "The essence of, ah . . ."—what they've already done.

———. "Three Things." On *Ray Gun Suitcase* (Tim/Kerr, 1995).

Pickford, Mary. Quoted in Kevin Brownlow, *The Parade's Gone By . . .* New York: Ballantine, 1969. P. 667.

Powers, Richard. *The Time of Our Singing.* New York: Farrar, Straus and Giroux, 2003. Pp. 275, 383, 40, 233, 276–77.

Pressler, Charlotte. "All the deepest." See Heylin, p. 217.

———. "Those Were Different Times: A Memoir of Cleveland Life, 1967–1973 (Part One)" (1978); first published in *CLE #3,* 1980. A quietly screaming essay, and word for word so fragile you can feel as if by reading it you'll break it. "Everybody was feeling pretty good," it ends, after pages of foreshadowing, which only makes it harder to accept that parts 2 ("Getting in Shape") and 3 ("Extermination Music Night") were never written.

Puckett, Riley. "Nobody's Business" (Bluebird, 1940). On the anthology *When the Sun Goes Down: East Virginia Blues* (Bluebird/BMG, 2004).

Rand, Ayn. *Atlas Shrugged*. New York: Random House, 1957.

Ravenstine, Allen. "I used to take my Sony TC55 recorder down to the railyards." E-mail to GM, 1 May 2005.

———. "Music Lessons" (c. 1988–90). In *The Penguin Book of Rock & Roll Writing*. Ed. Clinton Heylin. London: Penguin, 1992. Pp. 444–45, 446, 452–53, 454.

Reagan, Ronald. Farewell address, 11 Jan. 1989. Recording courtesy Sarah Vowell.

Reed, Ishmael. *Mumbo Jumbo*. Garden City, NY: Doubleday, 1972. P. 135.

Reznikoff, Charles. *Testimony*. New York: Objectivist Press, 1934. Citation from Michael Davidson, "On *Testimony*," *Modern American Poetry*, english .uiuc.edu/maps/poets/m_r/reznikoff/Davidson.htm.

Rick (Showtime, 2004). Directed by Curtiss Clayton, written by Daniel Handler.

riot grrrl. "Manifesto." See Emily White, "Revolution Girl Style Now," *LA Weekly*, 10–16 July 1992, p. 20.

riot grrrl (Olympia, WA, c. 1990).

Rocket from the Tombs. "Sonic Reducer." On *The Day the Earth Met the . . . Rocket from the Tombs* (Smog Veil, 2002; recorded 1975) and *Rocket Redux* (Smog Veil, 2004).

Rodley, Chris. *Lynch on Lynch: Revised Edition*. London: Faber and Faber, 2005.

Rosie and the Originals. "Angel Baby" (1960). On *The Best of Rosie & the Originals* (Ace, 1999). After Rosie, Pam Brown did it best.

Roth, Philip. *American Pastoral*. Boston: Houghton Mifflin, 1997.

———. *The Ghost Writer*. New York: Farrar, Straus and Giroux, 1979. Pp. 4, 14.

———. *The Human Stain*. Boston: Houghton Mifflin, 2000. The unabridged audiobook (Houghton Mifflin, 2000), read by Arliss Howard with Debra Winger, may be better than the book itself. Howard finds infinite shadings not only between the many characters he inhabits but within them: different voices for the same person at different times in his life, reflecting not only age but state of mind, not only identity but disguise, until the last words are like night falling, for good.

———. *I Married a Communist*. Boston: Houghton Mifflin, 1998.

———. *The Plot Against America*. Boston: Houghton Mifflin, 2004.

Rourke, Constance. On "Goliath" (from the minstrel routine "Ole King David and the Philistine Boys"). See *American Humor: A Study of the National Character* (1931). New York: New York Review Books, 2004. P. 89.

———. "Half magnification." In *American Humor*, p. 48.

———. "Theatrical managers." "The Rise of the Theatricals." In *The Roots of American Culture*. Ed. Van Wyck Brooks. New York: Harcourt, Brace & World, 1942. P. 156.

Rushdie, Salman. *In Good Faith* (1990). Collected in *Imaginary Homelands: Essays and Criticism, 1981–1991*. New York: Viking Penguin, 1991.

Savage, Ann. "Edgar snapped his fingers." Quoted in Eddie Muller, *Dark City Dames: The Wicked Women of Film Noir*. New York: HarperCollins, 2001. P. 161.

Savio, Mario. "An End to History" (2 Dec. 1964). In Hal Draper, *Berkeley: The New Student Revolt*. New York: Grove Press, 1965. Pp. 6, 179, 181.

Scaggs, Boz. "Loan Me a Dime." On *Boz Scaggs* (Atlantic, 1969). Included on *Duane Allman: An Anthology* (Capricorn, 1972).

Scholtes, Peter S. "Tomb Raider." *City Pages* (Minneapolis), 26 Nov. 2003. P. 63.

Scott, Jane. "Fan records Laughner Tapes." Cleveland *Plain Dealer*, 16 July 1982.

Simkins, Modjeska. Notes on the Book of Job: "Speech on back of campaign flyers." Quoted in David Chappell, *A Stone of Hope: Prophetic Religion and the Death of Jim Crow*. Chapel Hill: University of North Carolina Press, 2004. P. 229, n. 60.

Spann, Otis. "Hotel Lorraine" and "Blues for Martin Luther King." Recorded 4 April 1968. On the anthology *Rare Chicago Blues, 1962–1968* (Rounder, 1993).

"Stagger Lee." See Moore.

Stough, Mary L. "Centralia's Union Mural." *Columbia* (Fall 1999). See washingtonhistory.org/wshs/columbia/articles/0339-a2.htm.

The Strange Love of Martha Ivers (1946). Directed by Lewis Milestone, written by Robert Rossen.

Taylor, Charles. "Haunting New Orleans" (on the movie *The Skeleton Key*). Newark *Star-Ledger*, 25 Sept. 2005.

Thomas, David. "Artifact." Notes to Pere Ubu, *Datapanik in the Year Zero*.

———. "The bellhop in 'Heartbreak Hotel.'" E-mail to GM, 26 December 2000.

———. "Compact, informed . . . people had jobs." *Datapanik in the Year Zero*.

———. "Elvis in our time will never be critiqued seriously." Script for *Mirror Man—Surf's Up in Bay City*, 2000. Courtesy David Thomas.

———. "Ghoulardi: Lessons in Mayhem from the 1st Age of Punk." Talk delivered at Pop Conference: Music as Masquerade: Poseurs, Playas, and Beyond, Experience Music Project, Seattle, 15 May 2005. Revised version 15 Oct. 2005, courtesy David Thomas.

———. "I chose it." (On "Shape of Things to Come.") E-mail to GM, 14 November 2000.

———. "I don't think anyone should sit around." (On Laughner.) Interview with Julere and David Deluca, *Search & Destroy*, no. 6 (1978). Collected in *Search & Destroy #1–6—The Complete Reprint*. Ed. V. Vale. San Francisco: V/Search, 1997. P. 134.

———. "I'm like Saddam Hussein." Conversation with GM, 17 February 1998.

———. "The Inward turning, defiant stance of a beleaguered few." Notes to "Pere Ubu Rarities (Terminal Drive)." In *Datapanik in the Year Zero*.

———. "I went through high school." (On dada and surrealism.) E-mail to GM, 14 November 2000.

———. "The media always lie." E-mail to GM, 14 November 2000.

———. *Mirror Man—Act 1: Jack & the General* (Cooking Vinyl, 1999). Recorded 3 April 1998 in London.

———. "Pere Ubu exists in an alternate universe." Pop Conference, Experience Music Project, Seattle, 15 May 2005.

———. "Pere Ubu is not punk." E-mail to GM, 15 November 2000.

———. "This business of sexuality and adolescent rebellion." Conversation with GM, 17 February 1998.

———. "Was a nexus for all music." (On Cleveland.) Interview with David Keenan, *Mojo*, 2002, unpublished; taken from the archives section of the Pere Ubu Web site, ubuprojex.net.

———. "We did the first record not as a beginning." Imago Records press release for Pere Ubu's *Story of My Life*, 1993. Found, after twelve years of searching, between two other Pere Ubu albums.

———. "We want to make the listener feel as if he is the narrator." See Heylin, p. 221.

———. "We were drawn to art." To Keenan.

———. "The whole scene in 1974." *Datapanik in the Year Zero*.

———. "You have to bear in mind that I personally consider Pere Ubu to be a pop band." To Julere and David Deluca.

———. "Your only reward is a genuine shot at being the best." To Keenan.

Thomas, David, and two pale boys. "Little Sister," from *18 Monkeys on a Dead Man's Chest* (Smog Veil, 2004).

———. "Night Driving." On *Surf's Up!* (Thirsty Ear, 2001). Notable for its graphics: movie stills of a hard-looking middle-aged woman, standing in front of a bright red 1960 Chevy station wagon and a corral in the mountains behind L.A., then watching with approval as her deadly-looking husband and son fire pistols.

———. "Nowheresville," recorded in Rennes, France, 1996. On *Meadville*, disc five in the five-CD set *david thomas, monster* (Cooking Vinyl, 1997).

———. "Runaway." On *Surf's Up!*
———. "Surfer Girl"/"Around the Fire." On *Meadville.*
Thomson, David. *Suspects.* New York: Knopf, 1985.
———. "Were these actors." Entry on Edgar G. Ulmer, *The New Biographical Dictionary of Film.* New York: Knopf, 2002. P. 888.
———. *The Whole Equation: A History of Hollywood.* New York: Knopf, 2004. P. 17.
Toole, John Kennedy. *A Confederacy of Dunces.* Baton Rouge: Louisiana State University Press, 1980. P. 105.
Tucker, Corin. "I was eighteen." Conversation with GM, 8 June 2000.
24 (Fox, Season Four, Episode 24, 6 a.m.–7 a.m., 23 May 2005). Created by Joel Surnow and Robert Cochran.
Twin Peaks (ABC, 8 April 1990–10 June 1991). Produced by David Lynch and Mark Frost.
Twin Peaks: Fire Walk with Me (New Line, 1992). Directed by David Lynch, written by Lynch and Robert Engels.
Twin Peaks: Fire Walk with Me—Music from the Motion Picture Soundtrack (Warner Bros., 1992).

Ulmer, Edgar G. See Bogdanovich.

The Virginian (TNT, 2000). Directed by Bill Pullman, written by Larry Gross.

White, Emily. "Revolution Girl Style Now." *LA Weekly,* 10–16 July 1992. "During performance," p. 23.
Wild in the Streets (American International Pictures, 1968). Directed by Barry Shear, written by Robert Thom.
Williams, Hank. "Lost Highway" (MGM, 1949). Written by Leon Payne. Best heard on Williams, *Alone and Forsaken* (Mercury, 1995).
Wilson, Edmund. "Abraham Lincoln: The Union as Religious Mysticism" (1953). In *Eight Essays.* Garden City, NY: Doubleday Anchor, 1954. P. 202.
Wilson, Woodrow. "Address of Woodrow Wilson at Lincoln's Birthplace." In *From Lincoln to Coolidge.* Ed. Alfred E. Logie. Chicago: Lyons and Carnahan, 1925.
Winthrop, John. "A Modell of Christian Charity" (1630). In *American Sermons.* Ed. Michael Warner. New York: Library of America, 1999.
Wolitzer, Meg. *The Position.* New York: Scribner, 2005. P. 63.
Wright, Lawrence. *Remembering Satan.* New York: Knopf, 1994. Pp. 7, 61, 121, 111, 198–99.

Young, Neil. Quoted in Greil Marcus, "Artist of the Year: Neil Young." *Spin,* Jan. 1994. P. 82.

ACKNOWLEDGMENTS

This book found its form over many years. There are many people to thank at many turning points.

The first of those was a week spent as Regents' Lecturer at the University of California at Berkeley in 1997. That was where I went to school, and the school I left; the talk I gave, on Winthrop, Lincoln, King, and Ginsberg, became the frame for themes I've tried to pursue here. I have been trying to live up to Kathleen Moran's introduction from that night ever since.

Not long after, Sean Wilentz of Princeton University invited me to apply for the Anschutz Distinguished Fellowship in American Studies, a teaching fellowship, and I am grateful to the Anschutz Family Foundation for the opportunities that followed. For Princeton, I developed an undergraduate seminar called Prophecy and the American Voice, which I taught there in the fall of 2000, at Berkeley the previous spring, and again at Berkeley in the spring of 2006. At Berkeley, I thank Kathleen Moran and then–Dean of Undergraduates Carolyn Porter, and, as visitors to the 2000 class on the 1978 remake of *Invasion of the Body Snatchers*, director Philip Kaufman, Rose Kaufman, who played the Outraged Woman, and Tom Luddy, who played Ted Hendley, the lead pod. Most of all I thank the students in the Berkeley classes, whose discussions of the likes of Philip Roth's *American Pastoral*, Bob Dylan's 1979 sermons and his

1997 *Time Out of Mind*, Ishmael Reed's *Mumbo Jumbo*, Lee Smith's *The Devil's Dream*, and Nick Tosches's *Hellfire* left me reeling: in 2000, Molly Brevis, Hiriti Belay, Alyce Kalmar, Arianne Sambrias, Donna Stone, Jude Fletcher, Juan Pablo Ferrer, Sara Stroud, Kalina Grabinska-Marusek, Amy Vecchione, Celeste Janssen, Megan Keane, Joseph Quinn, Erika Ault, Mark Bowman, and Kati Williams; and in 2006, Bridget Brew, Jonathan Haynes, Ramzi Fawaz, Kristin Loutensock, Megan Pugh, Paul Schwochow, Kristofor Lofgren, Alex Toledano, Mark Farrier, Ben Urwand, Sam Sckramski, and Katie Simon ("It's so American . . . It has to be everyone"). At Princeton I thank Sean Wilentz, Judith Ferszt of the American Studies Program for her unfailing support and quizzical smile, Carol Rigolot of the Council of the Humanities, and Hal and Sandy Foster, Tom Levin, Michael Wood, Paul Muldoon, and Mike Jennings, all of whom made me feel welcome. The class broke open with the assignment to cast a movie version of Roth's *American Pastoral* (my friend Steve Block's idea); in my book on *The Manchurian Candidate*, I've written about what happened during the class centering on that picture, when, after the projector broke, Jenny Martin, Andrew Garland, Milano Miodini, Joe Cipolla, Tanya Kalivas, Liz Baker, Genevieve Yue (uncredited correspondent on listening to "Wichita Vortex Sutra" on I-5), Olivia Ford, Anastasia Nowacki, Carmen Breslin, Sara Isani, Ryan Martin, Chris McParland, David Whitelaw, Joel Conkling, Lee Williams, Henley Holmes, Cameron Siewert, and Sarah Stoneking squeezed into a space between the seminar table and the wall to watch the last scenes on a tiny TV monitor. Bruce Springsteen attended the last class, on Ginsberg's "Wichita Vortex Sutra"; he came with an idea he wanted to put across, about the poem as Ginsberg's claim that as an American he belonged in any part of America, but by making his argument only by playing off arguments others in the class were making, he made himself both a catalyst and nearly anonymous. As an Anschutz Fellow at Princeton, I was invited to give a public talk; the David Thomas chapter here grows out of that night.

This book took shape in pieces and fragments, stabs in the dark, keywords popping up again and again long before I had any idea why. As far back as 1978, I was lucky to work with people who gave me room: at *New West* (later *California*), Jon Carroll, Janet Duckworth, and Bill Broyles; at *Rolling Stone*, Jann Wenner; at the Whitney Museum of American Art, David Ross and Elisabeth Sussman; at *Threepenny Review*, Wendy Lesser; at the Walker Art Center in Minneapolis, Philippe Vergne; at the Skirball Cultural Center in Los Angeles, Robert Kirschner; at the University of Minnesota, Karal Ann Marling and Colleen Sheehy; at *Du*, Georg Brunold; with the Music and Media series at the Museum of Modern Art in New York, Barbara London; at *Interview*, Ingrid Sischy, Graham Fuller, and Brad Goldfarb; at *Salon*, Bill Wyman; at LaSer in Paris, Philippe Lemoine, Eric Barchechath, and Isabelle Félix; at the Institute of Contemporary Art and the Spiegel Symposium at Penn, Claudia Gould, Ingrid Schaffner, Anita Gelburd, and Johanna Plummer; at the *Los Angeles Times Book Review*, Steve Wasserman and Tom Curwen; at the New York *Times*, John Rockwell, John Darnton, Martin Arnold, and Olive Evans; at *City Pages* in Minneapolis, Steve Perry and Melissa Maerz (the friend who caught Sheryl Lee on Lifetime); at *La nouvelle revue française*, Michel Braudeau and Julia Dorner; at the *Village Voice*, Doug Simmons; at the Southern California Institute of Architecture, Margaret Crawford, and at *Offramp* at SCI-Arc, Caryl Kinsey; at *World Art*, Ashley Crawford and Sarah Bayliss; Jim Miller and Robert Polito at New School University in New York; at *Artforum*, Ida Panicelli, Jack Bankowsky, and David Frankel; at *Esquire*, David Granger, Peter Griffin, Adrienne Miller, and Dave Eggers; at the Experience Music Project in Seattle, Eric Weisbard and Ann Powers; at *Representations*, Jean Day; for the release of Ginsberg's 1994 performance of "Wichita Vortex Sutra" on Artemis Records, Peter Hale and Bob Rosenthal of the Allen Ginsberg Trust, Hal Willner, and Rani Singh.

Many other people helped me with encouragement, ideas,

phrases, tapes, CDs, books, facts, movies, friendship, and, in their way, making sure the sun rose the next day, or allowing me to believe it would. My thanks go to Ihsan Amanatullah, the always gracious and responsive Polly Armstrong and Bill O'Hanlon of the Department of Special Collections at Stanford University, Gina Arnold (for now impossible to find riot grrrl fanzines), William E. Bernstein, Dean Blackwood of Revenant Records, David Bowman, Carrie Brownstein, David Byrne, Robert Cantwell (for allowing me to read his "Twigs of Folly"), Peter Carey, Curtiss Clayton, Bruce Conner, the staff of DC Comics, Steve Erickson (for diving so deeply), Ken Friedman, Barry Gifford, Howard Hampton, Niko Hansen, Clinton Heylin, Sean Howe, Richard Hutson, Steve Indig of Landmark Theatres, Lisa Kennedy, Christian Marclay, Cecily Marcus, Daniel Marcus, Emily Marcus, Ann Marlowe, the Mendoza Line (for their name, for "It's a Long Line [But It Moves Quickly]," and for their press releases on the aftermath of the 2000 election), B. K. Moran, Eddie Muller, the New Pornographers (for "Letter from an Occupant," the only song that from 12 September 2001 through at least the next two weeks I could bear to listen to), Geoffrey O'Brien, Chuck Pirtle, Allen Ravenstine, Jerre Redecker of the *Olympian*, Jeff Rosen and Lynn Okin Sheridan of Bob Dylan Music, Salman Rushdie, Charles Taylor, David Thomson, Greg Tomeoni and Greg Schmalz of Copy Central in Albany, Corin Tucker, Eric Vigne, Janet Weiss, and Sarah Vowell.

I was lucky to have the chance to develop this book with Jon Riley, Lee Brackstone, Helen Francis, and Stephen Page at Faber and Faber in London, with David Rogers of Picador USA and with Jonathan Galassi and Linda Rosenberg at Farrar, Straus and Giroux, where I also benefited from the dedication of production editor Wah-Ming Chang, designers Susan Mitchell and Jonathan Lippincott, and the extraordinary fact-checking of copy editor Ingrid Sterner. I had the sustenance, as always, of Wendy Weil and Emily Forland of the Wendy Weil Agency in New York and Anthony Goff of David Higham Associates in London. My greatest debt is to Frances Coady of Picador USA and Farrar, Straus. As a publisher, she is a spring of enthusiasm and encouragement; as an editor, she is close to omniscient, never losing sight of a book's argument (or finding one when the author could not) without forgetting a slight redundancy back on page 58. She's the motor of these pages, if not the wheels, the gas, and the credit card. Thank you, Frances.

There is a way in which this book, like my first book, *Mystery Train*, which was published in 1975, is an attempt to keep faith with John Schaar, Norman Jacobson, Larzer Ziff, and the late Michael Rogin, the great teachers I had at Berkeley. The questions they asked in their classes forty years ago got under my skin; they still bother me. And in all ways these words are an attempt to keep faith with Jenny Marcus, who was there then and is here now.

INDEX

Address to the March on Washington (King), 21–22, 30–37
Agee, James, 54
"Ain't It Fun" (Rocket from the Tombs, Laughner), 229, 230–31, 233
Alewitz, Mike, 56n
Allman, Duane, 272
Altman, Robert, 75
The Amazing Transparent Man (Ulmer), 132
American Beauty, 71, 72
The American Jeremiad (Bercovitch), 147
American Pastoral (Roth), 15, 43, 44–45, 46, 59, 61, 64, 66–74, 81–86, 99, 100
The Americans (Frank), 114
An American Tragedy (Dreiser), 132
Amos, Book of, 7, 19, 25, 29–30
"Amphetamine" (Laughner), 229
The Anatomy Lesson (Roth), 60
Anderson, Ernie, *see* Ghoulardi
Anderson, Marian, 35–37
"Angel Baby" (Rosie and the Originals), 173, 175
Angley, Ernest, 265, 265n
Apocalypse Now (Coppola), 71, 72, 219

Arbella (ship), 19, 20, 197
Arendt, Hannah, 98
Arquette, Patricia, 108, 111, 125, 136
The Asphalt Jungle, 158
Atlas Shrugged (Rand), 3
Avedon, Richard, 138–39
Avengers, 232
Ayers, Bill, 4

"Baby's Gone" (Heavens to Betsy), 189–90
Badalamenti, Angelo, 116, 148
Baez, Joan, 30
Baker, Josephine, 30
Baldwin, Alec, 143
"The Ballad of Davy Crockett" (Parker), 263
"The Ballad of the Green Berets" (Sadler), 268
Baretta, 129n
Barnaby (Crocket Johnson), 160n
Baron, Art, 270
Beach Boys, 236, 237
Beatles, 227, 233, 267
Beavis and Butthead, 72
Bening, Annette, 72

Benton, Thomas Hart, 157
Bercovitch, Sacvan, 147
Berry, Chuck, 260
Beymer, Richard, 161n
Beyond the Time Barrier (Ulmer), 132
The Big Heat, 158
The Big Money (Dos Passos), 48
Bikini Kill, 183–88
Birch, Thora, 72
Black, Frank, 240, 241, 242
Blackburn, Alan, 91n
The Black Cat (Ulmer), 132
Blair, Linda, 72
Blake, Robert, 109, 128n–29n
"Blue and Lonesome" (Little Walter),
    35
Blue City (Macdonald), 158,
    160–62
"Blues for Martin Luther King"
    (Spann), 34
Blue Sky Boys, 155–57, 251
Blue Velvet (Lynch), 107, 108,
    115–17, 118–19, 121, 122, 131,
    243
"Blue Velvet" (Vinton), 116, 175
Bogart, Humphrey, 160, 225
Bogdanovich, Peter, 132
Boggs, Dock, 156, 251
Bolick, Bill, 155–57
Bolick, Earl, 155–57
Booth, John Wilkes, 20, 26
Bourke-White, Margaret, 159n
Bowman, David, 265n
Boys Nation, 57
Brando, Marlon, 72, 160n
Breakaway (Conner), 118
"A Brief Recognition of New-
    Englands Errand into the
    Wilderness" (Danforth), 150–51
Brown, John, 79
Brown, Norman O., 147
Bryan, William Jennings, 50–51

Buckley, William F., 47
"The Building" (Mekons), 189
Bullock, Sandra, 139
Burbank, Luther, 52
Burroughs, William, 160n, 267
Burton, Richard, 223
Buscemi, Steve, 72
Bush, George H. W., 15, 183
Bush, George W., 43, 282
Byrne, David, 265, 265n

Cage, Nicolas, 106
Caldwell, Erskine, 159n
Cantwell, Robert, 25, 44
Capote, Truman, 128n
Captain Beefheart, 208, 237
Car Accident—U.S. 66, Between
    Winslow and Flagstaff, Arizona
    (Frank), 114
Carr, Lucien, 267, 271
Carter, Jimmy, 205
Cassady, Neal, 267
"The Celestial Railroad"
    (Hawthorne), 68–69
Chandler, Raymond, 158, 210, 228,
    247, 248
Chaplin, Charlie, 227
Charles, Ray, 118
Cheers, 240
Children of Israel, 7, 8, 11
"Chinese Radiation" (Pere Ubu), 89
Chomsky, Noam, 4
Chrome, Cheetah, 232, 233
Clarence Lippard, drifter, Interstate
    80, Sparks, Nevada, August 29,
    1983 (Avedon), 138
Clash, 267
Clinton, Bill, 15, 46–48, 57, 99, 216,
    266
Cohn, Norman, 202
Colbert, Stephen, 129n

A Color and Activity Book (Bikini Kill), 184, 186, 187
"Come Softly to Me" (Fleetwoods), 173
A Confederacy of Dunces (Toole), 245
Conner, Bruce, 117, 118–23, 270
Conrad, Joseph, 210
Cooper, Gary, 102
Corman, Roger, 132
Corso, Gregory, 267
Corwin, Norman, 75
Cosmic Ray (Conner), 118
Coulson, Catherine, 106, 163
The Counterlife (Roth), 44, 60
Cream, 233
Crossroads (Conner), 118
Cruise, Julee, 148, 163, 172–76, 180
Crumley, James, 4

"Daddy's Li'l Girl" (Bikini Kill), 186
The Daily Show, 129n
Danforth, John C., 196
Danforth, Reverend Samuel, 150–51
Dangerfield, Rodney, 72
Daniels, Jeff, 139
Danner, Mark, 282
Dante, 150
"Danville Girl" (Boggs), 156
Darnall, Steve, 259
Daughters of the American Revolution, 36
Davis, Angela, 70, 74
Davis, Miles, 160n
Day the Earth Met the . . . Rocket from the Tombs—Live from Punk Ground Zero, Cleveland 1975 (Rocket from the Tombs), 228, 234
The Day the Earth Stood Still, 236
Dean, James, 110, 111, 113, 160n

Debs, Eugene, 52
Declaration of Independence, 10, 11, 13, 26, 30, 50, 87, 88, 266
DeFeo, Jay, 118
Detour (Ulmer), 130, 130n, 132–36, 136n, 144
DeVito, Danny, 72
Diddley, Bo, 243
Disastodrome!, 108, 206, 232, 239–44
Disordo, Joe, 3
"Don't Worry Baby" (Beach Boys), 236
Dos Passos, John, 48–56, 56n, 57–59, 62, 63, 64, 65, 66, 89, 100, 197–98
Double Indemnity, 112, 132, 158, 225
Douglas, Kirk, 158–59, 160
Douglas, William O., 55n, 56n
Douglass, Frederick, 8, 12, 26
"Down by the River" (Pere Ubu), 250–51
"Down by the River" (Young), 251
"Down on the Banks of the Ohio" (Blue Sky Boys), 156, 157, 251
Drifters, 111
Dukakis, Michael, 71
Duke, Patty, 73
Duncan, Isadora, 52
Dune (Lynch), 106
Duyckinck, Evert, 88
Dylan, Bob, 6, 11–12, 30, 43, 116, 118, 250–51, 267, 268, 279

Eastwood, Clint, 125
Ecclesiastes, 75
Edison, Thomas, 52, 235
Electric Prunes, 208
Elephant Man (Lynch), 106

Ellison, Ralph, 210
Emerson, Ralph Waldo, 8, 88
"The End of the Innocence"
  (Henley), 147
The End of Violence (Wenders), 138,
  140
Eraserhead (Lynch), 105–106, 114,
  172, 222
Erickson, Steve, 125, 225
Evans, Walker, 54, 114
Everest, Wesley, 54–55, 55*n*–56*n*, 56
The Exorcist, 72

"Fair Eyed Ellen" (Blue Sky Boys),
  156
"Falling" (Cruise), 163, 173
Falwell, Reverend Jerry, 5
Farber, Manny, 159, 204, 205, 210
"Final Solution" (Pere Ubu), 211,
  233
Fiorentino, Linda, 143
The Firm (Grisham), 259
Fitzgerald, F. Scott, 7
Fleetwoods, 173, 175
"Floating" (Cruise), 173
The Flower Carrier (Rivera), 77–78
"Flowers on the Wall" (Statler
  Brothers), 269
The Fog of War (Morris), 281, 282
Fonda, Henry, 48
Ford, Henry, 52
Ford, John, 48
Ford, Olivia, 72–73
Ford, Richard, 142
Ford, Tennessee Ernie, 202, 203
The 42nd Parallel (Dos Passos), 48
Foster, Hal, 5
Frank, Robert, 114
Freed, Alan, 214
Freeman, Morgan, 74
Fugitive Days (Ayers), 4

Gabel, Martin, 75
Gandhi, Mohandas K., 82
Garrison, William Lloyd, 13
Getty, Balthazar, 110, 112
Gettysburg Address (Lincoln), 63,
  76, 96
The Ghost Writer (Roth), 45–46, 60
Ghoulardi, 217–20
Gifford, Barry, 108, 122, 124, 124*n*,
  139, 144
Gingrich, Newt, 43, 216
Ginsberg, Allen, 14, 16, 160*n*,
  267–84
Girl Power (Bikini Kill), 184, 185
Girls in Chains (Ulmer), 132
Glass, Philip, 270, 277, 279
The Godfather (Coppola), 225
Go East, Young Man (Douglas), 55*n*
Gonzales, Albert, 14
Goodbye, Columbus (Roth), 85
"Good Vibrations" (Beach Boys),
  236
Gould, Jay, 48
Grant, Linda, 66
The Grapes of Wrath (Ford), 48–49
Grateful Dead, 267
Gray Shirts, 90, 91*n*
The Great McGinty (Sturges), 205
Greer, Jane, 163*n*
Griffith, D. W., 109
Grisham, John, 259–60
Gross, Larry, 145
The Guilty (Waller), 138, 140, 142
Gulliver's Travels (Swift), 22

Hackman, Gene, 73
Hagelin, John, 103
Hail the Conquering Hero (Sturges),
  204
Hall, Donald, 81
Hamilton, Ann, 80–81

Hamilton, Suzanna, 223
Hammett, Dashiell, 158
Hampton, Howard, 89
Hanks, Tom, 142–43
Hanna, Kathleen, 183–88
Harrison, George, 103
Hauptmann, Bruno, 94
Hawthorne, Nathaniel, 8, 47, 66,
    68–69, 83, 84, 152, 153
"Heart of Darkness" (Pere Ubu), 209,
    210–11, 212, 228, 245
Heavens to Betsy, 15, 188–91
Heflin, Van, 158, 159
Hemingway, Ernest, 159*n*
Hendrix, Jimi, 189
Henley, Don, 147
Herman, Tom, 221
Herrmann, Bernard, 75, 116
"Highlands" (Dylan), 250–51
High Sierra, 225
"High Water (For Charley Patton)"
    (Dylan), 6, 11–12
"High Water Everywhere Part II"
    (Patton), 5
Hild, Daved, 108, 130, 239–40
Hill, Joe, 52
Hiss, Alger, 78–79
Hitchens, Christopher, 5
Holman, Bob, 240, 242
Homes, A. M., 11
Hopper, Dennis, 72
Hopper, Edward, 242
"Hotel Lorraine" (Spann), 34–35
House Un-American Activities
    Committee, 45, 62, 78
"Howl" (Ginsberg), 267, 268
Hubley, Georgia, 240, 242
Hudson, Rock, 72
Hughes, Langston, 197
The Human Stain (Roth), 43, 45, 46,
    59, 61, 64, 65, 66, 82, 99, 100,
    147

Hurok, Sol, 36
Hurt, John, 223
Hussein, Saddam, 207

I Am a Fugitive from a Chain Gang,
    144
Ice-T, 74
Ickes, Harold L., 36
"If I Lose, Let Me Lose" (Poole), 222
Igby Goes Down (Steers), 138, 139,
    140, 141–42
"I Had Too Much to Dream (Last
    Night)" (Electric Prunes), 208
I Love a Mystery, 121
I Married a Communist (Roth), 43,
    45, 59, 60–61, 62–66, 78–81, 99,
    100
I Married a Communist (Stevenson),
    77–78
In Cold Blood (Capote), 128*n*
Independence Day, 22, 139
"Independence Day" (McBride), 15,
    181–82
Industrial Workers of the World
    (IWW), 50, 54–55, 55*n*–56*n*
Inferno (Dante), 150
In Good Faith (Rushdie), 5
Ingram, Ericka, 192–93
Ingram, Julie, 192–93
Ingram, Paul R., 191–93
*In Retrospect: The Tragedy and Lessons
    of Vietnam* (McNamara), 282
In the American West (Avedon), 138
Intolerance (Griffith), 109
"Into the Night" (Cruise), 173
Invasion of the Body Snatchers
    (Kaufman), 88
Invasion of the Body Snatchers
    (Siegel), 78, 88, 192
Invisible Man (Ellison), 210
Isaak, Chris, 165, 180

Isaiah, 34
Isani, Sara, 74
Island of Lost Souls, 210
It Can't Happen Here (Lewis), 6, 89,
    90–93, 104
"I Wanna Be Your Dog" (Stooges,
    Pere Ubu), 212
"I Wish I Was Your Mother" (Mott
    the Hoople), 233

Jackson, Mahalia, 32
Jackson, Phil, 214n
Jarry, Alfred, 216
Jefferson, Thomas, 13, 14, 26, 50,
    65, 80
Job, Book of, 38
"Johnny B. Goode" (Berry), 260
Johnson, Lyndon B., 216, 272, 273
Johnson, Philip, 90, 91n
Johnson, Robert, 242
Jolie, Angelina, 72
Julius Caesar (Shakespeare), 68

Kalivas, Tanya, 72, 204
Kaufman, Philip, 88
Kaye, John, 21
Keaton, Diane, 225
Keinholz, Ed, 246
Keinholz, Nancy Reddin, 246
Kennedy, John F., 46, 57, 67, 94,
    195, 197, 226, 227, 266, 273
Kennedy, Lisa, 186
Kennedy, Robert F., 98
Kerouac, Jack, 160n, 267
Kerry, John, 197, 198
The Kid from Tomkinsville
    (Tunis), 46
Kidman, Nicole, 143
Kidney, Robert and Jack, 240,
    242–43
King, Ben E., 236

King, Martin Luther, Jr., 7, 19, 21,
    30–37, 57, 82, 269, 270
Kiss Me Deadly, 144
Krauss, Scott, 208

La Follette, Robert, 58, 89
Lang, Fritz, 125
"Last Fair Deal Gone Down"
    (Johnson), 242
The Last Good Kiss (Crumley), 4
The Last Seduction (Dahl), 138, 139,
    140, 142, 143
Laughner, Peter, 207, 212, 217, 221,
    228–30, 230n, 231–35
Law & Order, 156
Lawrence, D. H., 17, 156,
    194, 204
Lee, Sheryl, 15, 17, 148–49, 154,
    164, 165, 170, 176, 178, 180
Lennon, John, 103
"Let America Be America Again"
    (Hughes), 197, 198
"Letter from Birmingham Jail" (King),
    57
Letterman, David, 142
Let Us Now Praise Famous Men (Agee
    and Evans), 54, 114
Lewinsky, Monica, 46–48
Lewis, Juliette, 72
Lewis, Sinclair, 6, 89–93, 104
"Life Stinks" (Rocket from the
    Tombs, Pere Ubu), 212, 229
Lincoln, Abraham, 7, 8–9, 12–13,
    14, 17, 19, 20, 20n, 21, 25–29, 30,
    33, 34, 37, 42, 55, 63, 70–71, 74,
    76–81, 87, 100, 201, 263, 266
Lindbergh, Anne Morrow, 94
Lindbergh, Charles, 89, 91n, 94–98
Lindsay, Arto, 270
Lipton, Peggy, 163n, 243
"Little Sister" (Thomas, and two pale
    boys), 248–49

The Little Sister (Chandler), 158,
    247–50
Little Walter, 35
Lloyd, Richard, 232
"Loan Me a Dime" (Scaggs), 272
Loggie, Robert, 111
"Lonesome Cowboy Dave" (Pere
    Ubu), 205–206
Long, Huey, 90n–91n, 92, 216
The Long Goodbye (Chandler), 210
Lost Highway (Lynch), 102, 107,
    108–14, 122, 123–28, 124n, 128n,
    128–30, 135, 136, 136n, 137, 139,
    142, 143–44, 145, 243
"Lost Highway" (Williams), 130
"Louie Louie," 208
Love, Courtney, 73
"Love and Theft" (Dylan), 11
Lynch, David, 6, 16, 101–45,
    147–99, 242, 243
Lynch, Jennifer, 148, 151
Lyons, Arthur, 137n

M (Lang), 125
Macdonald, Ross, 158, 160–62
MacLachlan, Kyle, 160, 198
Madansky, Johnny, 232
Madison, James, 26, 139
Maharishi Mahesh Yogi, 103
Malice (Becker), 137, 143
The Maltese Falcon, 223
The Manchurian Candidate
    (Frankenheimer), 42, 78, 144
March on Washington for Jobs and
    Freedom (1963), 21, 30–37
Marclay, Christian, 270, 278–80
Marcus, Emily, 6
Martin, Steve, 125, 241
Mason, George, 13
Massachusetts Bay Company, 7, 19,
    22
The Masses, 49

"The May-Pole of Merry Mount"
    (Hawthorne), 83
McBride, Martina, 15, 181–82
McCartney, Paul, 103
McClure, Michael, 270
McKenna, Kristine, 103, 126, 175
McNamara, Robert, 274, 275,
    281–82
McPherson, Aimee Semple, 16, 137n
Meadville (Pere Ubu), 236
"Meditation on the Divine Will"
    (Lincoln), 27
Mehlman, Steve, 232
Mekons, 189
Melville, Herman, 6, 8, 66, 84, 88,
    107, 203, 271
Mercury Theatre, 75
"The Minister's Black Veil"
    (Hawthorne), 83
The Miracle of Morgan's Creek
    (Sturges), 204
Mirror Man (Hild), 108, 130, 241–44
Moby-Dick (Melville), 6, 82, 141,
    203–204
"A Modell of Christian Charity"
    (Winthrop), 7, 19–20, 20n, 22–25,
    63
"Money (That's What I Want)"
    (Beatles), 233
"Monsters" (Heavens to Betsy),
    188
Monty Python, 240
"Moondog Show" (Freed), 214
Morgan, J. P., 52
Morris, Errol, 281
Mott the Hoople, 233
A Movie (Conner), 118
Mudeiris, Sheikh Ibrahim, 202n
Mulholland Dr. (Lynch), 107, 113,
    243
Muller, Eddie, 158
Mumbo Jumbo (Reed), 115
Muni, Paul, 144

Murnau, F. W., 125, 132
"Music Lessons" (Ravenstine), 211,
212–13
Myein (Hamilton), 80–81
"My Red Self" (Heavens to Betsy),
189
"My Secret" (Heavens to Betsy),
190–91
"Mysteries of Love" (Cruise), 175

Nance, Jack, 105–106, 111, 128n,
149, 222
Natural Born Killers (Stone), 131
Neal, Tom, 130n, 132, 133, 136,
136n–137n
Neal, Tom, Jr., 130n
"Never Gonna Kill Myself Again"
(Laughner), 229
Newman, Randy, 214, 214n
New York Times, 9, 90n, 129n, 214n
Nicholson, Jack, 102
Nighthawks (Hopper), 242
Night People (Gifford), 124n
1919 (Dos Passos), 48, 54, 55n
1984 (Orwell), 223
1984 (Radford), 223–24
Nirvana, 28
Nixon, Richard, 125, 260
"Nobody's Business" (Puckett), 124
Nochimson, Martha, 113, 131
"No One to Welcome Me Home"
(Blue Sky Boys), 156
Notes on the State of Virginia
(Jefferson), 13
"Nowheresville" (Thomas, with two
pale boys), 252, 253
Numbers Band, 240, 242

O'Connor, Sandra Day, 196
On a Note of Triumph (Corwin),
75–76, 86–87

"Once in a Lifetime" (Talking
Heads), 265, 265n
The One Day (Hall), 81
"On Top of Old Smokey" (Blue Sky
Boys), 156
Orbison, Roy, 119, 243
Orwell, George, 223
Oswald, Lee Harvey, 46, 226

Palm Springs Life, 137n
Parker, Fess, 263
Parks, Van Dyke, 240
The Partner (Grisham), 259
Patton, Charley, 5
Payton, Barbara, 137n
The Pedicord Apts. (Keinholz),
246–47
Pennies from Heaven, 125, 242
Pere Ubu, 89, 205–55
Permian Strata (Conner), 118
Peter Gunn, 125
Peters, Gretchen, 181
Peyton Place, 106
Pickford, Mary, 180
Pierre (Melville), 107
"Pink Western Range" (Lynch and
Neff), 6
Pixies, 240
The Plot Against America (Roth), 15,
89–90, 93–99, 159n
Plymell, Charlie, 270
PM, 159n–60n
Poe, Edgar Allan, 8
Poole, Charlie, 222
Portman, Natalie, 72
Posey, Parker, 72
The Position (Wolitzer), 47
Poster, W. S., 204, 205
Potter, Dennis, 125
Pound, Ezra, 91n
Powell, Dick, 160
Powers, Richard, 21, 35–37

Preminger, Otto, 125
Presley, Elvis, 134, 175, 216, 242, 244
Pressler, Charlotte, 215, 217
"Pretty Polly" (Boggs), 156, 251
Producers Releasing Corporation, 130
Pryor, Richard, 255
Puckett, Riley, 124
Pullman, Bill, 15, 22, 101–102, 108–14, 123, 124–30, 137–45, 243
Puritans, 7, 19–20, 22–25, 26, 83, 150–51, 152
The Pursuit of the Millennium (Cohn), 202
"Pushin' Too Hard" (Pere Ubu), 211–12
"Pushin' Too Hard (Seeds), 208

"Questions in a World of Blue" (Cruise), 172, 165

Radford, Michael, 223
"Rainy Day Women #12 & 35" (Dylan), 118
Rand, Ayn, 3
Ravenstine, Allen, 211, 212–13, 221
Ray, James Earl, 34
Ray Gun Suitcase (Pere Ubu), 246, 251
Reagan, Ronald, 103, 195–97, 207, 260
Rebel Without a Cause, 111, 113, 225
Redford, Robert, 71
Reed, Ishmael, 115
Reed, Lou, 111
Reid, Harry, 14
Remembering Satan (Wright), 192
Report (Conner), 118

The Resurrection of Wesley Everest (Alewitz), 56n
Revolution Girl Style Now (Bikini Kill), 186
Rexroth, Kenneth, 48
Reznikoff, Charles, 80, 80n
Rhames, Ving, 143
Ribot, Marc, 270
Ricci, Christina, 72
Rick (Clayton), 138, 140–41
Rimbaud, Arthur, 224
Ringold, Ira, 74, 79
riot grrrl, 185
Ritter, Thelma, 160
Rivera, Diego, 77–78
Robeson, Paul, 63, 77
Rocket from the Tombs, 207, 217, 227–31, 233, 240
Rockwell, Norman, 49
Rodley, Chris, 104, 107, 175
Rolling Stones, 268
Roosevelt, Eleanor, 36
Roosevelt, Franklin, 63, 89, 90n, 92, 97
The Rose (DeFeo), 118
Rosie and the Originals, 173
Ross, Alex, 259
Rossen, Robert, 159n
Roth, Philip, 15, 16, 43–46, 59–100, 101, 159n
Rourke, Constance, 211, 236
Rove, Karl, 216
Ruby, Jack, 226
The Runaway Jury (Grisham), 259
Rushdie, Salman, 5
Ruth, Babe, 94
Ryan, Meg, 72, 74
Ryan, Robert, 77, 78

Sandburg, Carl, 75
Savage, Ann, 132, 134, 134n, 135, 144

Savio, Mario, 31n
Scaggs, Boz, 272
The Scarlet Letter (Hawthorne), 83
Schaar, John, 23
Scholtes, Peter S., 214
Scott, Jane, 230
Scott, Lizabeth, 158
The Sea Came in at Midnight
    (Erickson), 225
Second Inaugural Address (Lincoln),
    20, 21, 26, 27–29, 63, 79, 80
The Secret Diary of Laura Palmer
    (Lynch), 148, 151
Seeds, 208
Seuss, Dr., 159n
Sex Pistols, 254
Shakespeare, William, 68, 88
The Shape of Things (Pere Ubu), 255
"Shape of Things to Come" (Max
    Frost and the Troopers), 254, 255
Siegel, Don, 88
Siewert, Cameron, 71–72
Simkins, Modjeska, 37–38
Sinatra, Frank, 144
Sinatra, Nancy, 268
Siodmak, Robert, 125
Sleater-Kinney, 28, 187, 188
Sleepless in Seattle, 101, 139
Smith, Reverend Samuel F., 32
"So Cold" (Laughner), 229
"Sonic Reducer" (Rocket from the
    Tombs), 217, 233
Spacey, Kevin, 72
Spann, Otis, 34–35
Spears, Britney, 254
Spice Girls, 186
"Spoonful" (Cream), 233
Spy Games, 139
"Stand By Me" (King), 236, 238, 239
Stanton, Harry Dean, 166
Stanwyck, Barbara, 112, 158, 159, 225
"The Star-Spangled Banner"
    (Hendrix), 189

Stars Screaming (Kaye), 21
Star Wars, 72
Statler Brothers, 269
Stewart, Martha, 72
Stone, I. F., 159n
Stone, Oliver, 131
Stone, Sharon, 72
Stooges, 208, 212
Story of My Life (Pere Ubu), 232
"Story of the Knoxville Girl" (Blue
    Sky Boys), 156
Stowe, Harriet Beecher, 8
The Straight Story (Lynch), 107
The Strange Love of Martha Ivers
    (Milestone), 159–60
Straw, Syd, 240, 242, 243
Sturges, Preston, 204, 205
"Suck My Left One" (Bikini Kill),
    186, 187
Sunrise (Murnau), 125, 132
"Surfer Girl" (Beach Boys), 236,
    237
Surf's Up! (Thomas, and two pale
    boys), 248
Suspects (Thomson), 225–27, 252
Sutherland, Kiefer, 165

Take the 5:10 to Dreamland
    (Conner), 117, 118, 119–22
"Take Up Thy Cross" (Blue Sky
    Boys), 156
Talking Heads, 265, 265n
Taylor, Charles, 53
Taylor, Frederick, 52
Terkel, Studs, 75
Testimony (Reznikoff), 80, 80n
"The House Where We Were Wed"
    (Blue Sky Boys), 156
Them!, 117
"These Boots Are Made for Walkin'"
    (Sinatra), 268
13th Floor Elevators, 208

"30 Seconds Over Tokyo" (Pere Ubu), 209–10, 211, 216, 228
"This Magic Moment" (Drifters), 111
This Must Be the Place: The Adventures of Talking Heads in the 20th Century (Bowman), 265*n*
Thomas, David, 16, 108, 205–55, 270
Thompson, Jim, 158
Thomson, David, 123, 225, 252, 253
Thoreau, Henry David, 147
"Three Things" (Pere Ubu), 246
Thurmond, Strom, 57
The Time of Our Singing (Powers), 21, 35–37
Time Out of Mind (Dylan), 43, 250
To Kill a Mockingbird (Lee), 71
Tone, Franchot, 137*n*
Toole, John Kennedy, 245
"Transfusion" (Laughner), 229
Truman, Harry, 63, 273
Tucker, Corin, 187–91
Tucker, Maureen, 209
Tunis, John R., 46
24, 41–42, 48
"Twigs of Folly" (Cantwell), 25
Twin Peaks, 106, 148–49, 154–55, 160, 161*n*, 162–63, 164, 173, 175, 183, 186, 190, 191, 192, 199, 242, 243
Twin Peaks: Fire Walk with Me (Lynch), 107, 124*n*, 148, 149–51, 162–99

Ubu Roi (Jarry), 216
Ulmer, Edgar G., 130, 131–36
Uncle Sam (Darnall and Ross), 259–67, 283
"Under My Thumb" (Rolling Stones), 268
U.S.A. (Dos Passos), 48–56, 58, 59, 62, 63, 64, 65, 66, 100, 197
U.S. 285, New Mexico (Frank), 114

Valentino, Rudolph, 52
Valse Triste (Conner), 117, 118, 119, 121–22
Veblen, Thorstein, 52
Velvet Underground, 208, 209, 237
Vertigo, 116
Vinton, Bobby, 116, 117
Virginia Declaration of Rights, 13
The Virginian (Pullman), 103, 138, 145
The Virginian (Wister), 103, 145
The Visiting, 88
von Ribbentrop, Joachim, 97

Wagner, Natasha Gregson, 110
Wallace, Henry, 63, 77
Washington, Denzel, 74
Washington, George, 50
Wayne, John, 57
Weegee, 159*n*
Welles, Orson, 75, 241
Wendt, George, 240, 241
West Side Story, 161*n*
"What'd I Say" (Charles), 118
"What Goes On" (Velvet Underground), 209
Wheeler, Robert, 235
"Where the Soul (of Man) Never Dies" (Blue Sky Boys), 156
While You Were Sleeping, 101, 139
White, Emily, 187
The White Rose (Conner), 118
"Who Do You Love" (Diddley), 243
The Whole Equation (Thomson), 123
"Wichita Vortex Sutra" (Ginsberg), 14, 267–80, 281, 282, 283–84
Wild at Heart (Lynch), 106, 131
Wilder, Billy, 125
Wild in the Streets (Shear), 254–55
Williams, Hank, 130
Williams, Robin, 73

Wilson, Brian, 236
Wilson, Edmund, 201, 202
Wilson, Woodrow, 132
Winchell, Walter, 89, 94
Winthrop, John, 7, 19–20, 20*n*, 21, 22–25, 26, 32, 34, 63, 150, 152, 194–95, 196, 197
Wire, 232
Wister, Owen, 103, 145
Wolitzer, Meg, 47
Wood, Natalie, 111, 113, 161*n*, 225
"Woolie Bullie" (Pere Ubu), 253–54
"The World Spins" (Cruise), 173

Wright, Lawrence, 192, 193
Wright, Robin, 72
Wright, Wilbur and Orville, 52–53

Yo La Tengo, 240
Young, Neil, 206, 250, 251
"Young Goodman Brown" (Hawthorne), 152–53
"You're Gonna Miss Me" (13th Floor Elevators), 208

Zhang, Yan, 253
Zuckerman Unbound (Roth), 60